JAMES AVERY JOYCE is an international lawyer and writer who has spent much of his career at diplomatic and disarmament conferences. He studied political science under Harold Laski at the London School of Economics, taught at various London colleges and was called to the bar in 1943. He ran for Parliament in 1951 and 1955 and subsequently became a consultant to the UN and UNESCO. He is well known as the author of several articles and some two dozen books on major social questions of our time.

THE WAR MACHINE

JAMES AVERY JOYCE

 A DISCUS BOOK/PUBLISHED BY AVON BOOKS

The cover photograph shows the United Nations Peace Keeping Force in Cyprus, 1973.
Cover photograph courtesy of United Nations/NAGATA

AVON BOOKS
A division of
The Hearst Corporation
959 Eighth Avenue
New York, New York 10019

Copyright © 1980 by James Avery Joyce
Published by arrangement with Quartet Books
Library of Congress Catalog Card Number: 82-90276
ISBN: 0-380-59915-5

First Discus Printing, August, 1982

DISCUS TRADEMARK REG. U. S. PAT. OFF. AND IN
OTHER COUNTRIES, MARCA REGISTRADA, HECHO EN
U. S. A.

Printed in the U. S. A. 100747

OP 10 9 8 7 6 5 4 3 2 1

Dedicated in admiration and respect to
Lieutenant-General Ensio Siilasvuo of Finland,
former commander of United Nations peace forces
in Jerusalem and the Middle East.

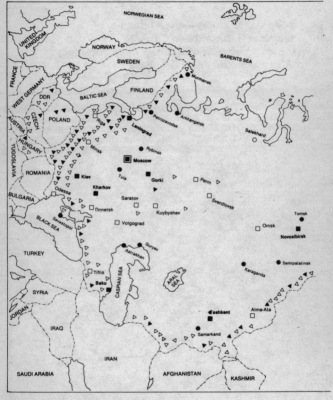

Map 1   Defending the Motherlands
Source: Phoebus Publishing Co/BPC Publishing Ltd 1975

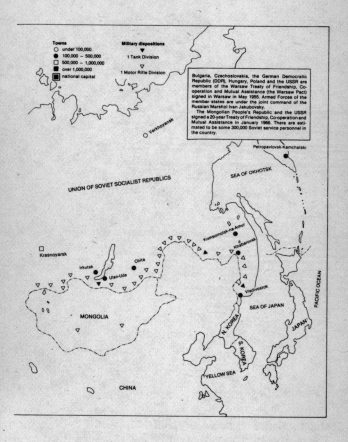

Towns
- ○ under 100,000
- ● 100,000 – 500,000
- □ 500,000 – 1,000,000
- ■ over 1,000,000
- ■ national capital

Military dispositions
- ▼ 1 Tank Division
- ▽ 1 Motor Rifle Division

Bulgaria, Czechoslovakia, the German Democratic Republic (DDR), Hungary, Poland and the USSR are members of the Warsaw Treaty of Friendship, Co-operation and Mutual Assistance (the Warsaw Pact) signed in Warsaw in May 1955. Armed Forces of the member states are under the joint command of the Russian Marshal Ivan Jakubovsky.

The Mongolian People's Republic and the USSR signed a 20-year Treaty of Friendship, Co-operation and Mutual Assistance in January 1966. There are estimated to be some 300,000 Soviet service personnel in the country.

○ Verkhoyansk

Petropavlovsk-Kamchatski ●

SEA OF OKHOTSK

UNION OF SOVIET SOCIALIST REPUBLICS

□ Krasnoyarsk

Komsomolsk-na-Amur ●

Khabarovsk ●

● Irkutsk ● Chita

Ulan-Ude ▼

PACIFIC OCEAN

MONGOLIA

Vladivostok ●

SEA OF JAPAN

N. KOREA

S. KOREA

JAPAN

CHINA

YELLOW SEA

Contents

Preface to Third Edition

The years 1981 and 1982 have sparked an unexpected and unrehearsed people's movement that can be seen, in longer perspective, as a European rebellion against the war machine, now under construction in both Washington and Moscow. This sudden shift in popular attitudes was foretold in the two earlier editions of this book. It now assumes a primary place in this third edition. For the 1980s *must be different!* or else...?

This massive protest against foreign bases and nuclear weapons on European soil has put a decisive spanner into the machinery of the war machine and thrown it out of gear. The whole phony vocabulary that has been spawned by military minds during the last thirty years of "first strike," "deterrence," "flexible response," "arms control" and whatnot—analyzed in these chapters—has to be looked at afresh in the light of a fast-spreading movement of disenchantment and disengagement.

Why is this? The aim of the NATO official deterrence policy for these three decades has been to frighten the Russians. Its quite unanticipated result has been to frighten the Europeans. This revelation dawned on Washington politicos only in the late summer of 1981, when Europe's revolt against the Pentagon's plan to plant 572 new U.S. supermissiles on the split continent—with a neutron bomb thrown in for good measure—could no longer be swept under the nuclear carpet. A spontaneous all-European people's movement, burgeoning in city after city—Bonn, Brussels, Paris, London, Madrid, Rome—was so unscheduled in Pentagon contingency plans that no one there could think of what to do about it. None of the backroom experts' gloomy scenarios of World War III had arranged a tidy little spot for it. So the United States President had to improvise at short notice a public rebuttal. Verbal reassurances that all was really well with the arms race then began to follow from the State Department, many of them inconsistent with each other.

Meantime, the usual run of hard-line Washington columnists had to get to work in the fall of 1981 "explaining" what they called an "orchestrated" chorus of Moscow's dupes to deflate NATO defence strategy. The simple truth, however, was that some 300 million people did not want to be killed. To accept 572 U.S. nuclear supermissiles in 1983, in addition to the vast weaponry already there, would be to acquiesce in signing their own collective death warrant. It proved, also, that the existing boasted weaponry was already out of date. It was just too much; especially for young people who had never asked for genocidal weapons to "defend" them in the first place. They rebelled. And it didn't need the Russians to tell them what to do—i.e., to get out from under the NATO "umbrella" while the going was good.

James Reston summed up this new alignment of moral forces on 30 November 1981, when the Geneva meetings opened: "The people of Europe are demanding the right to be heard and insisting that this subject is too important to be left to secret negotiations in Geneva between the two atomic giants. What started as a mathematical dispute about the balance of military power between Soviet missiles and NATO missiles has turned into a philosophic question involving the universities, the churches, and the rising young generation that has no memory of the two world wars."

That same day, in fact, a symbolic demonstration was parading the streets of London, organized by Britain's 15-million-member Trades Union Congress under the slogan: "Give us a Future!" Thousands of unemployed young people carried placards: "JOBS NOT BOMBS!"

12

James Reston is correct in saying: "There seems to be agreement in London and in Bonn that this is not an anti-American movement. It may be anti-Reagan, but is certainly not pro-Communist, despite Moscow's efforts to exploit it." And the real reason? "The European young have their grievances. The economies of their countries are in decline, and many of the younger generation are afraid of not getting into universities or of not getting out of them with jobs. They are afraid of Moscow, but bewildered by the casual nuclear rhetoric out of Washington. And beyond this, they are terrified by the elemental power of atomic weapons and find an outlet for their emotions in their cries for a nuclear-free Europe."

Rereading those earlier off-the-cuff analyses of what was supposed to be going on in European minds, one gains a sense of the pity and sorrow that the biggest foreign-policy miscalculation since the end of World War II had not been seen even on a clear day across the Atlantic. Those current press "explanations" make no sense any more. A large and influential section of European opinion had thrown NATO weapons out with the Atlantic bath water. NATO policy was back in the melting pot.

The stress that the present book puts on a return to the principles of the U.N. Charter, signed by all the belligerents in 1945, is not only because of the fact that a Special Session on Disarmament had been convened in New York in the summer of 1982, but rather because thirty years of sabotage of those U.N. principles has brought mankind to the brink of mutual extermination.

Some fourteen years ago, the present author published *End of an Illusion*,* a detailed study indicting NATO as an illegal and dangerous anachronism. Today, an inveterate American conservative, William Pfaff, writes: "NATO is in more serious danger from Washington, these days, than from Moscow. Ignorance, bad temper, and prejudice are driving the Western allies apart. Before this ends, if it ends, NATO could be finished as an effective alliance." He concludes:

> It may be that NATO deserves to end, that it has outlived its usefulness. You will not hear that in Washington; but some people there are acting as if they believed it. Even if NATO has served its purpose—as I think may be true—it

*J. Avery Joyce, *End of an Illusion* (Bobbs-Merrill, New York, 1969).

13

deserves to be ended in an intelligent and constructive manner. . . . Two over-armed nuclear alliances now confront one another across the mine-field that separates the two Germanys. Neither has anything to gain from attacking the other. Both know it. (*International Herald Tribune*, 10 November 1981)

"Toughness" has failed, both morally and diplomatically. It is one of the purposes of this present book, therefore, to show how the effete and moribund policies of NATO can and must be replaced by genuine peace programs under the less-spectacular and long-neglected U.N. security system.

The important long-term effects of this European revolt on world opinion we shall also take up in this edition. A new "peace movement" has begun in America's nuclear backyard. But what was the short-term result in the United States? The writing was so clearly on its wall that the White House had immediately to reverse gears—with or without NATO's tacit consent. For there was no time to consult all the "allies," especially as, in mid-November 1981, President Brezhnev was on his way to Bonn for so-called conciliation talks with West German Chancellor Schmidt and a U.S.–U.S.S.R. parley had already been fixed in Geneva. So President Reagan challenged the Soviet Union to turn away from enlarging its own military arsenal and to join the U.S. in *reducing* nuclear and conventional forces. But how did he do it?

In his first major foreign-policy address in Washington (incidentally directed to newsmen) Ronald Reagan took on a surprisingly conciliatory tone toward Moscow, while carefully reassuring his European allies that it was the Soviet Union, not the United States, that stood in the way of reducing tensions. His epoch-seeking speech consequently received a lot of publicity. Had peace really broken out?

His calling for mutual "zero" reduction of weaponry was an extraordinarily skillful effort to reach Europeans—but not the Russians. The Europeans had been dismayed and alienated by his machismatic and bellicose statements a few weeks before, not least his unfortunate gaffe that a nuclear war *limited to Europe* was in the works. In fact, the United States government paid the costs of broadcasting this after-dinner speech by satellite to Europe—which helped to explain why the Russians did not take it too seriously, as not being directed for their own benefit. His proposal was that the United States would be willing to *cancel its plans* to deliver the 572 new Cruise and Pershing-2 missiles to Europe, if the Russians would *dismantle* the 600 SS-20, SS-4 and SS-5 intermediate-range missiles they had already deployed in the west of the Soviet Union.

This offer seemed to mean to most people that the Soviet Union was being asked to abandon an *existing* asset in exchange for a promise that the United States would scrap *future* deliveries. A typical comment from Oxford, England (by Mr. Ian McKelled), was: "Whereas the new proposal demands a withdrawal of *existing* Soviet medium-range missiles, it offers only a slashing of *planned* positioning of U.S. Cruise and Pershing missiles. The asymmetry here is obvious. You think up something terrible, then offer not to carry it out in trade for some real reductions on the Soviet side. . . . The logic of the U.S. proposal rests on belligerency in foreign policy; it is not very likely to result in fruitful arms reduction talks."

Then, to support his offer, Reagan introduced the dubious concept of a military "balance"—a concept which we shall examine closely in this book. "The Soviets assert that a balance of intermediate-range nuclear forces already exists; that assertion is wrong," Mr. Reagan said. Hence, "to reduce the dread threat of nuclear war which hangs over the people of Europe," the U.S. would be willing, in practice, to *cut* nothing. Leaders of Western Europe, however, where the nuclear buildup had touched off all those street demonstrations, called for mutual *reductions* of both U.S. and Soviet missiles *now*. Statesmen cannot "bargain" with megaton warheads like little boys playing with glass marbles. But they *think* they can!

An intermediate-range missile reduction plan was actually put on the table on November 30, 1981, when U.S. and Soviet negotiators sat down in Geneva for their first talks after many years. So the rebelling Europeans had at least shamed the two sides to begin talking. But it was still talk. What *cuts* was Reagan offering? Did anybody know?

Moscow denounced his Washington speech as a "propagandistic" effort to stem the growing antinuclear movement in Western Europe, while preserving U.S. military superiority "through the back door." *Tass* (the voice of Moscow) said that, by excluding other U.S. weapons—missile-carrying submarines and warplanes already stationed in the region—Mr. Reagan was giving the West clear military superiority in Europe. *Tass* also asserted that NATO countries currently had 986 medium-range nuclear weapons systems in Europe, compared with 975 for the Soviet Union. It added moreover that, with multiple warheads on the weapons, NATO has a 50-percent edge over the Russians. (*International Herald Tribune*, 19 November 1981.) In other words, the U.S. leader was only "pretending" to renounce deployment of *new* U.S. medium-range nuclear missiles in order to win over European public opinion. So we were soon back to square one. That is where the Reagan gesture got stuck.

There is, of course, another view. Lawrence S. Eagleburger, Assistant Secretary for European Affairs, stated before the North Atlantic Assembly (a NATO affiliate) on 15 October 1981: "Precisely because the prevention of nuclear war is so terribly important, we are concerned about pressures—some well intentioned, some not so well intentioned—to change a policy which has prevented war for over thirty years. Many of my countrymen wonder whether the debate now taking place here (in Europe) is a fundamental challenge to the principles which have guided us for over thirty years [on] the traditional premises about Western security." Millions of Europeans— including the cream of its professions and universities and many top names in religious, political and military leadership—have given him a fundamental answer: "Thirty years of traditional 'security' is enough—we can't take it any more!"

But what proposals did some other Americans want their President to advocate? Only a small advance selection of this fast-expanding grass-roots opinion—hardly noticed in the media—can be featured in this Preface. Across the country prominent persons are calling on the White House to support a bilateral nuclear-weapons "freeze," also to reduce the military budget, and *stop* the production of the MX missile, the B-1 bomber, and other nuclear systems. In Minneapolis, a phone-in campaign was expanded to contact state senators every fifteen minutes throughout October and November 1981. Five "Caravans for Human Survival," organized by the World Federalists from locations in New England, Canada, Miami, and Minneapolis, arrived in New York recently at the United Nations headquarters. The Women's Strike for Peace also planned a march to join them there, led by Ramsey Clark, former U.S. Attorney General, and Professor Richard Falk from Princeton University. A group of Buddhist monks had begun a trans-America *walk* from Pasadena, California, to arrive at the United Nations Special Session on Disarmament in June 1982. Americans want their government to move at last beyond after-dinner speeches to ACTION.

Some commentators on the previous editions have noted that my book has been based solely on Western source materials. One reason for this deliberate selection is that the majority of Western writers on the arms race have exhibited a sort of built-in cold-war stance that *assumes* that any initiative to slow or reverse it must come from the Russians. This attitude, in the view of this writer, can only add to our dilemma, since it encourages a fixation on Moscow, instead of promoting the many positive initiatives and options, as adumbrated in these chapters, which the West can employ in breaking through the stranglehold of those fears and apprehensions that have for too long been the curse and bane of Western policy.

Worldwide protests in Europe, Japan, Canada, and Australia against nuclear weapons are being reflected by mounting campaigns all over the United States, too. Many peace groups, including the American Friends Service Committee, Clergy and Laity Concerned, Women's International League for Peace and Freedom, and the Fellowship of Reconciliation, are promoting local activities. They are coordinating their activities in the "Call to Halt the Nuclear Arms Race." This proposes a freeze between the U.S. and U.S.S.R. on the production, testing, and deployment of nuclear weapons and their delivery systems. To start with, state legislatures in New York, Massachusetts, and Oregon have all passed resolutions supporting the freeze. Governor Brendan Byrne of New Jersey, for instance, proclaimed a Mutual Nuclear Arms Freeze Week in his state during October 1981. (Other such activities are described in Chapter V.)

The time has long passed, however, for merely repeating peace ideals and antiwar slogans. We are concerned first and foremost in this book to present some of the hard realities of human survival, amidst the man-made threat of nuclear death for billions of ordinary people across the earth.

American historian and diplomat George F. Kennan can be cited, as we close this Preface, as representative of that "other America," which holds the peace of mankind in stewardship. He proposed on 19 May 1981 that a start be made in Washington for "an immediate across-the-board reduction by 50 percent of the nuclear arsenals now being maintained by the two superpowers". He is no Communist or terrorist. He is no "star-eyed peacenik." But a life-long realist. Like every other modern thinker, he warns that oblivion is the only alternative to world disarmament. He points out (our italics):

> I see this competitive buildup of armaments conceived initially as a means to an end, but soon becoming *the end itself*. I see it taking possession of men's imagination and behavior, becoming a force in its own right . . . leading both parties, invariably and inexorably, to the war *they no longer know how to avoid*.

Drawn from his long experience as former U.S. Ambassador in Moscow, and as a leading scholar on Russian affairs, George F. Kennan underlines the main thesis put forward in the pages of the present book, by characterizing the arms race as "a species of fixation, brewed out of many components. There are fears, resentments, national pride, personal pride. There are misreadings of the adversary's intentions—sometimes even the refusal to consider them at all. There is the tendency of national communities *to idealize themselves and to dehumanize the opponent*. There is the blinkered, narrow vision of the professional military planner, and his tendency to make war inevitable by assuming its inevitability."

Could anyone but Kennan have so deftly summed up the cruel absurdities of the arms race and the confused minds of those who encourage, plan, and support it?

> Tossed together, these components form a powerful brew. They guide the fears and the ambitions of men. They seize the policies of governments and whip them around like trees before the tempest.

JAMES AVERY JOYCE

Geneva, April 1982

Introduction

This book cannot be read in a hurry because it is full of the politics of survival, the politics of peace. It is packed with facts and covers many controversial subjects. It tries to give answers to questions that millions of citizens are raising about their future and the future of our planet. The first edition (in Britain) was called by Lord Fenner Brockway, a life-long member of Parliament and peace campaigner, the "Bible of the Peace Movement."

But sometimes individual judgment in politics may err. This book can be no exception. Perhaps we shall overstate our case against the promoters of the arms race; perhaps we shall overlook the pressures of *realpolitik* on political decision makers; perhaps we shall over-estimate the conservatism of the powers-that-be; perhaps we shall underestimate the impact of the media or the emotional reaction of the crowd that pushes them on or holds them back. But of two things in this arms business we are certain: that the ordinary people of this planet want and need peace, and their national politicians believe, with few exceptions, that they are providing it—in their own way. "I think that people want peace so much that one of these days, governments had better get out of their way and let them have it."—Dwight D. Eisenhower, 1959. Yet what must by now be as plain as daylight to increasing numbers of thinking people in all countries is that the arms race is *not* the way to get it. The arms race is a nonwinner; it is a blind alley with a holocaust at the end of it.

For the first time in human history this fact is being increasingly recognized all over the world; but the world's statesmen seem incapable or unwilling to cope with an entirely new challenge to the traditional doctrines of national defense. That is why, in our Preface and in later pages, we have drawn special attention to the unexpected people's movements in Europe in 1981 and 1982. Is this the breakthrough we are waiting for? "We fought World War I in Europe, we fought World War II in Europe, and if you dummies will let us, we will fight World War III in Europe." Such is the advice of ex-Admiral Gene La Rocque, former U.S. strategic planner. The common people of Europe seem to have heard the message.

Karl von Clausewitz, the great strategist, said: "No human affair stands so constantly and so generally in close connection with chance as War." Of all the branches of human activity, he added, war was "the most like a gambling game." That is why we cannot dodge examining political attitudes when we expose and condemn, as we do in these pages, the lies and shams and misconceptions in this gigantic balance of error that the arms race has become today.

For the arms race is not basically about guns or strategy or money; it is about political attitudes. It is about political decisions on "security" that have got out of hand. It has been spawned by a military contest between the United States and the Soviet Union, and their respective allies and satellites. Though both sides talk about national security, the contest is really about military superiority—not equality but *superiority*.

Early in the new 97th Congress a bi-partisan coalition, pulled together by the American Security Council, put forward a resolution to commit the United States to nuclear arms *superiority* over the Soviet Union. In view of the conservative make-up of the Congress and with President Reagan in office, proponents of the resolution assumed a large majority for a national policy to increase military spending. But former Secretary of State Muskie, advocating SALT II ratification, told a Washington audience on 16 October 1980:

If at the same time our nation were proclaiming a new strategic doctrine—a doctrine of "superiority"—the prospects of those negotiations would evaporate. Whether it is called "superiority" or "margin of safety," this doctrine rejects the central principle of this treaty—that the greatest safety comes from an overall balance in our forces. It proclaims, in effect, that we would accept no treaty . . . unless an edge for the United States is locked in.

Unaware that Europe was fast slipping away and that the old magic was fading from American arms domination, Defense Secretary Caspar Weinberger prepared for President Reagan on August 14, 1981, a comprehensive proposal to expand America's strategic nuclear deterrent forces well beyond previous plans to strengthen those forces. The plan, costing about $200 billion, would encompass intercontinental ballistic missiles, long-range bombers, Trident submarines armed with more accurate missiles, and a vast rebuilding of the extensive communications apparatus through which strategic forces are controlled.

The pro-Western press had for over a year been fed by Pentagon stories of the Soviet "build-up" of tanks in Eastern Europe; but a study of the Weinberger plan, especially its new Trident submarine with its 100 kilotons of explosive power aimed at 408 separate targets (which we describe in this book) leaves no doubt whatsoever that the U.S. aims at overwhelming superiority. "Equality" has lost any meaning today. A balance of terror turns out to be merely the politician's slapstick in a tragicomedy of errors. Jeane J. Kirkpatrick, U.S. representative to the United Nations, admitted this in a speech she made to the American Enterprise Institute on December 8, 1981, when she said:

Even if the Soviet Union does not now hold military superiority over the United States, the United States and the West have definitely lost the superiority they once had.

There are lesser aspects to be considered, of course—since there are many lesser armed struggles going on. Since 1945 it is estimated that 133 "local" wars have occurred, costing 25 million human lives and producing 13 million refugees. But the United States and the Soviet Union's military rivalry is primary. We shall never lose sight of that; not even when we seek to explain, toward the end of this book, that the only viable solutions to this insane rivalry lie outside the areas of conflict altogether, namely, within the whole world community, acting through the United Nations system. For was not the U.N. Charter set up (as it says): "to save succeeding generations from the scourge of war" and "to practice tolerance and live together in peace with one another as good neighbors?"

Having started in 1945 from that common pledge to live and let live, how did we get onto this dreadful treadmill to oblivion? This evil cult of far-more dreadful weapons is the main answer. The fear of being "outmaneuvered" by the Soviet Union has so long dominated the minds of political leaders in the West that normal people have been seduced into believing that it can go on and on like this. But, as we enter the 1980s, we are living on borrowed time. Scientists, calculating the mathematical risks of the unthinkable happening, while megatons are being piled on megatons of mass-murder, spread across five continents, know that our days are getting close to zero.

Someone, sooner rather than later, will pull the wrong trigger, press the wrong button on this man-made inferno. Or someone will bump by accident into this monstrous network of military make-believe. The day before Armistice Day 1979, we were six minutes away from a nuclear war, when the United States went (by accident) on "red alert." For six incredible minutes, the United States' "red alert" signalled a nuclear war to begin at 3:40. Jet fighters took to the air. B-52 bombers were readied for take-off.

But it was all a ghastly mistake. The press reported next day: "World War III could have begun in six minutes of madness"—meaning that the arms race had slipped into top gear. Apparently, "they" did not know that their computer machine was connected to the early-warning system across the Western Defense Bases, which received a clear warning that the United States was *under attack*! It took six minutes before the North American Air Defense Command (NORAD) in Colorado realized that an error had been made when feeding in details of a phony missile attack coming from over the North Pole. Prime Minister Thatcher was never told about it, it seems. The mistake was discovered by the RAF before "she needed to be informed!" Within 30 seconds they had received the reassuring answer: "Computer error."

22

John Bradley is a fifty-six-year-old American. Between 1972 and 1974 he was the chief tester of the computer network which alerts the United States to a nuclear attack. He alleges that in 1973 he warned of serious defects in this computer, and was given the sack as a result. American officials later decided that the computer was indeed faulty. So much so that in June 1980 it had twice sounded the alarm warning of a Russian attack on the United States. On one of these occasions the entire American strike force was put on a three-minute alert.

Who will answer "computer error" next time, when a flight of wild geese across the North Pole sets all the bells ringing across this Heath-Robinson contraption that we have built in the name of "security?" Questioned in the British House of Commons two days later about why "the Americans have the right [sic] to initiate the use of these weapons without consultation" (i.e. the new 572 "upgraded" warheads for NATO), the then Defense Minister, Francis Pym, replied: "This is not a dual key, it is a single key, but there are consultative processes, long established, which successive governments have thought to be adequate in all circumstances for the purpose." So the Americans hold the key to Britain's becoming involved in a nuclear war! This knowledge has not brought our two countries together, but led in 1981–82 to a powerful movement, within all the political parties, to get rid of the U.S. bases, which house the nuclear weapons under American control.

Unfortunately, that was not Mr. Pym's last word. On 9 June 1980 he was again explaining away the two further "false computer warnings of a Soviet attack," happening within four days of each other. He assured the House that "the computers are interlinked on both sides of the Atlantic." With a single key?

Nuclear bombs are unreliable servants. Even under controlled situations, specialized bombs dropped on the ill-fated *Torrey Canyon*, adrift near the English coast in 1968, failed to explode in the damaged ship, thus creating an additional hazard to the Channel shipping. In 1978 the accuracy of the bombing of another foundering oil-tanker depended on which way the winds were blowing.

We are asked to believe, however, that Cruise missiles are made to drop within a few feet of their selected targets after traveling several thousand miles. But this military guesswork is nonsense. Clausewitz was right. Modern war is an instrument of imprecision—a fool's game of chance.

Referring to the Soviet satellite which went astray in Canada in 1978, Frank Allaun MP drew attention in the House of Commons to the accidental discharge of a nuclear-carrying missile. "Sooner or later it is going to happen," he said:

There are more than 10,000 of them poised for instant action East and West of the vertical frontier through the heart of Europe. The United States deploys over 30,000 nuclear warheads throughout the world. The Soviet Union also has a vast, though smaller, arsenal. Then there are the submarine-carried nuclear missiles on both sides. Electronic accidents have occurred, fortunately for us all without calamitous effects—so far. However, a crazy submarine commander could misinterpret or disobey a signal. And though there are electronic locks on some of the weapons, even electronic locks can be picked.

But the six minutes to zero did not happen in a vacuum. The Pentagon-planners and their Johnnies-come-lately in the Kremlin have been filling up the earth's vacuums with military hardware as fast as they can on the first-come-first-served principle. The Indian Ocean—proclaimed a zone of peace by Africans and Asians and most of the U.N.—is being festooned with nuclear bases from Somalia to Pakistan. Britain callously turned out the native islanders of Diego Garcia to make room for a new United States base, which is expanding fast now that the Russians are in Afghanistan. Somalia is actually switching over a former Soviet-occupied naval port to the Americans. United States warships and aircraft carriers went speeding to the Arabian Gulf when Iran impounded the 52 U.S. Embassy staff; but now we complain that the Russians are swarming in!

It is in *this* starkly irrational context (not as featured in colorful scenarios of James Bond) that the fate of millions is being put at the mercy of military computer errors. The European rebellion against this madness is now being duplicated in Africa and Asia. "To hell with both your houses!" is a current version of the black man's burden.

We know all too well today that when religious fanaticism compounds public fears with political arrogance, as it does across the Middle East, it can take only a handful of unstable bigots to imperil the common peace. Little wars are not local anymore. Today they are the spark-plugs for Armageddon.

"We are in a war situation," proclaimed an enraged ayatollah: "It is a struggle between Islam and blasphemy." Inevitably, the arms race has since produced an over-reaction that has reached the limits of the absurd. One intransigent zealot can play on Russian fears and block a peaceful Middle East settlement which millions of unhappy people want and which the United Nations has voted time and again with vast majorities.

On the other side of chaos, however, a statesman of wider vision and deeper acquaintance with Russian problems, George Kennan (former U.S. Ambassador to Moscow), can tell his fellow citizens: "In the official American interpretation of what occurred in Afghanistan, no serious account appears to have been taken of such specific factors as geographic proximity, ethnic affinity of peoples on both sides of the border, and political instability in what is, after all, a border country of the Soviet Union." (See Map 1)

During the last three decades, mankind has several times approached the brink of oblivion. But "brinkmanship" did not start with Stalin. It became almost a way of life before that with John Foster Dulles. Richard Nixon is reported to have once said: "I have only to press that button . . ." and, idle threat though it may have been, took us pretty close to it more than once. How many more times can this happen, until the lemmings follow each other over the brink?

International efforts to "control" the mad momentum of a hair-triggered arms race have so far produced no significant results. They founder on public ignorance and national egotism, which become obvious to the serious student who draws his facts and figures—as we shall do in the chapters that follow—from impartial sources such as SIPRI (the Swedish International Peace Research Institute) and the statistical services of the United Nations. These world-based institutions have no incentive to "cook" their data to bolster up some forthcoming war budget against an outside enemy.

The year 1980 ushered in a decade of cynicism, when—always on the pretext of some newly discovered "Russian threat" to Europe—eleven members of NATO introduced 11,270 new weapons. Moreover, the governments of what is called the Eurogroup announced that their defense spending had risen by $20 billion in 1979; and they predicted that their contributions to world suicide would rise still higher in 1980. (They had already spent $50 billion on defense in 1978 and

$70 billion in 1979.) Did Mr. Reagan forget this big NATO weapons expansion when he met the Russians head-on in December 1981? Clearly the Russians had not forgotten it.

Meantime, military technology advances as rapidly as human ingenuity and the stock market allow. Yesterday's science fiction becomes today's reality—and tomorrow's doom. It is no longer only a competition in quantity, but also quality; not numbers of weapons, but "capacity" for indiscriminate destruction. This mad race has already become a war of technologies; of robots, not men. This is what was meant by "updating" NATO's "theater" weapons in the 1980s (no James Bond scenario about *this* theater!), meaning 572 super-super-warheads (each 20 times more terrible than Hiroshima). The Pentagon, *who holds the keys*, has decreed to Brussels that 160 of these should be planted on British soil by 1983.

Yet, if nuclear war came in Europe, our national societies would cease to exist. Nuclear deterrence is a nihilist doctrine, without morality, without reason, without hope. But it has become an article of Western faith; and the whole population of Europe—East and West—is trapped by it. Mutual assured destruction (MAD) has become the most morally indefensible strategy ever devised in the history of warfare. But today it is the established policy of the big powers—a Satanic ideology legalized by treaties such as NATO. And the Russians, who are always behind the West in overall throw-weight, have followed suit. The Warsaw Pact was formed in 1955, *after* West Germany was brought into NATO (1949). There are plenty of battlefields on which to fight the good fight against the Soviet ideology and its contemptible totalitarian conception and mispractice of human rights, but a nuclear battlefield is not one of them.

Exactly what human values, we ask, what national interests, are worth defending with weapons of genocidal destruction? Where are human rights, when millions of human beings are reduced to mathematical coefficients on nuclear targets? We are so mentally paralyzed by the false rhetoric of the arms race that the horror weapons we shall study in these chapters have to be given innocent-sounding names. And our whole "defense" psychology today is being promoted by statesmen who do not know where they are going. We have become so inured to violence—impersonal, automated violence—that our moral judgment has become impaired by the apocalyptic calculations of a new breed of deterrence strategists, who are now asking:

26

"How many million deaths would be 'acceptable' in a nuclear war? How much megatonnage would be *needed* for national defense?" But no one answers, because there are no answers.

In a speech to UNESCO in Paris on 2 June 1980, His Holiness John Paul II said:

> . . . reasons of geo-politics, economic problems on a worldwide scale, dreadful misunderstandings, wounded national pride, the materialism of our age and the decline of moral values have brought our world to a state of instability, a delicate equilibrium which is liable to be upset at any moment as a result of errors of judgment, information or interpretation.

We have become the Age of Violence. When a British Member of Parliament stands up in the same House of Commons debate mentioned above, and asserts: "The decision of Brussels with the statement of President Carter on substantially increasing the American defense budget is the best news for peace and freedom since the Soviet Union deployed the SS-20 against us; I thank Mr. Pym for his courage in giving leadership to the alliance"—are he and his supporters aware of the contribution they are making to the banked-up violence and moral degradation that is destroying our society?

This cancer of endemic military war runs through all lands and all social systems like a collective death wish. "Whom the Gods would destroy, they first make mad" can be seen today on every level of national and international life. Dr. Eric Martin, a Swiss, formerly President of the International Red Cross, says: "For the last 20 years, violence in all its forms has been spreading over the planet in a frightening manner." And he adds: "Contrary to what might have been hoped or claimed, it is now evident that torture is not a remnant of a barbaric age, destined to disappear with the progress of civilization. Virtually eliminated from European States by the end of the nineteenth century, it has come back in full force, even within nations that claim to be in the forefront of social and legal progress."

From the Third World, Judge Keba M'Baye, President of the Supreme Court of Senegal and President of the U.N. Human Rights Commission, has probed even deeper into our common sickness: "The execrable crimes of the Second World War seem to have accustomed the human soul to the worst forms of cruelty. It is as if the barbarity sleeping in every man has been liberated in some individuals. Those among them who hold a scrap of authority giving them the power to subdue or destroy their neighbor do not fail to use it."

No one could have described the psychotic springs of the arms race in a shorter sentence. The psychotic personality may well have some genuine grounds in his original derangement: it is simply that he has lost touch with reality. Whatever its earlier moral motivation, that is what the arms race has become today. It has passed beyond moral or political control. When governments officially plan and support the crime of genocide in their foreign policies, can they hope to suppress crimes of violence in their own communities?

Not only big wars are the building blocks of violence. From an unexpected quarter, an Irishman of vision, Dr. Desmond Moran, the coroner at the inquest into the deaths of Earl Mountbatten of Burma and three other members of his boating party in August 1979, urged politicians to make greater efforts to achieve peace in Ireland. At the end of the inquest, Dr. Moran said: "It is now unfortunately obvious to us all that outrages of this sort are one of the main problems society has to face in the latter half of the twentieth century." And he added some simple but deeply moving words:

> I believe it is necessary to stress again the great responsibility that parents and teachers of any nation have in the way they interpret history and pass it on to the youth of their country. I believe that if history could be taught in such a fashion that it would help to create harmony among people rather than division and hatred, it would serve this nation and all other nations better.

The worldwide campaign to stop the arms race and combat the violence that sustains it will be reflected in the positive proposals that find a central place in these pages. Yet at the outset we must admit that there can be found no panacea that can be compressed into a single rallying cry or presented in a neat political capsule. Wars can be won on national slogans, but peace can only be won on international understanding. And that is a hard discipline which cannot happen at once. There can be no higher form of patriotism than the kind of world loyalty for which this book pleads. That undoubtedly must start in our schools; but it must eventually run through the whole of life.

Behind the arms race are a mass of group loyalties, of national traditions, and of emotional commitments that cannot be shifted by a few slogans. The stress laid in this book on disarmament *education* and the whole process of our seeking *alternatives* to the present world anarchy, is fundamentally a call to a new way of life for individuals and nations. And that will not be easy.

Our immediate problem is that ordinary people are utterly bewildered. They do not know where to turn. Leadership—except for war propaganda—is non-existent. But the real dangers are not outside us. They are inside us. In November 1980, 50 percent of the voters in the West's most powerful democracy did not vote at all. They returned, with barely a quarter of their votes, a retired film actor for President who now possesses enormous constitutional powers of peace and war and who selected as his Secretary of State a man well known as an anti-Russian hawk and a top NATO general during the worst years of the Cold War.

Yet the thrust of this book is to remember all the time that we are dealing with human beings—good and bad, but human. We are surely intelligent enough today to surmount the barricades of fear and misunderstanding that war-oriented chauvinists of yesterday have erected between nations in the minds of their peoples—and thus to turn the tide of this growing WAR hysteria to grind the mills of hope? Mankind cannot surely be so self-condemned. Addressing the U.N. Special Session on Disarmament in 1978, the then Prime Minister Desai of India said: "If all this power of destruction came from the human intellect, surely that intellect can create something more compassionate and benevolent."

It is in the minds of people that the institutions of peace must be constructed. And the first step is to find out what are the facts—to define the disease that has corrupted our minds and imperils our society. No cure can be easy or swift. But the time to stop the arms race leading to the "execrable crime" of a third world war is *NOW*. For we shall not pass this way again.

I
The Meaning of Overkill

Thirty-seven summers ago an American bomb with an explosive no larger than a baseball was dropped on the city of Hiroshima. Three days later Nagasaki too lay devastated under mass killing that had no parallel in our history. The long-drawn-out dying from radiation sickness is not yet over in Japan.

This first chapter states in plain language that nuclear weapons are illegal, immoral and unworkable as instruments of defense. This view is not based on idealistic or ideological theory. It is supported by facts as shown in statistics, charts and diagrams adduced by acknowledged experts working in their professional fields. As the Russians have pressed long and hard for such a plan, the U.S. and Britain should immediately stop testing, begin to scale down their nuclear weapons and destroy all stocks forthwith. Chapter VII takes these half-forgotten proposals further; but, for the time being, we must study the main facts of the nuclear menace to all mankind.

(1) What World War III would be like

A third world war would be the *final* phase of the present contest for world hegemony between the so-called capitalism of the U.S.A. and the alleged communism of the U.S.S.R., with everyone else dragged in. But neither system would survive it. For the arms race does not have a winner. The following pages try to explain why.

"Limited" nuclear war is pure fantasy. If we cannot stop it from beginning, how can we stop it halfway from accelerating? Speaking at Dartmouth College recently, George Kennan said that "there is no way in which nuclear weapons could conceivably be employed in combat that would not involve the possibility—and indeed the probability, high probability—of escalation into a general nuclear disaster." This American view has been supported by a study from the prestigious Institute for Strategic Studies in London, which concludes that the use of nuclear weapons, *once begun*, could not be "controlled."

Nobody knows how many people would be left on earth. Estimates vary. But, if any at all, they wouldn't be very many or very healthy. In fact, "overkill," as now being planned by NATO and WAPO (the rival North Atlantic Treaty and Warsaw Pact Organizations) will take care of everything—leaving, as the saying is, "not a wrack behind."

So why are politicians and opinion-makers in the West so keen on backing overkill? Why are some of them now proclaiming its inevitability? Yet they have nothing to say about stopping it from *beginning*! They are mesmerized by Moscow. Lord Chalfont in England, like Richard Nixon, bluntly says that World War III "has already *begun*". British Air Marshal Sir Neil Cameron, visiting China recently, hinted as plainly: "We both have an enemy at our door, whose capital is Moscow." Mrs. Thatcher, then leader of the British Conservative Party, when in Peking in 1977, urged the Chinese to increase their overkill capacity against the Soviet Union. She launched into an anti-Russian crusade in Brussels on 23 June 1978 with this advice:

The NATO Alliance will always be our best source of security. Indeed the United States, who will remain the foremost member of that Alliance, has taken the lead in increasing her own contribution to our joint defense . . . Unless we learn, as the Soviet Union has learnt, to look at the

31

landscape as a whole, we shall be consistently out-maneuvered.

The present book, in tracing the causes and consequences of the arms race, will have much to say about allowing the Russians to decide our defense programs for us. This pragmatic approach is bound to upset a lot of people who take the arms race for granted. They *assume* that they can somehow "live" with the threatened holocaust. They call this "security." So the more the merrier. But an increasing number of people in America and Britain are paying fantastic prices for shelters to protect them from the effects of a nuclear attack. So they can't be very convinced about what their Government is saying about "security." Nor can the Government, either.

Few overworked politicians can give much time or thought to what will really happen to Planet Earth if their national arms build-ups continue at the present rate. They are too wrapped up in saving their faces and keeping an eye on the next election. They are in office for five or six years, or less. So are presidents. But the arms profiteers and the Russians-are-coming military complex have their programs already fixed, covering the whole of the 1980s and beyond. Cabinets never have time to discuss the perils of the arms race in depth, least of all what can be done to *stop* it.

Mrs. Thatcher was not quite a lone horse in encouraging this supplementary arms race, roping in China as a new untried ally. At the height of the Afghanistan crisis, the Carter administration, too, was revealed as seeking China's co-operation in boosting both China's and Pakistan's defenses against Soviet military "pressure." Proposals for arms increases came from both governments, but on their own terms. U.S.-Chinese efforts to strengthen Pakistan's defenses were seen as a step towards closer "security" collaboration between Washington and its inveterate enemy Peking! Washington even asserted that "the Soviets have *forced* us and the Chinese to see the world in the same way." What sort of non-policy is this? Do Peking and Moscow now make our major decisions? Let us look at the figures of the so-called "balance" at the beginning of the 1980s.

Hence, closer security ties with Peking had become a new-fangled way for the United States to respond to Moscow's irresponsible military actions in Afghanistan. In other words, the more unstable the situation, the more arms are poured into

32

	NATO	Warsaw Pact	People's Republic of China
Population	554,800,000	365,700,000	900,000,000
GNP	$3,367 billion	$1,240 billion	$309 billion
Military spending	$175 billion	$139 billion	$23–28 billion
Military manpower	4,900,000	4,850,000	4,300,000
Strategic nuclear weapons	9,400	4,500	200?
Tactical nuclear weapons	22,000?	15,000?	N.A.
Tanks	25,250+	59,000	9,000
Anti-tank missiles	200,000	N.A.	N.A.
Other armored vehicles	48,000+	62,000+	3,500
Heavy artillery	11,400+	22,600+	20,000
Combat aircraft	8,900+	10,400	5,900
Helicopters	12,300	4,550	350
Major surface warships	522	247	22
Attack submarines (all types)	211	239	66

Table 1   Military resources of NATO, Warsaw Pact and the People's Republic of China. (The U.S. Defense Department estimates of Warsaw Pact manpower include 750,000 uniformed civilian personnel, making the total Warsaw Pact manpower 5.6 million.)

Source: U.S. Department of Defense

Note: The figures presented in these tables are the latest available. They may vary slightly from year to year but, being long term in incidence, comparisons between them would not substantially change until real disarmament reduces them.

it. This piecemeal hit-and-miss management (or non-management) of the arms race has merely shifted the beginnings of World War III from central Europe or the Middle East to the Far East. Where next? Japan is being pressed to violate its "peace" constitution and introduce a 9 percent war budget increase in 1982, a topic we take up in Chapter VI.

So what this book sets out to do first of all is "to look at the landscape as a whole" and ask what World War III would be like if this suicidal helter-skelter death game is not halted in time. Its conclusions, as will be seen, are very different from those of the sophisticated hawks, British and American, who get all the media publicity but who contribute nothing to our sanity or safety. In this book we shall call the arms race not just a spade, but what Lt. General E. L. M. Burns of Canada has defined it as: "*megamurder*". Megamurder means that we have now stored up three tons of TNT for every person on earth—all at the mercy of that *one key* in Washington.

Nothing in this book will seek to minimize the threat of nuclear war that hangs over us. Nothing in this book will lessen the need to prepare ourselves against it. Nothing in this book proposes a no-win policy or no-defense program on the part of any government. Nothing in this book will underestimate the peril facing the ordinary people if their government takes the wrong action or no action. Nothing in this book condones the military aggression in Afghanistan by a country that is constantly calling for a "Treaty on the Non-Use of Force in International Relations."

What this book does propose is action that is quite the reverse to our present posture of defense and defiance, based upon theories and traditions that have had their day and can no longer work. What this book does advocate is an abandonment of alleged "defense" measures which are determined by *unilateral* national decisions and based on military alliances which, by their nature, are bound to fail. What this book does do is to call for a fundamental revision of these attitudes and procedures so that, step by step, the present anarchy of states is replaced by a global order based on the principles of the U.N. Charter.

There is nothing illegal or unpatriotic about that approach. Members of the U.N. are committed to act in accordance with those specific procedures and to pursue *universal and complete disarmament*. It is precisely because we have reneged or sidestepped the U.N. that we are in the mess we are in. A deliberate decision to stop rearming and turn all the mental and material energies of the arms race into a world system of international co-operation through the U.N. is the moral duty of all citizens and a legal obligation of all governments. Not all citizens will see this as plainly as others, nor will all governments act as resolutely as others. But there can be no question that the Western nations, now dominated by the United States military hierarchy, must lead the other nations in establishing action programs to implement their commitments to *stop* arming and work jointly and singly for a disarmed world. *That* is our challenge today: not Russia, not communism (nor capitalism), but *megamurder*.

This book should leave no doubt that by repudiating the national policies that make the arms race inevitable, the responsible citizen is fulfilling his most sacred responsibilities to his own country and to the world community. That this step demands a fundamental change of personal attitudes and national postures goes without saying. We have long passed the point where orthodox excuses for inaction or trivial goodwill gestures can accomplish great ends. It has been well said: "For big ills, small remedies are no remedy at all." And we are not proposing in this book small remedies to stop megamurder.

The reason why the senior Canadian General E. L. M. Burns calls all the subterfuges of a "limited" nuclear war—even "winning" a nuclear war—"megamurder," is simply because, in a single short sentence: "War has *become* megamurder." Under the Hague Convention of 1907 the civilized nations agreed that the right of belligerents to adopt means of injuring the enemy "was not unlimited." The laws of war did not permit unarmed civilians to be killed deliberately.

However, in the fifty years that followed the Hague Convention, all that has been changed . . . If the mass of nuclear weapons which now exists is used in war, it will mean the killing of millions of women, children and old men who bear no arms and who bear no responsibility for warlike decisions. Megaton bombs will cause mega-deaths. Is it wrong to call this not war, but mega-murder? (*Megamurder*, 1966).

When he left the Canadian service, Lt. General Burns joined the U.N. Truce Supervisory Service operating in Palestine between Jews and Arabs. He confesses that this assignment was the toughest in his career, i.e. keeping peace in a cauldron of fear and hatred and miscalculation. He says in his book *Megamurder*: "The nightmare of the Western world and of the Soviet Union is that any day instantaneous death may come to millions upon millions of their populations, with the simultaneous destruction of the cities, the structures, the machines and the stored knowledge upon which civilizations depend."

He is not alone in this belief. Herman Kahn, a conservative American scholar and leading research analyst on war, brought these fears into the open years ago in a way that shocked many people. In his 1959 book *On Thermonuclear War* he estimated with scientific detachment the results at that time of the destruction of 43 of the greatest metropolitan areas of the United States, as could well happen in so-called "nuclear exchange" with the Soviet Union. The casualties which the American people would suffer might amount to 90,000,000. If, however, 70 percent of the population of the 43 great metropolitan areas were *evacuated*—a vast undertaking requiring many months and many billions of dollars to build fall-out shelters in the less populated parts of the country—and *if* large stocks of everything needed to enable the survivors to live and rebuild the shattered country were laid by, then perhaps only 5,000,000 "would need" (*sic*) to die outright. This scenario was indeed over-optimistic in view of the much later data we shall deal with in this book. And Professor Kahn omitted to mention what sort of society would follow "survival." We shall refer later on to a British scholarly inventor of war games, General Sir John Hackett, who also fails to favor us with a picture of a *liveable* world, after all his own "ifs" have come out to the satisfaction of mice and men, i.e. when the good guys have won a nuclear war against the Russians.

Lt. General E. L. M. Burns points out, however, that all these dubious prophets of a nuclear war do not, and cannot, know what they are talking about. He says: "There have been only two occasions, separated by a couple of days, when overkill weapons were used in actual warfare; hence it is necessary to imagine what will happen when the thousandfold more powerful and more numerous thermonuclear weapons of today are used." A distinguished soldier himself, he reminds us:

As no general or admiral has any *real* experience of nuclear warfare, the pre-1945 theory of military tactics and strategy, built up from military history and criticism, provides little guidance. Thus the scientist, by his training, is probably as well able to determine how these new weapons systems should be used as is the military man.

Since the 1950s, however, scientists have been spending more energy publishing books warning us about the catastrophe to be expected than on devising practical policies *to avoid it*. So there exists a triple gap in public awareness—the active generals tell us it is all right, the scientists tell us it is not all right, and the politicians tell us nothing. In the United States, successive administrations, hoping somehow to reduce the danger which the mere existence of nuclear arms creates, have developed comforting theories about "arms control." Of course, it never works. But the basic idea is that nations having nuclear armaments should limit, by treaty or convention, their numbers and even their *use in war*—but without abolishing them. The word "control" is never defined. It is preceded by adjectives like "effective" or "adequate." Thus the fantasy of "arms control" has become the enemy of disarmament, which means something quite different from control.

To improve the nation's strategic posture, the Reagan Administration will consider building an anti-ballistic missile defense system and basing a new mobile offensive missile at sea. Secretary of Defense Weinberger has said that extension of the anti-ballistic missile (ABM) treaty with Russia beyond 1982 is not automatic. In order to protect U.S. land-based missiles now threatened by Soviet rockets, the new Administration might want to build an anti-ballistic missile system larger than the two sizes permitted under the treaty signed with Moscow in 1972 (SALT I). It must be remembered that Russia has signed SALT II. America has turned it down.

Only a handful of people, relative to this massive arms build-up, are standing up to be counted against such iniquities. Yet they include some of the most respected and intelligent leaders of our time. We shall cite their testimony in the course of this book. But public opinion is no longer intimidated by the Pentagon bully boys. In 1981, the Reagan administration's discussions of nuclear strategy and its emphasis on building up U.S. defenses have brought the specter of nuclear annihilation nearer to many people for the first time.

According to a recent poll, seven of 10 Americans fear that nuclear war could erupt between the superpowers, and

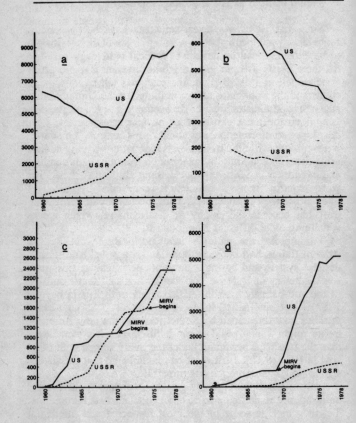

Fig. 1 (a) Total strategic nuclear weapons. United States and
U.S.S.R.; (b) number of long-range bombers, U.S. and U.S.S.R.;
(c) nuclear weapons on land-based missiles, U.S. and U.S.S.R.;
(d) nuclear weapons on submarine missiles, U.S. and U.S.S.R.
These graphs cover *strategic* nuclear weapons; they do not include
the even larger number of *tactical* nuclear weapons on both sides.
The U.S. has approximately 30,000 nuclear weapons, the Soviets
approximately 20,000.
Source: U.S. Center for Defense Information

that fear has invigorated arms control groups. The nation-wide Nuclear Freeze campaign, which began in March at Georgetown University and since has established petition drives in 20 states, attracts nearly 100 people to monthly educational meetings in Northern Virginia. (*Washington Post*, December 4, 1981.)

This bi-polarization of nuclear destruction between the U.S. and U.S.S.R. is more and more seen to be a criminal conspiracy by two superpowers and their hangers-on, and completely irrelevant to the real pressing problems of our planet in the 1980s and beyond. The Brandt Commission, which reported in the spring of 1980, put this into perspective. They said:

We are increasingly confronted, whether we like it or not, with more and more problems which affect mankind as a whole, so that solutions to these problems are inevitably internationalized. The globalization of dangers and challenges—war, chaos, self-destruction—calls for a domestic policy which goes much beyond parochial or even national items. We see signs of a new awareness that mankind is becoming a single community; but so far they have not been strong enough to stem the drift. In the short period since our Commission first met, in December 1977, the international situation has gone from bad to worse. It is no exaggeration to say that the future of the world can rarely have seemed so endangered.

The Third World and the non-aligned countries represent more people than are now being pitted against each other by their leaders in an unwinable Armageddon. The North-South Dialogue, which aims to feed the world's 500 million hungry children and to reduce the poverty and misery of undeveloped peoples, is a more viable guarantee of peace and security than NATO's and WAPO's rival arsenals. The abomination of an East-West suicide pact overshadows a better life for the Earth's peoples with a mushroom cloud.

The hypocrisy of a NATO *versus* WAPO hara-kiri projected into the 1980s was brilliantly summed up by a speech to American scientists in Philadelphia on 8 November 1979, by Lord Zuckerman. The British Government's Chief Scientific Adviser from 1964 to 1971 stated that:

the so-called "missile gap" turned out to have been a myth. [This was an earlier form of the "Russian threat."] Indeed, the Russians then started pressing hard to close the gap which *they* had perceived. This added another dimension to the arms race . . . But even at the worst moments of the Cold War, neither side was prepared to risk hostilities which would result in what was euphemistically called "a level of unacceptable damage."

And what were his conclusions? Lord Zuckerman continued: "The process of the nuclear race clearly has no logic. In the early 1970s, when Dr. Henry Kissinger occupied high political office, he declared that no meaning could any longer be attached to the concept of nuclear superiority." And he added:

> More recently, at a meeting in Brussels last September, when talking about the "modernization" of NATO's nuclear armory, he [Kissinger] is reported as having said that the European allies of the United States should not keep asking the United States "to multiply strategic assurances that we cannot possibly mean, or if we do mean, we should not want to execute, because if we execute we risk the destruction of civilization."

Nuclear weapons have not been used in war since August 1945. So all the hard-core facts about both their short-term and long-term effects relate to that horrendous month. There are varying estimates of the casualties at Hiroshima and Nagasaki. It has proved difficult to estimate the exact numbers of exposed people who may have died after *escaping* from the city. Some 45,000 of the fatal casualties at Hiroshima died on the day of the explosion, and some 20,000 during the following four months, as a result of traumatic wounds, burns and radiation effects. There are no estimates of the numbers who may have died from the effects of induced radioactivity experienced during rescue work in the city.

Most of the medical facilities in Hiroshima were in the devastated area. Next to immediate medical problems, the most serious challenge to those who survived the direct effects of the explosion were problems of water supply, housing and food. To those who did not suffer immediately, these difficulties compounded the profound psychological effects of the disaster. Twenty years after the bombings there was still an excessive sensitivity to the thought of radiation hazard. As late as September 1978 a 75-year-old Hiroshima atomic bomb survivor despondent over her lingering illness caused by exposure to radiation jumped to her death from the fifth floor of a nursing home in Tokyo where she was being treated for radiation-related lumbago, while a day later another survivor committed suicide because of radiation poisoning.*

Apart from the effects which ionizing radiation had on the victims of the explosions, the survivors were also exposed to the hazards of radiation both in terms of latent diseases occurring in the individual (somatic effects) and of changes in hereditary material (genetic effects). Exposure to repeated moderate doses of nuclear radiation is conducive to leukaemia—a disease which is associated with a malignant over-production of white blood cells. The incidence of leukemia in the survivors of Hiroshima and Nagasaki was observed to be increasing in 1948 and reached a peak in 1952. It still remains much higher than in the population of the rest of Japan. While the incidence of the disease increased in all age groups, it did so more sharply in young people.†

Since every city has its own individuality, communications and food supplies, a realistic picture of what *would* happen cannot be derived unless one considers a real city. One such study was made in 1968 by U.N. specialists of a city with a population of just over one million people. It was assumed that a one-megaton nuclear weapon had burst at ground level. Using the experience of Hiroshima and Nagasaki, and estimating on the basis of the results of carefully designed weapons experiments, the following figures of casualties emerged:

Killed by blast and fire	270,000
Killed by radioactive fall-out	90,000
Injured (of whom 15,000 were in the area of fall-out and thus exposed to the effects of radiation)	90,000
Uninjured (of whom 115,000 were in the area of fall-out)	710,000

*UPI report, 3 and 4 September 1978
†U.N. Publication, A/6858

This report to the U.N. in 1968 was presented by a group of consultant experts, whose members were: Wilhelm Billig, Chairman of the State Council for Peaceful Uses of Atomic Energy, Poland; Alfonso Léon de Garay, Director of the Genetics and Radiobiology Program, National Nuclear Energy Commission, Mexico; Vasily S. Emelyanov, Chairman of the Commission on the Scientific Problems of Disarmament of the Academy of Sciences of the Union of Soviet Socialist Republics; Martin Fehrm, Director General of the Research Institute of Swedish National Defense; Bertrand Goldschmidt, Director of External Relations and Planning, Atomic Energy Commission, France; W. Bennett Lewis, Senior Vice-President, Science, Atomic Energy of Canada Limited; Takashi Mukaibo, Professor, Faculty of Engineering, University of Tokyo, Japan; H. M. A. Onitiri, Director, Nigerian Institute of Social and Economic Research, University of Ibadan, Nigeria; John G. Palfrey, Professor of Law, Columbia University, New York, U.S.A.; Gunnar Randers, Managing Director, Norwegian Institute for Atomic Energy; Vikram A. Sarabhai, Chairman, Atomic Energy Commission of India; Sir Solly Zuckerman, Chief Scientific Adviser to Her Majesty's Government, United Kingdom. This is what they also said:

The enormity of the shadow which is cast over mankind by the possibility of nuclear war makes it essential that its effects be clearly and widely understood. It is not enough to know that nuclear weapons add a completely new dimension to man's powers of destruction. Published estimates of the effects of nuclear weapons range all the way from the concept of the total destruction of humanity to the belief that a nuclear war would differ from a conventional conflict, not in kind, but only in scale.

The situation, however, is not as arbitrary as opposing generalizations such as these might suggest. There is one inescapable and basic fact. It is that the nuclear armories which are in being already contain large megaton weapons every one of which has a destructive power greater than that of all the conventional explosive that has ever been used in warfare since the day gunpowder was discovered. Were such weapons ever to be used in numbers, hundreds of millions of people might be killed, and civilization as we know it, as well as organized community life, would inevitably come to an end in the countries involved.

We now learn that a *single* nuclear bomb exploding in the atmosphere over the United States could lead to a *nationwide power blackout* because U.S. power stations are too vulnerable, according to an official study prepared in January 1981 for the Government by civil defense and energy experts.

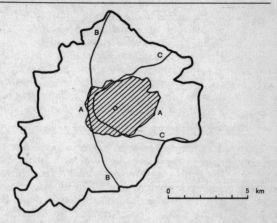

Fig. 2   Distribution of casualties following a nuclear attack. A is a line enclosing central area of 6 × 5 km., where practically the whole population would be killed. B is a line through a point 2.5 km. west of bomb-burst, marking limit of fall-out. C marks the area inside which a person would receive a lethal dose from fall-out in 48 hours if he stayed in the open.
Source: U.N. Report, 1968

Those, fortunately only a few, who talk glibly about "winning" a nuclear war have not looked at what the geneticists are saying about the changes that ionizing radiation induces in plants, animals, and human beings. What kind of survival they propose to "win" at the end of it is discreetly ignored. The aforementioned U.N. report is modest, but it concludes:

In general, the long-term genetic effects of nuclear radiation in living organisms are cumulative. While no visible injury would accompany the induction of genetic changes in the exposed individuals, undesirable consequences would arise in succeeding generations. It is reasonably certain that a population which had been irradiated at an intensity sufficient to kill even a few percent of its members, would suffer important long-term consequences. (U.N. report)

Countless dead bodies and seriously wounded people, who barely breathed, were left on the road or the river-banks of the city. Medical supplies were used up immediately because of the unimaginable number of wounded. The un-treated people took their last breath moaning, "Give me water." What is now called radiation sickness soon ap-peared. People began suffering from diarrhea as if they had dysentery, losing clumps of their hair, and developing pur-ple colored spots on their skin which made them look like a map. Such people soon died, their bodies full of big mag-gots they were too weak to remove. (Eyewitness at Hiro-shima, 1945)

The word "defense," however, has recently taken on a mean-ing appropriate to the Stone Age—or at least the battle of Waterloo. The British Government's civil defense plans are to be given greater priority now that SS-20 Russian missiles will carry pre-targeted warheads, and the supersonic Backfire bomber is to be added, "counterpoised" to Britain's agreed installation of 160 "upgraded" American-built and manned ground-launched Cruise missiles. Hence the Government is likewise thinking of "upgrading" civil defense, instead of downgrading the missiles due to arrive in 1983. Has it not occurred to any government that "defense" can no longer be so "civil"? As a document on Britain's "civil defense" plans clearly shows:

One megaton is the equivalent of one million tons of TNT. The effect of a single one-megaton air-burst over County Hall, London, would be the complete destruction of brick structures in a radius of one and three-quarter miles, ignition of fabrics in a radius of eight miles; blistering burns in a *radius of nine miles* on those who had not taken proper shelter [sic] and light damage to buildings in a radius of 11 miles.

London's plan is based on the assumption that a megaton-nage of between 180 and 200 could be "delivered" to the United Kingdom by about 200 weapons, in the one-megaton range.

44

Such an attack would probably be delivered within 24 hours, the planners think, and would comprise a mixture of both air and ground bursts (*Observer*, 16 January 1980).

In February 1980 70 MPs signed a motion in the Commons urging the Government to reconstitute the World War II Civil Defense Corps. One of the signatories, Miss Janet Fookes, Conservative MP for Plymouth, Drake, said: "We are living in a dangerous world. I am a hawk as far as the Soviet Union is concerned. I don't trust their Government at all" (*The Times*, 8 February 1980). So the British people now know what the hawks are thinking. We can trust our shelters, but we can't trust the Russians. These people still think they are planning for the Second World War.

Perhaps the most apposite commentary on this renewed "civil defense" debate in the 1980s was also the shortest. It appeared from a correspondent (Mr. B. J. Greenwood) in *The Times* in these terms:

> Sir, I must thank you for your fascinating series of articles on Civil Defense. It is indeed a great comfort to learn that, when the holocaust arrives, our Government will be safely housed in a three-story bunker deep under a wooded hill in the country. What a shame that they will no longer have a population to govern!

A parallel voice in the United States is just as pungent. I. F. Stone, in *Resist Newsletter*, says: "Billions needed to rebuild our cities may go for more and bigger ratholes in which to cower."

But has anybody during twelve years of discussion on measures for universal and complete disarmament heard the ringing tones of British delegates announcing *British* disarmament plans or, at any time, accepting and approving the many Soviet and Eastern European and Third World proposals, tabled again and again at the U.N.? The tactics in negotiations are always the same—delay and postpone! Wait for the Russians. The game is called "arms control." But where has Britain stood on those crucial U.N. debates for banning of nuclear weapons? Will Britain's acceptance of 160 of NATO's new 572 mega-murder weapons compensate for a shameful decade of neglect and silence? Cannot the British yet see that the only form of "civil defense" in the 1980s *is to stop the arms race*?

"Britain's vulnerability," says Councillor Ronald Huzzard of London:

> arises from our so-called defense policy which causes nuclear weapons targeted on other countries to be stationed in these islands. There is no conceivable protection against nuclear weapons, whether they are of the size which obliterated Hiroshima or the larger type now stockpiled by the two super-Powers. The 1978 United Nations special session stressed that the only security today lies through disarmament (*Observer*, 2 April 1980).

Why the silent back-room scientists are no match for the strident militarists is because 50 percent of them are now working for the military-industrial complex itself. The military man, it is true, whether soldier, sailor or airman, still thinks of himself as the defender of his country. He assumes that in carrying out this duty, there should be no limits to the degree of force which he can employ when under the authority of his government.

The TV on both sides of the Atlantic is now bringing into our homes simulated war games and uniformed men *enjoying* various staged actions of World War III; but the program-makers suppress the truth that matters most—what happens afterwards on an irradiated earth unfit to live any more? We *know* *this* to be true. The evidence is given later in this book. But the war-propaganda merchants (some supported by NATO or our military budgets) dare not tell the truth about nuclear war.

But if we ask the simple question: "What, in any country, *is* the principal requirement of the military?" the answer is, bluntly, "*an enemy*." Since World War II, the United States has never lacked an enemy. The expansion in Eastern Europe of communist political control, under the aegis of a victorious Soviet army as long ago as 1944, produced the initial psychological jolt. But, today, a million Americans, including their families, are stationed in West Germany—35 years after World War II *ended*. So is BAOR—a throw-back to World War I.

As mutual fears intensified, the U.S. focused on the possibility of nuclear war, to stop an implacable enemy at the gates. Yet the mythical syndrome of an undefined "world communist conspiracy" that dominated American thinking, was exploded when China was discovered to be the *real* enemy of Russia. But it had, meanwhile, bolstered up the armaments budgets of the United States and its allies. The bolstering still goes ahead, while China and Russia now exchange insults and threats with each other, as the West looks on helplessly.

Stating that "it has not been the most triumphant chapter in American diplomatic history," Professor Walter La Feber of Cornell University writes in his *America, Russia, and the Cold War* (1976): "The Cold War has dominated American life since 1945. It has cost Americans a trillion and a half dollars in defense expenditures, taken the lives of nearly 100,000 of their young men, ruined the careers of many others during the McCarthyite witch-hunts, led the nation into the horrors of Southeast Asian conflicts, and in the 1970s triggered the worst economic depression in forty years."

Recounting the successive phases of the Cold War since the deflation of the Cuban missile crisis in 1962 (thanks to the worldwide pressure exerted on both belligerents at the U.N. Security Council), Professor La Feber notes that "this step back from the brink set the tone for a Soviet policy line, which was epitomized in a June 1964 press announcement that in order to guarantee the final preponderance of the forces of socialism over the forces of capitalism, to win victory in peaceful competition, *peace is essential*."

Soon, however, the fetish of a "world communist conspiracy," which had dominated U.S. editorials and Senatorial speeches in the 1950s and 60s, began to fade. It could no longer be sustained by an educated opinion, when in the 1970s (again helped by U.N. decision-making) Communist China was admitted to the family of nations and thus broke down the monolithic myth. But that was not the end of fear for Americans. The conspiracy specter then shifted to the eastern reaches of Europe. The headlines varied from "Warsaw Pact buildup" to "Russian expansionism." Soon thousands of Russian tanks would come gallivanting through Poland and East Germany. This was the latest nightmare that called for the 572 new weapons. Heaven knows *where* they were going to, because no one could guess, after 35 years of peace in Europe. But, nevertheless, they called for an immediate counter-buildup of the dubious neutron bombs. The even more dubious appearance of Western books, articles, and films on *The Third World War* put the new nuclear militarism at the top of the best-seller fiction lists in the 1980s.

As time went on "the enemy" has become more and more *essential* to keep our defense system on its toes. The fear, threat or some other menace of "the enemy" has always had to be manufactured, even where it does not exist. Every Western arms budget increase is served up with Russian caviar to make it palatable. Britain spends more of its gross domestic product on defense than any NATO country except the United States, according to NATO figures published in December 1980. Britain allocated 5.2 percent of its GDP, which is the value of all goods and services produced in the country, to defense this year, compared with 5.5 percent for the United States. 4.2 for West Germany, 4.0 for France, and 3.3 for both Belgium and the Netherlands. Canada, at 1.8 percent, and Luxembourg, at 1.1 percent, are at the bottom of the list (*International Herald Tribune*, 10 December 1980).

The Pentagon spends millions of dollars in propaganda on inflating this enemy. The press, with its selective news coverage, has kept the ball rolling. As a result, the Russians—negatively, it is true—have become an essential part of the Western way of life. (Or death?) Is it not ironical that the Soviet Union should have produced America's greatest modern industry—the war industry, an industry that grows, financially and even geographically, all the time?

Paul Warnke, director of the United States Arms Control Agency, wrote in 1975 that:

> A new generation of tactical nuclear weapons would be an absolute disaster. New weapons with a lower yield and greater accuracy and presumably few collateral consequences would erode rather than strengthen deterrence, and could at worst increase the prospects of eventual nuclear war.

Yet a U.S. Air Force study reported in 1978 that the proposed new MX missile system for the 1980s will cost between $20 and $27 billion and need an area of between 4,000 and 6,500 square miles—about the size of Connecticut. "Full-scale engineering development is expected, however, to result in only 44,000 new jobs nationwide for workers in aerospace and related industries," according to an Air Force statement on the proposed IBM and its mobile launching system. As the Rev. William Sloan Coffin, a leading U.S. heretic has said: "The arms race provides more and more jobs for machines and fewer jobs for people." Meantime, the MX Muddle is back in the melting-pot. The local people—and the governors of their threatened states—did not want to lose their trees, their water, or their colorful landscape under millions of tons of cement.

How does this war-preparedness obsession work out on the official level? "NATO's strategy of flexible response," says the U.S. State Department (November 1979)—

is designed to enable the alliance *to respond to any level of initial action* by an aggressor, from demonstrations of force to full-scale hostilities. Our ability to *meet any threat* must pose a clear risk of unacceptable costs *to our potential enemies*—this is the crucial element needed to deter an aggressor from any level of initial action. This strategy requires a force structure—conventional, theatre nuclear, and strategic—which plainly shows that we have many options to influence the course of conflict. The logic of deterrence remains compelling; for 30 years it has helped preserve peace in Europe [our italics].

So what is Washington's conclusion? More and more and more: in other words: "The alliance must modernize in order not to encourage Soviet misperceptions about our capabilities." We notice how well the options worked over Iran and Afghanistan. Addressing senators, the Defense Secretary, Caspar Weinberger, called for a drastic rearming of the United States, and said social programs may have to be cut to pay for it. In February 1981 Mr. Weinberger told the Senate Armed Services Committee that military readiness was "the highest priority of the nation." He was testifying on the 1982 military budget, for which former President Jimmy Carter's request was $196.1 billion, $25 billion more than in 1981. He added: "We have to recognize that it will mean a slowdown in growth or a reduction in many programs."

In his November 1981 speech, the President contradicted the Soviet claims on the current balance of so-called "theater" (i.e., intermediate-range) nuclear forces. He stated that the Soviet Union had an overwhelming advantage on the order of six to one. The six-to-one ratio did not include allied systems on either side, but if such systems were included, he said, the Soviet Union would still enjoy an overwhelming advantage in intermediate-range nuclear forces. That left the really big boys out of account. The Washington view of this "balance" is as follows:

U.S. Systems		Soviet Systems	
F-111	164	SS-20	250
F-4	265	SS-4/SS-5	350
A-6/A-7	68	SS-12/SS-22	100
Subtotal	497	Backfire	45
FB-111 (U.S.-based)	63	Badger/Blinder	350
Total	560	Fencer/Flogger/Fitter	2,700
		SS-N-5	30
		Total	3,825

Source: State Department Bulletin No. 220

Whatever may still be Russian "misperceptions," after all this time, the biggest sleight-of-hand in this fragile house of cards is that it has kept peace in Europe for 30 years. That is what has always been said about past arms races. This is what the man who fell from the 50th floor window muttered as he passed the 30th floor. But there is nothing sacrosanct about 30 years. Generals who talk like this are mesmerized by the short span of 20 years between World War I and World War II. Such comparisons are fallacious. They ignore the fact that there was no major European war between 1814 and 1914 aside from the Franco-Prussian War in 1870.

What the arms race has actually done to Europe can be seen on three separate levels. First, it has split the continent into two insecure armed camps and has therefore diminished, not increased, the peace of Europe. Secondly, it has fed fear and hate into the minds of a whole new generation, who had no responsibility for the errors that led to World War II. Thirdly, its horror weapons and moral iniquity have spilled over into a hundred Third World nations outside Europe, so that Korea and China and Iran and Afghanistan, and a dozen African states, have all become the cat's-paws of both sides of a broken Europe; and the race is now reaching into the Indian Ocean and the Sea of Japan. The pretext is always the same; but no honest observer can fail to see whose ships and weapons got there first.

And as regards Europe itself, in 1957 NATO decided to include nuclear arms in its strategy, as a counterweight to a supposed conventional preponderance of Soviet manpower and tanks. Consequently, on the *Western* side, tactical nuclear arms were made available by the United States, under American supervision. Later, on the *East European* side, too, tactical nuclear arms, directed against Western Europe, were stationed. At the moment NATO has 7,000 tactical nuclear arms in Europe, the Warsaw Pact about 3,500. Together they are strong enough to destroy Hiroshima 50,000 times. That is surely enough!

We have demonstrated in this book how the concoction of colored lie-words, beginning with Dulles' "massive retaliation" and passing through "phased responses" and "deterrence" to the latest abomination called "nuclear capability," has been so built into the false rhetoric of political debate and columnists' jargon, that few people realize the intellectual degradation and spiritual corrosiveness of the brain-washing process to which they have been subjected these 30 years. For these reasons, the World Disarmament Campaign that is now gaining force around and through the U.N.—of which this book is a small harbinger—has to fight a Herculean battle over a terrain poisoned with ancient untruth and encumbered with the vestiges of man's savage ancestry.

The founders and joint-chairmen of this campaign are British. Lords Philip Noel-Baker and Fenner Brockway, and the campaign's secretary, Brigadier Michael Harbottle, can be under no illusion as to the immensity of the revolutionary task to which they and their supporters have set their hand. We shall return to their endeavors later in this book; but, by placing their world campaign within the framework of the United Nations programs and structures, to which over 150 governments are already *legally* committed, the organizers have confidently spelled out their policy as being directed:

> to achieve, by appropriate stages, the general and complete disarmament of all nations under strict and effective international control, together with the reallocation of the resources so released to world development, that is to say, to the ending of world poverty and for the promotion of social justice and human welfare in all countries, developed and developing. (*The Times*, London, April 2, 1980)

The "unilateralist" movements that have since sprung up all over Europe—and beyond—by no means derogate from this U.N.-oriented world campaign, but add, on the contrary, new vigor and drama to it, especially in enlisting millions of young people, who are thus discovering their world citizenship through common action against the war-mongers.

(2) Line-up of the nukes

Let us begin at the beginning. As the nuclear age has "unfolded" (according to a State Department brochure) the United States and the Soviet Union have procured new kinds of strategic systems to deliver nuclear weapons. First these systems were bombers. Then the bombers were supplemented by land-based intercontinental ballistic missiles (ICBMs) and submarine-launched ballistic missiles (SLBMs). In the 1970s both nations increased their nuclear capabilities by deploying MIRVed missiles—missiles with several warheads that can be independently targeted. Today, the U.S. and the U.S.S.R. both have vast arrays of sophisticated nuclear weapons aimed at targets in each other's territory. Both nations view the SLBMs as vital to their defense because, for the foreseeable future, they are virtually invulnerable to detection and attack.

Although the Soviets have about 950 SLBMs in 62 submarines [says the State Department], compared to our 656 in 41 submarines, MIRVing now enables us to deliver many more warheads than the Soviets can *from beneath the sea*. Also, our SLBMs are more accurate and most have greater throw-weight. Our submarines are quieter and harder to track, and we keep more of them on patrol at sea than do the Soviets [our italics].

The Soviet Navy has completed work on a new submarine described by U.S. Defense Department officials as the largest undersea vessel ever built. The huge vessel was spotted by U.S. surveillance satellites when it was moved out of a construction shed at the naval yard on the White Sea. Based on the satellite photographs, intelligence analysts concluded that the submarine is about 480 feet long and 57 feet in diameter, making it larger in volume than the U.S. Navy's new class of nuclear-powered Trident submarines.

Great Britain has, of course, been caught in this underwater net of terror weapons, and is locked there until the late 1990s. A decision has been made at the Ministry of Defense that Britain's "independent" (*sic*) nuclear deterrent should be replaced in the 1990s by a fleet of five submarines carrying American Trident missiles fitted with British warheads. This

52

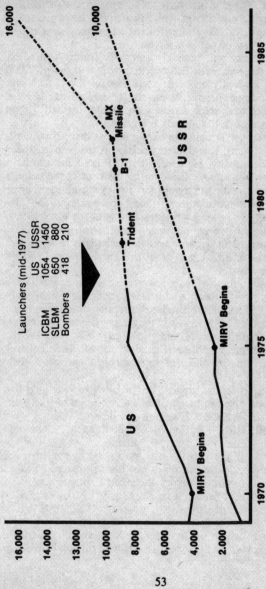

Fig. 3 Nuclear warheads and launchers possessed and projected by U.S. and U.S.S.R.
Source: U.S. Department of Defense

53

Trident proposed purchase is a direct successor to the older Polaris missile. The plan is to have the first of the new submarines in service by the mid-1990s, with a fleet of five boats eventually replacing the Royal Navy's four Polaris submarines, so as to have at least two boats on patrol at anytime.

Each of them will probably carry 16 Trident I missiles, which are three-stage ballistic rockets with a range of 7,000 kilometers, currently under development for the U.S. Navy. The Aldermaston Atomic Weapons Research Establishment may be asked to develop a new warhead carrying MIRVs, on which design work has already been done.

But the cost to Britain can hardly be less than £5,000 millions ($10 billion), if a Cabinet decision is made to go ahead with this monstrosity. However, the RAF are known to have some reservations about spending ten percent of the defense budget on a so-called deterrent farce (sic) during the four or five years of its development. One hope remains. The submarines will not be under construction until the early 1990s. *In 1982 the U.N. meets to seek a World Disarmament Convention. Meanwhile, vigorous public campaigns in support of it have begun in England to block this perversion of Britain's limited resources.*

Reverting to the two main adversaries, a third part of each country's strategic force is still intercontinental bombers. In 1980 the U.S. had 420 operational aircraft—more than twice as many as the U.S.S.R.—and they carry heavier armament, more advanced electronics, and greater payloads. Although the Soviet Union has emphasized air defense, the U.S. believes that it can count on most of its bombers to penetrate their defenses.

Some things never change. The "missile gap" warnings that John Kennedy used in his presidential campaign twenty years ago to attack President Eisenhower's defense policies were demonstrably false. Yet, once in office, Kennedy, along with his defense secretary, Robert McNamara, allowed an unprecedented U.S. military buildup to go on unchallenged, even though the missile-gap warnings had been shown to be false. This piece of forgotten history Desmond Ball analyzes in his book *Politics and Force Levels: The Strategic Missile Program of the Kennedy Administration* (University of California Press). He shows that the massive development of the U.S. strategic nuclear forces which began under the Kennedy administration was unwarranted, and yet was pursued with the full knowledge that the U.S. was *not* in danger of being left behind in an "arms race," that was just then beginning.

The present Reagan administration's campaign is a strong case of *déjà vu*. It reenters the arms race under the sobriquet of "control" to bring the U.S. back into a position of strategic superiority *before* resuming SALT negotiations. The Russians can see this too well. Professor Ball points out that if the first major "leap" into the arms race was predicated on political thinking and bureaucratic irrationality, then any decision to renew such a race on the basis of campaign promises and bureaucratic inertia must be challenged in America before new weapons are sent to Europe. McNamara's decisions on force levels were much higher than either he or Kennedy felt warranted, because of the confluence of political and bureaucratic pressures on the Administration. Are things different today in this futile "security" chase?

The mutually induced threats the two countries face are nevertheless somewhat different. For example, China, France and the United Kingdom, although not parties to the pre-Reagan SALT talks, have nuclear weapons of their own. Chinese missiles are at present too limited in range to pose a threat to the U.S., but not to the U.S.S.R. So all the talk about "balance" is irrelevant.

Given these differences, it is difficult to compare the nuclear forces of the two sides and decide whether one has an overall advantage. The United States leads in deliverable warheads, the Soviets in vehicles to deliver them; the United States leads in bomber payload, and (assumed) submarine quality; but the Soviet Union leads in missile throw-weight, and is developing more new systems. Since both sides have gone to great lengths to ensure the survival of their retaliatory forces, the balance between them is now alleged to be in "strategic equilibrium." The theory is that neither side should be *tempted* to gain an advantage by trying to destroy the other's forces. But—and this is a big *BUT*—the arms race goes on, because each side tries to upset this "balance" in its own favor.

This illusion that there can be a "balance" of existing armaments has received a similar mythical input when the Soviet Union in November 1981 released a study of the East-West military balance in rebuttal of a Pentagon pamphlet published in September outlining supposed Soviet military might. Soviet military doctrine, says the Kremlin, is interested only in "equality and equal security," and that poses no threat to Western

Europe or to the United States. The Moscow counter-pamphlet asserts that military parity exists between the forces of the Warsaw Pact and NATO. It says Europe is threatened not from the East, "but from the arms race started by the U.S.A. and other imperialist countries." (United Press International, 21 November 1981.)

The folly of this paper game with millions of people's lives was exposed recently by rumors that the U.S. civilian intelligence agencies were quarreling behind the scenes with the military about what that "balance" really was. The military contends that the job of comparing U.S. and Soviet forces in an atomic struggle is the prerogative of the Joint Chiefs of Staff and the Defense Department rather than the CIA. Other paper strategists have sensibly remarked that the total missilry is so vast that a few megatons one side or the other no longer matters.

An agreed overall limit of 2,400 ICBMs, SLBMs, heavy bombers, and air-to-surface ballistic missiles for each side was accepted at Vladivostok at the 1974 summit meeting between President Ford and (then) General Secretary Brezhnev. Within these agreed limits, each side would be free to choose whatever "mix" of forces it preferred. But two key issues—concerning the Soviet bomber known to us as Backfire and the U.S. Cruise missiles—were not settled. Disagreement on whether, or how, these weapons would be limited has played a large part in delaying a SALT II accord. President Reagan has the ball in his court.

Yet there has been other progress of a sort. On 6 October 1979 President Brezhnev announced an immediate and unilateral, though limited, withdrawal of 1,000 tanks and 20,000 Russian troops from East Germany. He also offered a reduction in the number of SS-20 medium-range missiles if NATO did not proceed with the Cruise and Pershing II missiles. But this opportunity was shuffled off. Then came the Afghanistan blunder. When an offer to negotiate comes, the sensible thing is to seize it quickly and put it to the test. Instead, NATO chiefs decided to manufacture and deploy the 572 new nuclear missiles, ignoring the Kremlin offer.

Mr. Caspar Weinberger, Secretary of Defense, said subsequently that the United States was prepared to negotiate in perfectly good faith and be very patient at the nuclear-missile-reduction talks with the Soviet Union in Geneva in December 1981. But, on receiving President Brezhnev's proposal in Bonn to reduce some Soviet medium-range missiles in Europe, Weinberger said that it seemed to be another version of the old moratorium proposal which Moscow had made on several occasions, beginning in 1979. "It contains nothing that is significantly new. At the same time, we would hope that President Brezhnev's willingness to consider reductions is a sign that the Soviets are beginning to see the advantages of pursuing genuine arms reductions in this area."

This is the normal Washington reaction to every Moscow proposal over quite two decades: "We hope that as negotiations proceed, the Soviets will take a forthcoming and fair position." The State Department statement reaffirmed President Reagan's proposal that *if* the Soviet Union dismantled its SS-20 and other medium-range nuclear missiles, the United States would forgo the deployment of 572 Pershing II and Cruise missiles in Western Europe. This has been widely called the "zero option" proposal. But we note—every time—the U.S. *if* transfers the initiative to the Russians. And *if* the Russians are not listening? But they *are*. In March 1982 Brezhnev repeated his freeze offer.

We recall Brezhnev's moratorium proposal, made in Bonn on 23 November, on medium-range missiles and, particularly, Soviet readiness to withdraw the SS-20s to behind the Urals. But Herr Schmidt repeated the agreed NATO view that a freeze of medium-range weapons at their present level was unacceptable, as it perpetuated the Soviet advantage. However, West German experts suspected that Mr. Brezhnev was making the moratorium proposal more attractive by his emphasis on withdrawing the SS-20s from European territory. Yet it appeared to differ little from earlier proposals *already rejected*, Bonn said. The West had argued that even from behind the Urals the SS-20s can still hit European cities. Period!

Yet chances of a direct aggressive attack across the Atlantic with nuclear weapons (labelled "first-strike") are precisely NIL. Neither the "West" nor the "East" have leaders so crazy as to press *that* button. But there are plenty of other buttons to press and that is where humanity's real peril lies. There exist buttons labelled "Afghanistan," "Poland," "Israel," "West Berlin," "Horn of Africa"—to name a few. And here the masters of the Pentagon or Kremlin are not masters of the local situation. The information they get is often wrong. To prepare them against first, second or third transatlantic strikes by piling on more and more counter-strikes labelled "deterrence" is a fool's game at best, since only fools believe that you can deter something that has already happened. What we do have to prepare against are the accidents, brainstorms or misjudgments of the little politicians who turn every local threat into a *casus belli* and call it a "pre-emptive" strike. This is happening under our eyes in the Indian Ocean, all the way from Nablus in occupied Palestine to the Hormuz Straits in the Persian Gulf. The premeditated brainstorm that destroyed a peaceful nuclear reactor plant at Baghdad in the summer of 1981 was at once condemned by both the U.N. and the European assemblies by virtually unanimous declarations. Such outrages against international law and the common peace call for the early establishment of the proposed code and court of U.N. criminal jurisdiction.

According to Rear-Admiral Gene R. La Rocque, director of the Washington Center for Defense Information, the traditional role of the military in all countries is to win:

> The military profession, to be blunt, has always sought superiority. Military men tend to be uncomfortable with notions of military balance or equilibrium...We feel reassured by big military establishments, we believe the security of our people is enhanced by spending for additional war-fighting and war-winning capabilities.

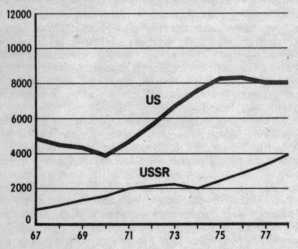

Fig. 4   U.S. and U.S.S.R. operational strategic offensive warheads/bombs, 1967–77.
Source: U.S. Center for Defense Information

Addressing the U.N. Special Session on Disarmament on 13 June 1978, the retired Admiral stated that the United States had added more nuclear weapons to its arsenal than the Soviet Union, increasing from 4,000 strategic weapons in 1970 to 9,000 in 1978. During the same period the Soviet Union increased from 1,800 to 4,500 nuclear weapons. "The U.S. has maintained a two-to-one edge in deliverable nuclear weapons throughout the period 1970–78," he stated, and added: "My experience in the United States military has convinced me that nuclear weapons have changed the traditional rules of warfare. To use an American phrase, 'it's a whole new ball game'."

That Rear-Admiral La Rocque does not underestimate the massive threat hanging over us was made clear in his address when he stated that a recent top-level U.S. Government study concludes that at a minimum 140 million people in the U.S. and 113 million in the U.S.S.R. would be killed in a major nuclear war. He concluded: "Almost three-quarters of their economies would be destroyed. In such a conflict, neither side could conceivably be described as a winner." Nor would those in the rest of the world be safe. Radiation would poison vast stretches of the planet not directly involved in the war. And the threat of ozone damage and ecological disruption leaves us no assurance that the earth would remain habitable for life as we know it. (Does Reagan prefer Europe instead?)

Doctors and other members of a Medical Working Group that took part in a recent Pugwash Conference in the Netherlands issued this statement on the medical aspects of nuclear conflict: "There is no possible effective medical response after a nuclear attack. In one major city alone there would be hundreds of thousands of people with severe burns, trauma and radiation sickness. Even if all medical resources were intact, the care of these immediate survivors would be next to impossible. In fact, most hospitals would be destroyed and medical personnel would be among the dead . . ." They continued:

Under the conditions of chaos and terror, the incidence of psychiatric disorders would rise sharply. The risk of long-term effects such as cancer would increase during their entire lifetime for many survivors—and possibly for their offspring as well.

The statement added: "Bomb shelters in cities would be useless owing to the blast, heat and radiation effects. Shelters as far as ten kilometers from the center of even a one-megaton nuclear explosion would become ovens for their occupants . . ."

(3) Piling on the agony
So, where do we go from here?

Later in this book we shall try to find some *new* answers. But for the moment, we must deal with the old answers. Such as: follow the logic of the bomb, go one better than the Russians or, simply, *more overkill*! That is just what the NATO summit conference decided in Brussels in November 1979. In fact, they said two things: (1) "We must raise our arms budgets another three per-cent a year" and (2) "We will accept and spread across Europe 572 new super-nuclear weapons from the Pentagon—*and under its control*."

These old answers amount to nothing less than "piling on the agony." They have added nothing to anyone's security. They involve a constant search for new "generations" of weapons. Advances in technology are all the time ushering in a new spurt in the arms race. The race for quantity has become a race for quality; and nuclear war becomes more "thinkable." Included in the current U.S. Defense Budget are proposed funds for:

(1) *The MX*, a mobile, land-based missile, and other "improvements" in the U.S. Minuteman III.
(2) *The Trident*, a huge submarine armed with 192 nuclear warheads.
(3) *The Cruise Missile*, a low-flying nuclear weapon aimed to land within 100 feet of the target after a flight of 8,000 miles.

If some warheads are to be smaller in size, more of them can be carried together in a large MIRV and then fired independently at different targets. With more warheads available and more accurate means of directing them at targets, military planners can program weapons to strike targets ranging from military installations and fortified missile silos to economic and industrial targets such as bridges, dams, power plants, and major storage areas. Anyone living close to these targets would be back in Hiroshima.

It is significant of the escape from reality of some governments in facing these qualitative changes in megamurder weapons that, according to Peter Hennessy, "the British Prime Minister has instructed her ministers to imitate her example and take a direct part in exercises designed to test plans for the transition to a conventional or a nuclear war." And Mr. Hennessy goes on to add:

> One of the more intriguing chapters in *The War Book*, Whitehall's highly secret and immensely detailed contingency plan, was promulgated in the early 1950s, when stock was first taken of the Soviet Union's capacity to launch an atomic strike against the British Isles.
>
> It deals with the role of the Chief Press Secretary to the Prime Minister in the transition period to nuclear war. He will be expected, according to *The War Book*, to take control of national newspapers and television (*The Times*, 26 February 1980).

Whether the authors of this secret war games compilation are to be taken seriously or not, it is to be noted that *The Times* correspondent concludes his astonishing revelations by pointing out that:

> the great weakness of the plan, according to an ultrarealistic official, is its touching expectation that anybody will be left in London to process the copy. "Can you imagine," he asked, "all your compositors and all the broadcasting technicians happily catching their usual trains to work in the knowledge that a bomb might be dropped on London at any moment?"

It is because ordinary people have been taught for years and years that there is a penny-in-the-slot remedy called "defense"—so that all they need in order to be safe is more and more nuclear bombs—that my present book concentrates most of all on the peril and *absurdity* of nuclear deterrence as a means of defense; on the contrary, the more bombs we build, the less hope we have to stay alive. Defense with nuclear bombs is not defense, but death! There are not two sides in a nuclear war; there is only one side, and that is the losing side.

World War III comes much closer because the temptation to strike such targets with these new weapons may persuade military planners to envisage "limited" attacks, intended to fall short of an all-out thermonuclear war. (We shall take up this grievous miscalculation when we examine General Hackett's horror fiction on World War III.) This is a highly dangerous speculation since, apart from the appalling destructiveness of any "limited" nuclear explosion, the other side would be most likely to respond with a counter-attack. So the whole situation would get out of control. *Who* would limit *what*?

Since the projected U.S. neutron bomb can, for the moment, be dubiously classified as a "conventional" weapon, we might look briefly at the other three nukes listed above. But, before doing so, we might remember how the United States Atomic Energy Commission describes radiation death caused by its newest weapon:

> A tendency to spontaneous internal bleeding towards the end of the first week . . . swelling and inflammation of the throat . . . a decrease in size and degenerative changes in the testes and ovaries; ulceration of the tonsils and of the mucous membrane of the large intestine . . . continuing to death.

That is if you are caught on the fringes. Death is much quicker at the center of the impact, and to that extent more merciful. The radiation disperses after a bit, allowing troops to move in.

MX (or "missile experimental") may be a land-based intercontinental ballistic missile (ICBM) designed to augment the existing force of Minuteman III. Besides being mobile, each MX would carry ten to 14 independently targeted warheads, each warhead possessing twice the explosive power and three times the accuracy of the Minuteman III. But its extra-special feature lies in an exotic subway system carved in the colorful deserts of the American Southwest, consisting of 300 covered trenches, each six to 25 miles long. At least, that was the main idea until the local populations realized that their homeland would be the first victim! This devil's subway was designed for *fighting a nuclear war*. Giant railway cars bearing the ICBMs would travel up and down the tunnels *so that the enemy won't know where they are*! Each missile would break through the earth and aim at enemy targets.

It is obvious that the MX is an extremely expensive system. Each missile is expected to cost $100 million, while the total costs for the system are estimated between $30 and $50 billion, if housed in 4,500 miles of tunnels, costing about $5 million a mile. The SALT II negotiations were held up because the

U.S. proposal for hiding land-based missiles among a cluster of empty, underground silos appeared to be incompatible with the terms of a new treaty *limiting* strategic arms until 1985. It met with great resistance from Moscow and also from Southwest Americans. (How can you "limit" missiles that are not there?)

Under such a U.S. "multiple aim point" idea, hundreds of missiles would be moved around thousands of empty launching silos in random fashion. The basic purpose of this "shell-game" would be to complicate any effort by the Soviet Union to destroy U.S. land-based missiles in a first-strike rocket attack. (The Russians are always assumed to strike first.) And then hardened (stationary) silos came into the argument. But the experts at once saw that that wouldn't work. The megatons would go through them like cheesecake.

The Air Force timetable puts the first MX missile flight in 1983, initial operation of the system in 1986, and completion in 1989. ("Completion" means what?) In 1981 the U.S. Air Force funding request would be about $2 billion for engineering development of the basing system. What the Air Force calls the largest construction project ever undertaken would strain the supplies of water, cement, electricity and construction materials available in the Southwest.

And what effect will this infantile game of hide-and-seek have upon the Russians? Its threat could plainly cause the Soviet Union to hasten its development of qualitative nuclear weapon improvements. But, as a vastly richer country, which, unlike the Soviet Union, gained considerable financial and commercial momentum as a result of the last war, the United States can pursue—and is pursuing—a beggar-my-neighbor policy against the Soviet Union, whose struggling economy has long been a figure of fun for American cold warriors and cartoonists.

Studies of the Soviet economy reveal that Moscow has been able to meet each new threat from the Pentagon only by heavy economic and social sacrifices. Nowadays almost half the machinery produced in the Soviet Union is military equipment of some sort. This represents an alarming diversion of resources from investment badly needed to modernize Soviet industry. The Soviet Union has already paid a high price to catch up militarily with the West. But it will have to pay an even higher price to hang on to that position if military competition continues at this rate.

Investment to maintain equality with America in such a new

round of weapons competition in the 1980s would have to be taken from diminishing funds. The Soviet Union is well behind America in such new technological development, as, for example, "miniaturization." What will happen to the Soviet economy over the next ten years is that it will grow at a slower pace. During the 1980s this could be between three and three and a half percent a year, which, as it happens, would be the same as is expected for the industrialized West. In other words, it will be Soviet citizens who will be the victims of the American build-up of these current weapons of mass destruction. But perhaps that is all part of the game? It will be noted that President Reagan did not include this already budgeted buildup in his November 1981 offer to Moscow. He only promised to forgo the 572 new "theater" weapons.

The depressing world economic outlook for the next two years or more, however, throws a deepening shadow over all the industrialized West. In Britain, for example, Treasury economists warned the Chancellor that output in Britain might fall by as much as three and a half percent in 1980, with a further drop in 1981. In one of the most depressing pre-Budget economic assessments ever made, they also gave a warning that the Government faces a possible deficit in 1981 of £9,500 million. The forecast for the drop in output foresees such a severe recession over at least three years ahead that it started a new round of soul-searching within the Treasury in 1980 about the forecasting techniques used to predict the future. While, in the United States, the new President, elected in November 1980, faces an economic challenge far more urgent and realistic than the perennial "Russian threat" to which he devoted his election speeches. The U.N. Economic Commission for Europe warned in March 1982 that tight-money policies were leading to a world depression.

The scientific ingenuity and the mammoth expenditure to which President Carter *had* to give the OK, was marked, though, in his farewell address in January 1981, when he called for an end to the arms race, which would have provided clinics, schools and shelter for the earth's 500 million sick and needy children.

There is a further forgotten aspect of this digging of future graveyards for our children. The current world population is about 4,000 million. Yet, if present population trends continue there will be double that number—8,000 million people—on earth *in only 35 years' time*. Our present diminishing land and food resources could not support them. This is because for many years thoughtless people and blind statesmen all over the world have been plundering and polluting the earth's natural resources on land, in the air, on the rivers, and in and under the sea at such a rate as to pose a serious threat to the environment, which supports all forms of life. While the U.N. Environment Program (UNEP) is starved of funds, equipment, and personnel, the military pollutionists are now driving up inflation in the U.S. by turning needed land into a vast cemetery.

And yet another forgotten aspect: pollution of the atmosphere and the reduction of the vital protective ozone layer around the earth present two other perils. Scientists warn that, if continued unchecked, these trends could so vitiate our biosphere that ultimately its capacity to support life might be destroyed. What happens to mankind when MX missiles and the rest of the man-made military poisons have eliminated the ozone layer protecting all life on earth?

The Trident is no mere sea-urchin! It is a nuclear-powered submarine over two football fields in length and five storys high, more than twice the size of the Polaris and Poseidon submarines. It will carry as many as 24 nuclear missiles, each equipped with 17 independently targetable warheads. It is designed to wreak thermo-nuclear havoc on 408 separate targets by hurling 75–100 kilotons of explosive power at each one with nearly pinpoint (90 foot) accuracy. The U.S. Navy plans 30 of these monstrosities to act for the rest of the century as a sea-leg of the strategic triad, ensuring American nuclear superiority over the U.S.S.R. and providing an integral component in a potential *first strike* nuclear capability.

Britain is being pressured to buy five of them, plus the 160 land-based killers under the 1979 NATO-Pentagon compact made in Brussels. There are, however, rumors of disagreement in the Cabinet and growing hostility from the Army as well as the RAF. The penny is now beginning to drop, in more senses than one. Given Britain's economic predicament, with three million unemployed, are the British now going to be able to afford Trident without huge cut-backs in equipment to the other two services? "The government remains convinced that no other choice but Trident-2 will provide a credible nuclear deterrent into the year 2000 and beyond," Defense Secretary John Nott said in a statement to Parliament in March 1982.

The relative invulnerability of submarines makes them an important part of the U.S. "defensive" arsenal, since submarines could survive a nuclear attack—in theory—and would be able to retaliate. So the Pentagon tells us. The existing Polaris and Poseidon submarines were *already* capable of obliterating scores of cities with their multiple warheads. The main difference between them and Trident lies in the greater number, power, and accuracy of its missiles. And the Trident missile will double the Poseidon's 2,000-mile range. But it won't stop even there—unless we stop the arms race.

And the effect on the U.S.S.R.? We have already noted that they are going one better. Trident will clearly be perceived by the Russians as transforming U.S. submarines from (so-called) retaliatory weapons into *offensive* weapons, with "silo-busting" potential. Submarines don't fight submarines, any more than tanks normally fight tanks; so the "balance" doctrine does not apply. The "balance of power" blew up with the First World War and left ten million dead. "They" are now trying to balance submarines, which alone would leave ten *billion* dead.

Each Trident will cost over 1.7 billion dollars. Total program costs are expected to exceed $30 billion. Some $8.8 billion has been spent to date. The U.S. program is already a year behind schedule, as well as 50 percent over its original budget! As with Britain, such massive costs threaten the U.S. Navy financially, for half its shipbuilding budget is being spent on this one ship alone. General Dynamics is building the Trident in Groton, Connecticut. But the major missile contractor is Lockheed. Over 25 other companies, including Westinghouse, GE, RCA and IBM have current contracts. Congressional hawks have many brokers among their constituents.

Finally, we come to the Cruise missile, which recalls a sinister memory for the British people, who—unlike the Americans—sat for ten months under the Nazis' V1 and V2 onslaught from the occupied Netherlands. No language was strong enough in the 1940s to excoriate these fiendish weapons, serviced so well by a certain Wernher von Braun, before his promotion to a more honorable spot in the U.S. rocket service. (Except that the Cruise missile will leave behind it, not just a crumbled housing block—as one saw in London streets—but a desolation wider than Hiroshima and Nagasaki combined!)

The Cruise missile is a small, subsonic, pilotless aeroplane, 14 to 20 feet long. It flies at tree-top level, eluding enemy radar, guiding itself to the target by means of a tiny computer which is supposed to match terrain features against computerized maps. It is relatively cheap and can be launched from almost any vehicle on land, sea or in the air. Yet Cruise missiles are expected to carry large warheads to within 100 feet of the target.

Critics have warned that Cruise missiles, like the neutron bomb, would lower the "nuclear threshold" and make nuclear war more likely and "thinkable," because they *look* less forbidding than a huge ballistic missile. Thefts and accidents would also be a risk if the missiles were dispersed widely. It is a perfect godsend to terrorists! Nations with a "nuclear capability" could use versions of the Cruise missile as delivery systems for nuclear bombs, so that, by the end of the century, a dozen countries could have them cheaply—mass-produced mass-murderers. A short-term American advantage could thus turn into a perilous long-term liability for everyone.

Safety questions have already been raised about this venomous missile, designed to duck below enemy radar and weave its way 1,000 miles over varied terrain to deliver a nuclear warhead. However, in December 1979, an unarmed missile weaved instead into a hillside in California and another veered into a cattle range. Both had been fired from a B-52 bomber about 400 miles off the California coast; both missiles were supposed to end up at a Utah test site. Three of five offshore launches crashed (one dropped into the ocean) and, in all, seven missiles had gone down out of the 16 in aircraft-launched tests.

These crashes raised questions not only about the effectiveness of the Cruise missile, but also about the safety of citizens living near its test path (*International Herald Tribune*, 4 January 1980). When Shakespeare warned: "Put not your trust in princes," he might have added, "nor generals." In this case General Dynamics might be appropriately listed, as the three offshore mislaunches had come from their workshops. (We might recall President Carter's unfortunate helicopters being caught in an Iranian sandstorm!)

Boeing and General Dynamics are currently building competing versions of the Cruise missile for the U.S. Air Force and Navy—and for faithful NATO. McDonnell Douglas has been working on the guidance system, and Williams Research Corporation holds a contract for Cruise missile engines. Many other companies will be involved. *If* the weapon goes into serious production.

The Cruise missiles that NATO proposes to station in Britain from 1983 may be housed on two of the seven existing U.S. Air Force bases, if they are still there! The individual missile launchers are mobile, so if war even *threatened*—or another six-minute "red alert" is sprung—they would be scattered across the countryside. But to minimize the environmental impact of this (to the British) too painfully nostalgic weapon, the deployment plans now being prepared in the Ministry of Defense have envisaged concentrating them in two or three locations from which U.S.A.F. F-111 bombers, armed with nuclear weapons, already operate.

Fortunately, there is a growing vocal opposition in Britain to these super-sized V1s and V2s. For example, 88 university faculty members wrote to *The Times* on 13 February 1980 in these specific terms:

> The likelihood of a nuclear war is now greater than at any time since October 1962. Both the super-powers have contributed to this terrifying state of affairs: the Soviet Union by its intervention in Afghanistan, the United States by its proposed installation of a "new generation" of nuclear weapons in Europe.
>
> Neither event is irreversible. While we can actively press for Soviet withdrawal from Afghanistan we can also repudiate the Brussels agreement to station Cruise missiles on British soil. These missiles multiply the lethal dangers of accident or miscalculation, make a "local" or "theater" nuclear war the most likely, and make it especially likely that this country will be a target in such a war.
>
> We, the undersigned, appeal to the Government to keep Cruise missiles out of the United Kingdom.

The signatories also state that "should the Government refuse to do so, we urge the British people to join us in contesting the installation of such missiles."

By the end of 1980, the public response was visibly growing. A mass demonstration of CND in central London was crowned by the leader of the Labor Party, Michael Foot, stating categorically that, if the present Government accepted the Cruise missiles from the Pentagon, a Labour Government, if elected, would send them back. The Barons of Brussels were dumbfounded, but couldn't blame the Communists this time!

A typical letter of protest ends: "Millions of us in Britain and the rest of Europe have come to realise that both Cruise missiles and the neutron bomb have been devised as "'first

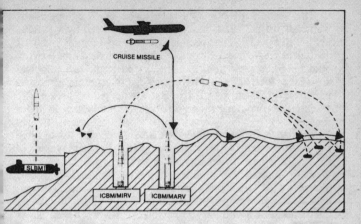

CRUISE MISSILE

SLBM

ICBM/MIRV ICBM/MARV

Fig. 5 The threat from land, sea and air.
Source: UNESCO Courier

strike'" weapons. Housing them here makes us vulnerable to
nuclear attack. If we allow our Government to be a party to
agreements with the United States which allow the possibility
of the use of "'theatre'" nuclear weapons, we are condoning a
moral outrage far worse than anything perpetrated by Hitler
and his Nazi supporters." (*The Observer*, London, 8 November
1981.) When, in March 1982, Trident was approved, the Labor
opposition immediately denounced the decision. "The next Labor
Government will cancel the Trident project," said John Silkin,
Labor's defense spokesman.

This is the voice of democracy. This is the voice of reason.
As it is echoed in more and more countries, the weight of added
fear will be lifted from people's minds. Belgium, Denmark and
Holland have already—and unilaterally—said "No."

President Reagan's bullish remarks about the possibility of
a nuclear war confined to Europe have increased suspicions
about the United States. The latest poll shows that a majority
(57 percent) thought Reagan's foreign policy was making nuclear war "more likely," whereas only 8 percent thought it was
making it "less likely." Distrust of the American military was
also reflected in answers to a question as to who was most
likely to *start* a nuclear war, if there were one. While Russia
emerged as the principal villain with 35 percent, 29 percent
thought it would be America.

The scandal of NATO's acceptance of 572 "upgraded" warheads for the 1980s has yet to be appreciated by a gullible public. But the U.S. had promised to start negotiating SALT III as soon as the Senate had completed SALT II: next time striving both for force *reductions* and for an end to the technological arms race. SALT II *could* have provided momentum for reaching these goals in SALT III. But strong public pressure is essential to encourage such initiatives. Will this happen under Reagan?

The 1980s plan to upgrade NATO's European missile force has been blamed, as we noticed, on Russia's deployment of the SS-20, a new rocket capable of striking targets throughout Western Europe from mobile bases in the Soviet Union. The 572 new NATO weapons are to be American-owned *and operated*, and are being produced to the usual refrain: to prevent the creation of a "military imbalance." In NATO eyes, however, America's .(somewhat suspect) commitment to defend Europe will be more credible, it is argued, now that its "forward" weapons are not on *American* soil, which the U.S. might be hesitant to use for fear of retaliation against its own heartland. Yet their presence, parked beside British motorways, would be a reminder of what America's *British* shield would suffer in even a "limited" nuclear war. This fact gives a new meaning to the despised word "unilateral."

These new proposals [points out the Committee for a Sane Nuclear Policy, Washington] undermine the spirit of agreements reached in the Strategic Arms limitation talks between the United States and the Soviet Union. For more than ten years now, American and Soviet negotiators have worked out agreements based on the principle that the nuclear forces they aim at other should be approximately equal. The Soviets have agreed to leave until later the complicated question of U.S. weapons systems able to reach the Soviet Union from bases *outside* the United States.

The military balance is not so fragile (says SANE) that the United States cannot afford to explore the possibility of negotiating limits on *new* nuclear weapons. And, in the light of Soviet President Brezhnev's own proposal at a WAPO summit held in Warsaw in May 1980 to *begin* such negotiations, "the

70

U.S. is obligated to pursue mutual arms reduction *before* deciding to go ahead with any major new plans."

But no-one can deny that there is a basic difference between the two systems. A detailed catalog of U.S. firms producing hard weaponry runs to many pages of fine print. A really substantial reduction in arms *at this point* would break the American economy; but it would bolster the Soviet economy. That is why arms *conversion*, not "control" has become the No. 1 priority for the United States economy. That elusive word "control" is being spouted by the media and the politicians as though it meant something real. It merely postpones decisions on *conversion*, which does mean *disarmament*. When our NATO leaders begin to discuss conversion, not before, we shall know that they are serious about arms *reduction*. (See Chapter V.)

Hardliner Professor Richard Pipes of Harvard University has stated: "the Soviet military take the prospect of strategic war with the United States seriously, and they are developing what is known as a 'war-fighting' and 'war-winning' strategy for it. This evidence, of course, has considerable bearing on our own strategic posture in general, and on our approach to SALT in particular." This reasoning seems incontrovertible, if we study in depth the development of Russian "defense" policy since World War II. It is the U.S. that is calling the tune, however, though insisting that it is all a reaction to Moscow.

Nonetheless, what we are more concerned with in this book is not to deplore and magnify the war threats of Moscow, but to ask whether the West has no wiser peace strategy of its own? There can be no doubt that the NATO decision in November 1979 to hit the jack-pot with these 572 "upgraded" weapons will leave the Russians little choice but to pursue their own suicidal policy to beat the winner.

This "beat the winner" mentality has for too long disastrously pervaded both sides. First, Moscow's brutal and ill-judged invasion of Afghanistan brought not only a rude shock to their self confidence about "détente," but more significantly an unexpectedly strong U.N. General Assembly solidarity of 104 votes, to only 18 against and 18 abstentions. But, second, poor Carter's intricate counter-move to placate his own back-woodsmen, to switch the seat of the 1980 Olympic Games, could hardly have revealed more pitifully the mess that the arms race has brought upon bewildered statesmen! The high purpose and ethics of this traditionally recurring event, involving all countries and peoples, was thus perverted and debased by being dragged into the NATO/WAPO cockpit.

The modern revival of the Olympic Games had already been exploited as a showpiece of tribal egotism and national glorification. That further degradation of the 1980 games by the U.S. government and some other countries was a salutary warning of how hysterical national statesmen can become when confronted by another nation's folly. Our television screens are resplendent with national flags and martial anthems sung *ad nauseam*, not to the glory of the individual champions (as Pindar did in timeless verse over two millennia ago), but to the governments which sponsor and finance them. Thus, an ancient festival of joy has become a modern theater of chauvinism.

It was the *individual* who won in the glory of his manhood; his crown of laurel had no economic worth. For a thousand years, beginning in 776 BC, the poets and dramatists of the whole Mediterranean world emblazoned his name in gold for posterity. The Games were, in fact, religious festivals. A Truce of God was proclaimed if wars between the city states coincided with them. Not only field events, but music and drama, sculpture and dancing—all the friendly arts—brought the cream of Hellenic culture together into a universal ceremonial, where the gods were the most honored spectators.

What a chance was missed, in this atmosphere of twentieth-century military rivalry, not to respond when the Prime Minister of Greece proposed that the Games come back to their neutral homeland! In fact, in November 1980, experts sent by the International Olympic Committee to evaluate President Karamanlis's proposal to give the Olympic Games a permanent home near their ancient birthplace chose Kaiafa, on a picturesque lagoon along the western coast.

As we approach the twenty-first century, are we not prostituting our common civilization and rich inheritance to the same martial slogans and nationalist anthems that emerged along with the sovereign states and greedy empires of the 18th and 19th centuries? Is there not richer music that "We the peoples" can join *together* in? For example, Beethoven's Ninth ("Ode to Joy") or in the United Nations anthem that world citizen Pablo Casals has composed? In calling the Olympics back home to Greece, a former British athlete, Christopher Brasher, tells of his personal vision, far beyond the cold-war-mongers of the 1980s, when he writes: "They carried no flags, they represented no nation, no ideology, no political system. Each was an individual, entire unto himself . . . These individuals spoke many languages, but they understood one another, for they spoke the common language of sport" (*Observer*, 3 February 1980).

(4) Non-proliferation at risk

In a decision on 3 August 1978 that could affect thousands of former soldiers, the U.S. Veterans' Appeals Board decided to award service-connected disability benefits to an Army veteran suffering from leukemia, who claimed that his illness resulted from exposure to radiation during 1957 nuclear weapons tests. He was one of 300,000 servicemen who took part in nuclear weapons tests in Nevada or in the Pacific between 1948 and 1958. Other soldiers were witnesses to nuclear explosions. Moreover, according to the *Washington Post*, about 2,400 former soldiers, who participated in the tests, reported to the Defense Department that they had subsequently become ill either with leukemia or some other form of cancer.

The Veterans' Appeals Board found that "it is reasonably probable" that the radiation exposure during the 1957 weapons test, called "Smoky," was a competent causative factor of disease, even though the leukemia appeared many years after exposure and after the veteran's retirement from service.

The cases of Donald Coe and of Paul Cooper, another ex-GI at the Smoky test, had been the first to focus public interest on a connection between low-level radiation exposure of nuclear test participants and subsequent development of leukemia and other forms of cancer. Mr. Cooper died of leukemia in February 1978.

The "peaceful" uses of nuclear energy fall beyond the scope of this book, but Dr. Keith Suter of the University of Sydney makes another relevant point: "In the continuing search for new dimensions in terror, for new vulnerabilities and pressure points, terrorists may find an unexpected ally in the growing nuclear power industry. Special nuclear materials and facilities offer terrorists the potential for considerable political leverage. Indeed, already nuclear installations have been attacked" (*Uranium, the Law and You*, 1978).

This brings us, again to consider the steps now being taken

in the broader political field by the U.N. The Non-proliferation Treaty (NPT) of 1968 to stop "proliferation" of nuclear weapons, sets up safeguards against even assumed "peaceful" uses of the perilous atom. Alas, the line between war use and peace use is becoming an increasingly thin one!

Britain began producing its own highly enriched uranium in 1980, suitable for use in nuclear weapons. A special plant ·is· to be built for the Ministry of Defense by British Nuclear Fuels at Capenhurst, Cheshire, subject to planning permission. The purpose of the new facility is allegedly to produce fuel suitable for the propulsion of the Navy's nuclear-powered submarines. But it is arguable that the Government is considering a new generation of nuclear weapons for the 1990s.

Uranium in its natural state contains only 0.71 percent of the isotope U-235. It has to be enriched until it contains about 4.5 percent for civil power plants—or about 97 percent for nuclear weapons. The Ministry has given several reasons for the sudden decision to switch to a home-made product. But outside experts think that the Ministry, in the long term, is more interested in developing Britain's nuclear weapons programs as less dependent upon the United States.

The International Atomic Energy Agency (IAEA) has the central responsibility for keeping the fragile war/peace line intact. As a result of safeguards agreements under the NPT, the Agency's safeguard coverage today is very extensive. There are only four states in the world, besides the nuclear-weapon states, that have significant nuclear activities *not* subject to Agency safeguards, namely India, Israel, South Africa and Spain. As already noted in the present chapter, it is ironic that one of these four noncooperative states—Israel—should have been guilty in 1981 of committing an unprovoked military outrage against one of the compliant and duly monitored signatory states, namely Iraq.

Nevertheless, any state that is not a party to NPT or the Tlatelolco Treaty is legally free to build or otherwise acquire unsafeguarded nuclear plants. The NPT requires each non-nuclear weapon state party to conclude a safeguards agreement with this U.N. Agency, covering all of the state's peaceful nuclear activities. Fifty-five states have wisely done so and have safeguards agreements in force. They are not perfect, but they advance the rule of law.

Small concessions to the new international order are thus steadily being made all the time. An agreement between the

74

United Kingdom, the European Atomic Energy Community (EURATOM) and the International Atomic Energy Agency (IAEA) for the application of safeguards in the United Kingdom under the Treaty, entered into force on 17 July 1978. By the terms of the agreement, the IAEA has the right to apply safeguards on sources of special fissionable material in nuclear facilities in the United Kingdom, subject only to exclusions for national security reasons. (The UK decides, of course, *what* the latter are!)

The spill-over of the nuclear weapons business is too complicated for us to follow here. But those few academics and retired generals who still envisage World War III, wearing World War II uniforms, might consider the *known* biological effects of ionizing radiation on human beings, even beyond the scope of their "defensive" weapons. There is growing alarm that hundreds of thousands of persons may risk long-term cancer from exposure to smaller doses of radiation than had previously been considered harmful.

For example, the U.S. Government restricts workers' annual radiation exposure to five rems, long believed to have been a safe limit. (Five rems equals more than 166 chest X-rays.) But scientists and Congress are now reassessing the occupational exposure limit. Several recent disclosures have raised a warning flag, because the cancer victims involved were supposedly exposed to less than five rems a year.

Meantime, a study of naval shipyard workers in Portsmouth, New Hampshire, has suggested that the nation's 36,400 nuclear submarine workers have six times more chance of developing leukemia than the general population. Again, at least eight cases of leukemia have been reported among the former military men involved in nuclear bomb test blasts between 1945 and 1962. Reports of harm to people employed in nuclear power plants will surely exacerbate fear of the plants to nearby communities. And then there are what are known as Three Mile Island risks.

What of the terrorist who imagines he can somehow cow or "control" his government, in the same way that the more sophisticated hawks imagine that they can stop communism or liquidate capitalism by a few well-placed warheads? Not least there are constant dangers to human rights, implicit in the development of nuclear power, particularly from fast-breeder reactors leading to a "plutonium economy." A plutonium bomb could be made from a few kilograms of plutonium, a material which can safely be handled with rubber gloves. Extraordinary precautions would have to be taken to prevent such material getting into the hands of "civilian" terrorists.

Professor Alan F. Westin has stated in a report published by the Office of Technology Assessment of Congress: "As incidents of non-nuclear terrorism have mounted world-wide, and as assaults have been made on nuclear facilities in several countries by various radical groups, there has been an increased program to safeguard such facilities from actions such as sabotage and deliberate release of radioactive materials." Excellent advice! Why should not governments institute a program to safeguard all of us from the infinitely greater terrorism of the nuclear arms race?

Only when the new "peace" movements have had time and capacity to build up a vigorous world public opinion that reacts to nuclear weapons and to nuclear-war policies with the same sense of outrage and repugnance with which normal people now reject cholera and other contagious diseases, will this planet be secure from these man-made inflictions.

In 1980 the second five-year review conference of the nuclear Non-proliferation Treaty took place in Geneva. However, the 107 signatories found little cause for self-congratulation. An assessment from the Swedish International Peace Research Institute (SIPRI) ran: "NPT is gradually being eroded, mainly because of the inconsistent policies of the nuclear material *suppliers* and the non-fulfilment of the disarmament obligations undertaken by the nuclear weapons Powers."

The most important clause of the 1968 Treaty declares that countries possessing nuclear weapons should not transfer them to anyone else. But by weapons the treaty means warheads, not their delivery systems. This type of vagueness has made the proliferation issue very easy to undermine. Non-nuclear powers wishing to purchase nuclear technology have to accept safeguards laid down by the NPT, and these safeguards include having their installations inspected by teams from the IAEA, as indicated above.

So there are two kinds of violation. One is *vertical* proliferation, whereby the superpowers increase their own arsenals, contrary to their obligations under the treaty to reduce them. Then there is *horizontal* proliferation—the acquisition of nuclear warheads by nations that previously had none. Third World countries without nuclear weapons have recently had some bad examples set them by such non-signatories as Israel and South Africa. (The names of these two countries were also linked together when a mysterious explosion took place in the Southern Indian Ocean in 1979.) But undoubtedly the first major setback to NPT took place on 18 May 1974 when India exploded a 15 kiloton device. The plutonium for this test had been acquired by circumventing restrictions imposed by the Canadians, who sold them a powerful research reactor, not subject to IAEA safeguards. Indian nuclear engineers then produced their own fuel, claiming that the Canadian fuel was their own.

The danger of civilian atomic energy programs leading to proliferation of nuclear weapons is the most important aspect of the nuclear power debate. According to a group of 35 eminent industrialists, politicians and academics from the EEC, America and Japan, the over-capacity in the nuclear construction industries in Europe and America, which are almost facing bankruptcy, is an inducement to export material that might lead to proliferation (*The Times*, 26 January 1981).

It was noted above that India is not a signatory of NPT. Since U.S. policy has—until the Afghan crisis—been wisely to prevent the spread of atomic weapons *horizontally*, uranium shipments to India were held up in 1980, to the consternation of the Indian nuclear planners. But to remove this source of limitation, while seeking Delhi's cooperation against Russia's Afghan invasion, President Carter gave the green light in May 1980 for 38 tons of enriched uranium to be shipped to Tarapur nuclear power station north of Bombay. Whether this is or is not a violation of the U.S. Non-proliferation Act is in dispute. Domestic politics and international law are poor bedpartners.

It is getting more difficult for other countries not to join the nuclear club. Pakistan is well on the way to having its first test. President Zia ul-Haq (just like the Indians) has insisted that his program is for peaceful purposes. Moreover, other Muslim states have been trying to acquire nuclear weapons to match the arsenal of atomic bombs that Israel is widely assumed to have manufactured out of a shipload of stolen uranium.

A U.N. report estimates that 150,000 people have been killed or will die from nuclear *tests* that have already taken place. The study, prepared by an international group of experts, says 90 percent of the victims are from the Northern Hemisphere. Professor Josef Goldblat, a scientist who worked on the Hiroshima bomb, points out that: "Nuclear tests, unlike medical X-rays, do not serve any useful purpose for man. On the contrary, these tests are part of the arms race, which will eventually lead to nuclear war." Later in this book we shall consider the case for the NTB—the nuclear test ban.

But the race goes on. Fridtjof Nansen, the Arctic explorer, humanitarian and founder of the world's first refugee organization, once said: "Though statesmen appear to their own people as moral men, when it comes to relations between nations, they behave like a den of thieves."

(5) How World War III might begin

Although old-fashioned generals would prefer World War III to begin at the eastern frontier of NATO to suit the expectation of the NATO war games, the event would be likely to be quite different. Some non-aligned world leaders are speculating, in fact, that World War III has already begun and that it has begun in their territories, where the big powers are now sparring for position. Iranian women were being trained to expect an invasion in 1980. But the invasion occurred next door! This bears out the warning of Clausewitz that war is like a "gambling game." That is why NATO's war games (and WAPO's) fall into the category of the lowest comedy.

Singapore's foreign minister, Sinnthamby Rajaratnam, told the 110-member Conference of Non-Aligned Nations at Belgrade in July 1978, that they should unite and block the nuclear giants from skirmishing on *their* territory. ("Workers of the Third World unite, you have nothing to lose but your wars!") He pointed out that the "nuclear balance of terror," following World War II, had *ruled out* Europe and North America as the battleground of a third world war. So the threat had been moved to other areas of the globe that had more or less been spared the first two wars. A plague-on-both-your-houses policy was therefore the most sensible way to prevent it from ever beginning. But this speculation was put out of serious circulation in 1981, when Reagan sprang his "limited"-nuclear-war surprise on an indignant Europe.

Yet World War III might not begin in the Third World at all. "The danger of war by accident . . . grows as modern weapons become more complex, command and control difficulties increase, and the premium is on ever-faster reaction." This was the verdict of Dean Rusk, U.S. Secretary of State, as long ago as 1962. And it can start any day of the week with someone's brainstorm. The *Guardian* reported (9 October 1975) that one young officer of the U.S. base at Omaha, Nebraska, put it this way: "We have two tasks. The first is not to let people go off their rockers. That's the negative side. The positive one is to ensure that people act without moral compunction."

Dr. John Cox comments in a timely book (*Overkill*, 1977) on this attitude:

> Imagine being cooped up in a submarine for three months on end, never seeing daylight and sleeping next to weapons of mass destruction. Such conditions are not normal and they can create special psychiatric problems. Similarly, those who man missile silos go down into the bowels of the earth each day to check missiles whose purpose is to kill thousands of people at the press of a button. These men undergo regular psychiatric checks and often become disturbed mentally.

A New York psychiatrist, Dr. Jonathan Serxner, has investigated the mental state of Polaris submarine crews. Despite lectures, classes, cinema shows, and other entertainments, religious services and a library, he found feuds and various minor psychiatric disturbances. About one in twenty of the men needed treatment. There was a chief petty officer who, after five weeks at sea, had delusions of persecution and heard voices. He was given heavy sedation and later transferred from the submarine service.

Where has the glory of war gone? The "spit-and-polish," the smart uniforms? Haven't we now entered a less-romantic age? Are we not calling for a new breed of men to face and conquer real problems? That is, to meet the challenge of world peace?

Nor is it only the people in charge of the missiles and submarines that could cause an inadvertent nuclear explosion. Thousands of tactical nuclear weapons are scattered around Europe under the control of field commanders. Although their working conditions are not as claustrophobic as those of the submarine and missile silo crews, they also can suffer mental disorders. In 1972 a homesick U.S. pilot climbed into a bomber aircraft at an H-bomb base in East Anglia, flew off and crashed in the English Channel, "pursued" by other American Air Force planes.

And it is not just the men subjected to these appalling conditions of stress who are in the psychological firing line. Lord Montgomery wrote in a professional services journal: "if we are attacked, we use nuclear weapons in our defense. That is agreed; the only proviso is that the politicians have to be asked first. That might be a bit awkward, of course, and personally I would use the weapons first and ask afterwards."

Then an early "warning" might turn out to be the real thing. The whole of the North Pole and Arctic is one network of sophisticated gadgets, any one of which may go wrong. Cases are on record where a moon echo has been interpreted as a Soviet movement of missiles and a flight of geese going to warmer climes for the winter has been mistaken for a hostile fighter bomber. These are small—some might say ridiculous—errors, but what used to be called "national security" now rests on flights of imagination in insecure individuals who, in normal relationships, would be treated as moonstruck and therefore to be avoided at all costs.

Freud had a good deal to say about this fetish called "national security"—a thinly disguised death-wish conveniently transferred on to the "enemy." "Throughout the life of the individual," he wrote in *Civilization, War and Death*, "there is a constant replacement of the external compulsion by the internal."

Professor Norman O. Brown in *Life Against Death*, says:

It is a shattering experience for anyone seriously committed to the Western traditions of morality and rationality to take a steadfast, unflinching look at what Freud has to say. It is humiliating to be compelled to admit the grossly seamy side of so many grand ideas . . . Freud was right: our real desires are unconscious. It also begins to be apparent that mankind, unconscious of its real desires and therefore unable to obtain satisfaction, is hostile to life and ready to destroy itself. [And he adds:] Freud was right in positing a death instinct, and the development of weapons of destruction makes our present dilemma plain: we either come to terms with our unconscious instincts and drives—with life and with death—or else we surely die.

The biggest of our modern fantasies, perhaps, is the belief that "military intelligence" *is* intelligent. Just fancy that the British should have once entrusted their safety, or our victory in war, to Philby, Burgess, and Maclean! The spate of books that have appeared recently—for James Bond still makes popular newsprint—on the past antics of these spies have also revealed that such cloak-and-dagger period pieces are *still* an essential part of our Foreign Office and MI6 diplomatic scenarios. Will it take another 20 years for the grotesque network of lies and spies and mutual deceit, that bolsters the continuing arms race, to be revealed as the best financed tragi-comedy of the 1980s?

The two most astonishing curiosities of our present pro-war window-dressing machine, however, are firstly that it is the enemy's successes that are boosted up and exaggerated to frighten us, while our own failures are featured most abjectly; and, secondly, that this propaganda-in-reverse is not directed against the enemy (for he has surely a surfeit of his own) but against our own citizens. So the common people, whose taxes support it, lose on both the swings and the roundabouts.

And where do our policy advisers get their facts? The International Institute for Strategic Studies, writes Andrew Wilson (*Observer*, 14 December 1980), has been severely criticized by Admiral Gene La Rocque for having erred over details of U.S. strength. "We have carefully examined the U.S. section of their *Military Balance, 1980–81*," said the retired Admiral. "There are numerous discrepancies between accurate official U.S. information and the numbers contained in the IISS publication. In this effort we have identified over 100 items of dubious accuracy."

Among the detailed corrections of fact, Admiral La Rocque gives the figure for the total of U.S. strategic nuclear warheads (which was wrongly given in the London publication as 7,301) as 9,200. The Institute also has since deleted the listing of 400 Hound Dog air-to-surface missiles under U.S. strategic air strength, as the missile was withdrawn from service two years ago. A third admitted error involved American servicemen in Europe: "We have a figure of 206,400. We have now been informed by U.S. official sources that the figure should be 214,165," says the Institute. We have long heard statistics defined as "damned lies." But how much of our nuclear "defense" is just that? Relying too on faulty computers?

Juggling with figures, to show that the other man is wrong, is an essential part of the war game. When experts differ, how can the public believe what they are told?

As David Halberstam, a former *New York Times* journalist, points out: "There is an unwritten law of American journalism that states that the greater and more powerful the platform, the more carefully it must be used and the more closely it must adhere to the norms of American society, particularly the norms of the American Government." Thus, much of the American media have kept pace with the politicians over such major calamities as McCarthyism, segregation and Vietnam, when a much more detached and critical relationship would have saved many lives, as well as the nation's peace of mind.

Do we expect to find these faithful camp-followers then, exposing the shams and mistakes of the arms race? No! The American press, with rare exceptions, presents a built-in segment of the arms race itself. Every passing crisis—Angola, Ethiopia, Cuba, El Salvador, Iran, Afghanistan, Poland—is dealt with in terms of pressing *military* response and brazen power politics. Diplomatic correspondents fall over themselves explaining what the *next* military moves should be. So the public always expect the worst. After all, what have the writers to lose? No one reads last month's columns; but they have planted their poison of fear and bellicosity in the public mind. One excellent result of the European peace protests of 1981–82, however, was to give American journalism a new moral stimulus and a new yardstick to check the gross excesses of the arms racket.

It seems at times almost futile for U.N. appeals and UNESCO declarations to deplore and condemn national war propaganda and biased news reporting, while the average citizen is being fed daily with the worst of all worlds and a mental conditioning of fear and apprehension. As a recent case in point, the very healthy and long overdue series of improvements in labor relations in Poland in 1980, and especially the legal vindication by Polish court decisions of trade union freedoms, was dealt with by the media as shot and shell against the Soviet Union. When martial law was declared (internally) in February 1982, the U.S. suspended international disarmament negotiations in Madrid and Geneva, thus cementing future Polish interests more firmly with Russia's.

The sparks that could ignite World War III spring today, not only from the orthodox machinations of foreign offices, but from the uncontrollable chaos of internal disruption in a second or third rate power, that has neither the purpose nor means to commit external aggression. The invasion of Russian forces into Iran's close neighbor, following the bloody collapse of the Shah's regime—and Washington's "gut" response— should also warn us that an arms race out of control could guarantee that once East/West war begins—however "incidental" the cause or pretext—nothing can hold back the holocaust. Disarmament must begin *NOW* and build into a world campaign of drastic all-round *reduction* to the levels of purely domestic security, until this powder-train can no longer be ignited by an "accident."

The Afghanistan invasion highlights, too, how vulnerable are the U.S. concepts of its manifest destiny across the globe. President Carter in Washington delivered another of his stern warnings to the Soviet Union: "Let our position be absolutely clear," he said. "An attempt by any outside force to gain control of the Persian Gulf region will be regarded as an assault on the vital interests of the United States. *It will be repelled by any means necessary, including military force.*" Evidently the United States now regards the Gulf area, like Western Europe, Japan and the North Pole as falling under its private defense umbrella! And what do the Russians think? Didn't Yalta offer them an umbrella? But it was at least confined to East Europe.

Several Arabian Gulf states, destabilized by the Iran and Afghanistan incidents, are seeking a common Muslim policy opposing the U.S. pretensions in the Middle East, especially over Israel. Frontier clashes also continue between Angola and South Africa. The latter attempted to foul up negotiated steps in both Namibia and Zimbabwe toward their non-racial statehood. In January 1980, a Geneva Conference for a ceasefire and Namibian elections was wrecked by South African intransigence. Then China is already a nuclear weapon state; while India hesitates to produce a nuclear arsenal because of Pakistan, who might immediately follow suit, now backed by the U.S.

And finally, when asked recently what was the implication of U.S. nuclear weapons *remaining* in South Korea, President Carter answered that the implication was that they would be used "in case of necessity." Did "necessity" mean "if North Korea committed any aggression against South Korea?"

Mr. Carter did not suggest that he meant "only in case of *nuclear* aggression." Yet he could have been interpreted as saying that, from now on, the U.S. would be the *first* to use nuclear weapons against an ally of the Soviet Union, i.e. North Korea, if the U.S. deemed that military aggression were committed even by a non-nuclear power using only conventional weapons. And even, we might add, if the conventional aggression were not committed against America but against any one of its many allies, large or small, around the globe. President

83

Carter confirmed that he did mean exactly that in the course of his key policy speech before the General Assembly of the United Nations on 4 October 1977: "I hereby solemnly declare on behalf of the United States that we will not use nuclear weapons except in self-defense; that is, in circumstances of an actual nuclear *or conventional* attack on the United States, our territories or armed forces, or such an attack *on our allies*" (*New York Times*, 5 October 1977).

We cite these postulates of U.S. policy because *they* form the backdrop of Soviet policy. They emphasize the argument of this book that there can be, on the facts of the case, only one way to change Russian policy, and that is to change our own. This was once called the "Golden Rule." Two thousand years later it was written into the U.N. Charter. It is still there.

The secret illnesses of statesmen can be more dangerous than their secret diplomacy. A Frenchman has written a book on "The Sick Men who Govern Us" and he selects his specimens from two or three decades ago. But who can truly size up the Sick Men of the Nuclear Age? In the area of most potentially perilous conflicts today—the Middle East—where religious fanaticism is compounded with tribal chauvinism, well-founded rumors have emerged whether 400 pounds of stolen uranium had found its way into Israel's secret arsenal.

There is an increasing anxiety in Western and Eastern governments alike, and also in the Third World, to seek a peaceful long-term solution through the United Nations in the interests of *all* the parties involved in the Arab-Israeli conflict. This must be obvious to every thinking person. But does the stolen uranium encourage this kind of solution? Does it add to anyone's security? Will the Israeli Government elected in 1981 decide to seek solutions based on the U.N. Charter and international law, on which the State of Israel was founded?

Beneath all these speculations on the "unknowable"—the accidents of "things"—lies the immaturity of man, as man. The mere fact that brains and formal education and specialized training are being deliberately misemployed to devise ever more elaborate means to outwit or to counter massacre devices of an assumed enemy calls for a new order of "peace intelligence" of urgent and exceptional quality. We pursue the vital topic of peace education in Chapter VIII.

Americans have been misled for years about the number of serious accidents involving United States nuclear weapons.

According to a Washington official, a B-52 bomber jettisoned a 24-megaton nuclear bomb over Goldsboro, North Carolina, in 1961. He claimed that five of the bomb's six safety devices were knocked out when it hit the ground and only one electric switch prevented a nuclear explosion nearly 2,000 times more powerful than Hiroshima (*Observer*, 7 December 1980). There have been hundreds of less dangerous nuclear weapons accidents, code-named "Bent Spears," but according to Pentagon officials they have been deeply classified because of their "political sensitivity." Some of these accidents resulted in the rupture of nuclear weapons and the spilling of radioactive, cancer-causing plutonium across the territory of U.S. allies. But the governments concerned have managed to keep the incidents secret. People don't like to hear these stories.

It was not a "shot in the dark," therefore, when the director of the International Atomic Energy Agency (IAEA) told the NPT Conference in Geneva in August 1980 that it was within the bounds of possibility that an *accidental* nuclear explosion could be expected to occur in the very near future. Is this appalling catastrophe something that our timid politicians are unconsciously waiting for? Has human intelligence become so atrophied by the arms race that only some vast, sudden and unprecedented slaughter of perhaps millions of people can bring the rest of us to our senses to DO something before it is too late?

The "shot across the bows" doctrine proposed by General Haig of dropping a "warning" nuclear bomb, which so shocked the newspapers in the summer of 1981, was "old hat" even in the 1960s. Three variations were then being considered by NATO: to explode a nuclear warhead in a remote area of NATO itself; to fire a nuclear warhead into an unpopulated area of the Warsaw Pact, such as the Arctic wastes of the Soviet Union; or to fire a nuclear warhead so high into the atmosphere that it would "cause no damage." In 1966, General Norsted, Supreme Allied Commander Europe, told the American Congress that in the event of a "small" Warsaw Pact attack, one of the several possible U.S. plans for dealing with the situation would contemplate the use of "some limited numbers of small atomic weapons against carefully selected targets." And in 1969, when NATO committed itself to be prepared to use nuclear weapons *first*, if conventionally attacked, a NATO planner suggested that one option would be a strictly "limited" nuclear strike. The enemy command-and-control system would be spared, he said, so that *enemy* commanders could continue to give and receive instructions and control their forces! In 1975, Defense Secretary James Schlesinger said that NATO plans included firing between 10 and 40 nuclear warheads—to facilitate "negotiations"! These are the crackpots who make life-and-death decisions behind the scenes for millions of human beings, without consulting them or their elected governments!

II
Conventional Killers

During the four conferences convened by the International Red Cross Committee, which took place in Geneva from 1974 to 1977 on humanitarian law, the question arose as to the nature of wounds inflicted on the human body by modern weapons. Since this was hardly a topic for 150 or so governments to pursue while negotiating new protocols on the laws of war, the Swedish Government has agreed to sponsor a separate conference on the "wounding effects" of today's *conventional* weapons in 1982–83—the grim results of which are awaited.

(1) New generations of weapons
The term "conventional," like other military shorthand, covers a vast range of weapons causing unnecessary human suffering, which have long been prohibited by international law. We might start off with a few, though it is rather an unpleasant subject.

Belligerents in modern warfare are today using weapons which inflict agonizing and terrible suffering. These are quite apart from the nuclear weapons, described in Chapter I, whose radiation causes either death or awesome diseases. Our modern armory includes incendiary weapons, containing napalm and phosphorus, which produces dreadful burning; and also fragmentation and cluster bombs.

The latest generation of the latter consists of bombs containing pellets of plastic, which, having penetrated the human body, cannot be traced by X-ray. The Swedish delegate at the Conference of Government Experts on the Reaffirmation and Development of International Humanitarian Law Applicable in Armed Conflicts held in Geneva, on 4 May 1972, described this weapon in the following terms:

> This is a bouncing anti-personnel mine filled with fifteen pounds of plasticized white phosphorus. When activated, the main part of the mine is propelled about four meters into the air where it explodes, spewing burning white phosphorus in all directions with a radius of about 25 meters. The phosphorus has the quality of gluing to the body when burning, and cannot be scraped off, but must be cut out, leaving frightful wounds. Furthermore, it is highly toxic, poisoning the liver, the kidneys and the nervous system after absorption through the wound.*

Atrocious wounds are also caused by hypervelocity rifles, whose bullets become unstable on impact, tumbling in the wound and producing a large cavity. One of these is a bullet fired by the U.S. M-16 rifle which was described by an Australian surgical team as follows:

> *Case 1:* A Vietnamese civilian was brought in dead after receiving a single projectile from an M-16 in the right thigh. Autopsy showed that the bullet had torn its way through the obturator foramen and disintegrated in the abdomen, only fragments of about 0.5 mm being recovered. Within the abdomen it had wrenched the whole small bowel from its mesentry and had perforated the pancreas, stomach and spleen. Such an injury is comparable to that produced by an explosive missile.

> *Case 2:* A Vietnamese civilian running away from an American received seven shots in the leg, the buttock, the

*Cited in A. Cassese, *Rivista di Diritto Internazionale*, 1975

chest and the arm. The injuries outside the abdomen were minor, but several bullets must have penetrated the buttock, leaving a hole in the sacrum which accepted a fist. The rectum was transected and the small bowel perforated in eight places. Once more no trace of the projectiles could be found at laparotomy.*

It will be noted that these two cases refer to *civilians*. There were untold thousands like them, left behind to suffer after the heroes had returned home. But we can well ask: what existing legal restraints have been imposed on these categories of cruel weapons? Specific bans have either developed as rules of customary law, or were formulated in treaty provisions that have later passed into customary international law. These prohibitions are therefore applicable to all members of the international community. We can list here only a few of them.

Customary rules have developed ever since the early 1800s specifying that poisoned bullets, projectiles filled with glass and caustic lime, minced lead and chain-bullets are to be proscribed among "civilized peoples" because they caused needless suffering. Specific prohibitions are embodied in the St. Petersburg Declaration of 1868 on explosive projectiles under 400 grams weight. Article 23(a) of the 1899 and 1907 Hague Regulations on Land Warfare prohibited poison or poisoned weapons. The 1899 Hague Declaration on expanding "dum-dum" bullets and the 1899 Hague Declaration on asphyxiating and deleterious gases were supplemented by the 1925 Geneva Protocol. The 1899 and 1907 Hague Regulations on Land Warfare specifically stated that "it is especially forbidden . . . to employ arms, projectiles or material which are such as to cause superfluous injury."

We are now approaching the 21st century, but "superfluous injury" has become an accepted principle of national foreign policy. Two U.N. conferences were held in Geneva in 1977 and 1979 to attempt to draft a Convention prohibiting these weapons designed to cause "unnecessary" injury and suffering. The ostensible purpose of shooting the enemy's soldiers was presumably to put them out of action. International law accepted that activity in the conflict of sovereign states. But these fiendish weapons are now being made *and intended* to cause

*Dudley, "Civilian Battle Casualties in South Vietnam," *British Journal of Surgery, 5, 1968*

torture and death by horrible suffering. The recent Geneva Conferences, dominated by military advisers of 100 governments, adjourned without having agreed on a Convention. But 1980 saw a further session. Does the public care if nothing more is done?

The swift approach of the 21st century does not rule out in the military mind the possible resort to a favorite elimination device of the Borgias, namely, *poison*. Deadly poisons, including enough shellfish toxin to kill thousands of people, were recently found in a secret cache maintained by the CIA. Senator Frank Church revealed that the CIA kept both the shellfish toxin and a smaller amount of cobra venom "in direct contravention" of presidential orders. The Senator said he would eventually find out who in the CIA was responsible, and promised that his Senate Committee on Intelligence Operations would hold public hearings on the matter in spite of White House objections. A macabre story lay behind this revelation.

These poisons were reportedly developed for the CIA under the code name of "Project Naomi" during the 1950s. Senator Church said that he had no reason to think any of the toxins were actually used; but his Committee was investigating "one particular mission" that apparently never came to fruition, because the object of it was assassinated by other means. He was familiar with an allegation that some toxin was sent to Africa to kill Congolese Premier Patrice Lumumba in 1961, but that the shipment did not arrive in time!

A bigger shock ran through the United States when television viewers in September 1975 actually watched a U.S. Army private trying unsuccessfully to cover an obstacle course while under the influence of a chemical code-named BZ. The soldier could not make his arms reach parallel bars to cross a stream, or even walk through a line of trees without bumping into them.

This film, shown by the Pentagon on the CBS Walter Cronkite show, was shot at the Army's chemical warfare center at Edgewood Arsenal, Maryland. Since 1953 the center has apparently carried out experiments on nearly 7,000 servicemen, using agents ranging from LSD to lethal nerve gases. Public anger was aroused and Congressional hearings revealed that the Army never told its "guinea-pigs" what was being tested on them. It was reported that there was no "after-care" program. Three people are known to have died during the experiments, with, as yet, no explanation in two cases. Several others experienced a "flashback phenomenon" of deep depression, which led to at least two attempted suicides.

It should be emphasized that President Nixon ordered the destruction of biological weapons in 1969 following the signing by the U.S. of the International Treaty limiting biochemical warfare. But it was recently disclosed, as noted above, that the CIA had kept two containers of poison—extracted from shellfish and cobra venom—in a warehouse at Fort Dietrick, Maryland.

It was for biological experiments before that ban, however, that the Army recruited 2,000 Seventh Day Adventists who, as conscientious objectors because of their beliefs, had opted to go to the Army medical training center at Fort Sam Houston, Texas. They were given a briefing session by the director of the Army Medical Research Institute of Infectious Diseases, and 95 percent of those briefed volunteered as guinea-pigs. The exact nature of the substances tested on them is not known, but those who declined to join the testing became medical orderlies, and many were sent to Vietnam.

The Soviet Union attempted to influence (then) President Nixon in 1969 to halt *all* chemical and biological weapons development. They have pressed for this ever since, as U.N. records show. Their technique then was, it seems, to transmit information through double agents working for the FBI. The aim of the agents' messages was to persuade Mr. Nixon that *if the United States continued its build-up of chemical weapons*, especially nerve gas, the Soviet Union would be compelled to start a "crash program" to match U.S. capabilities. Mr. Nixon's decision to renounce U.S. use of biological weapons in November 1969 and later to curb chemical weapons in the U.S. arsenal was in any case good on its own merits.

In March 1980, the British got into the act, as spectators. General Bernard Rogers, supreme NATO Commander, urged in a BBC interview in London that the United States should begin "producing chemical weapons to deter the Kremlin from using them." We have heard this immoral advice before. The road to Hell is paved with good deterrence! Also the Western European Union (a military organization) recommended in May 1980 that "NATO's chemical weapon stocks should equal the assumed offensive capability of the Warsaw Pact *as a deterrent.*"

The absurdity, once again, of this proposed "balance" of chemical products, one side against the other, could hardly be more obvious. Happily, the same report recommends that NATO should "encourage bilateral and multilateral negotiations to ban the production, stock-piling and use of chemical weapons with adequate verification." As to what is "adequate" has held up negotiations for 20 years. National sovereignty—and not merely Russia's—has consistently blocked U.N. verification measures. In 1982 "nerve gas" (binary weapons) crept back into Washington's black boxes.

The question of chemical warfare has, in fact, been discussed intermittently at the U.N. throughout the 1950s and 1960s, usually in conjunction with biological weapons. The argument whether biological and chemical weapons should be dealt with separately was settled in 1971 by a draft Convention on the Prohibition of the Development, Production and Stockpiling of Bacteriological (Biological) and Toxin Weapons and on Their Destruction.

The General Assembly adopted a resolution urging adoption of that Convention. It contains an undertaking by the parties to negotiate an agreement "on effective measures for the prohibition of the production and stockpiling of chemical weapons and for their destruction," also on measures concerning equipment and means of delivery. There things seem to have stuck. But it came up once more at a Special Geneva Conference in April 1980. Again, the West was dragging its feet. On the last day of this Conference (this author was present) a red herring was dragged across the final proceedings about an alleged exposure of toxic gas materials in a town in Siberia. The Soviet delegate heatedly denied that this was an escape of war-making materials. But the rest was silence and Russian secrecy produced a crop of hysterical assertions. Nevertheless, the U.N.'s new Committee on Disarmament was still working on the subject in 1981, with few signs of an agreement.

Professor René Wadlow, a Geneva disarmament specialist, in answer to Washington's fears, has stated:

A serious presumption exists that poison gas is being used against the hill tribes in Laos and more widely in Cambodia in violation of the spirit of the 1925 Protocol banning use of poison gas. Unfortunately, no dispute-settlement mechanism exists in the Protocol. An investigation carried out by only a single country—no matter how well done or well publicized—will be discounted as politically motivated . . . Therefore, what is necessary is the creation by the United

Nations of an ad hoc investigation into the complaint of poison gas use in Laos and Cambodia followed by steps to strengthen the 1925 Protocol by the creation of permanent verification and dispute-settlement procedure (*Herald Tribune*, 31 December 1979).

Vietnam proved to be—since no one could stop it—an ideal "laboratory" for testing the effectiveness of America's new techniques in (prohibited) chemical warfare. But, strange to relate, its long-term effectiveness on the *invaders*, no less than on the invaded, has only recently come to light in odd places. A statistical study has been completed in Australia, which reveals that one in four of Australian ex-servicemen exposed in Vietnam to the defoliant "Agent Orange" have fathered deformed children. The national average of one seriously deformed baby in every 1,000 is 250 times lower than the veterans' rate.

The study was carried out on 50 men who suffered from a variety of complaints, which they believed were caused by contact with Agent Orange in Vietnam between 1965 and 1970. The families of the veterans, all living in New South Wales, contain four children with deformed hands, including three cases in which all the fingers of one hand and half the thumb are missing, two with deformed legs, and including one of a baby girl's leg which had to be amputated.

Moreover, 11 of the men who reported deformed babies suffered themselves from extreme nervousness, and ten from a body rash which has been accepted as being linked to Agent Orange. (In New South Wales overall, only one baby in 2,000 usually suffers such deformity.) A research biochemist on fetal deformities for the Sydney-based Children's Medical Research Foundation said that a total of eight gross limb deformities were included in the ex-servicemen's group.

This group's statistics roughly conformed to those more recently compiled in the United States, where 77 birth defects were reported in the families of 538 ex-servicemen exposed to Agent Orange, a wartime code-name for a defoliant which is one of the phenoxy herbicides, containing dioxin, and a phenoxy-type drug that is reputed to bind itself directly to the victim's genetic material (*The Times*, 4 January 1980). The U.S. veterans' protest group has actually called itself "Agent Orange Victims International." It contends in its legal claim that the defoliant caused serious maladies in servicemen exposed to it and birth defects in some of their children. So the U.S. Government had begun (in 1980) a long-term study of the defoliant's deleterious health effects. But will they *stop* its use?

The head of the U.S. Veterans Administration has said that the cost of compensating Vietnam veterans for harm done them by the Agent Orange herbicide would be *hundreds of millions of dollars per year for many years*. At the same time, the doctor at the University of California who is planning the VA's study of Agent Orange in Vietnam said it may never be possible to determine exactly who was exposed to it and how much exposure they received. There is no evidence, however, of similar U.S. concern for the health of the survivors against whose farms and rice paddies this powerful war chemical was directed.

Meanwhile, Edmund Juteau, organizer of the campaign to link the herbicide Agent Orange with cancer, died in February 1980 at 30 years of age in a hospital in New Hartford, N.Y., where he was being treated for cancer. An Air Force staff sergeant in Vietnam in the early 1970s, he said that he had been sprayed with Agent Orange and he had won an appeal from the Veterans' Administration that his cancer was linked to his duty in Vietnam.

The British Army is, nonetheless, planning for the use of chemical weapons against Russia, even though their use has been banned in Europe since 1925. Officers at the Staff College at Camberley were recently briefed about "a terrifying chemical armory built up by the Soviet Union." They were reported as saying that they would like to see Britain develop a "deterrent"—according to a BBC television series called "War School" (*Observer*, 27 January 1980). Once more we meet the "balance" theory or eye-for-an-eye illusion that two wrongs make a right.

A platoon from a British infantry regiment were the first troops to arrive at Porton Down, Wiltshire, to inaugurate NATO's first officially designated battle training area for chemical warfare—just three months ahead of a Geneva conference convened in March 1980 *to re-confirm the outlawing* of similar inhuman and illegal weapons!

The Convention against Biological and Toxin Weapons entered into force on 26 March 1975 after ratification by the 22nd party, including the "depositaries" of the Convention, namely, the Soviet Union, the United Kingdom and the United States. Some 85 ratifications and 34 signatures have since been deposited. Under article I, states parties undertake:

never in any circumstances to develop, produce or otherwise acquire or retain:

Microbial or other biological agents, or toxins whatever their origin or method of production, of types and in quantities that have no justification for prophylactic, protection or other purposes;
Weapons, equipment or means of delivery designed to use such agents or toxins for hostile purposes or in armed conflict.

And under article II, states parties undertake "to destroy or to divert for peaceful purposes" all biological agents, toxins, weapons, equipment and means of delivery which are in their possession or under their jurisdiction or control.

When the Review Conference of the parties to the Biological Weapons Convention met in Geneva in March 1980 the Secretary-General said:

The significance of the Convention comes into sharper focus when one considers that the unceasing progress in science and technology leads to the development and production of newer and more dangerous weapons. The arresting of this ominous trend at least in one area is an achievement that resulted from long but persevering efforts of the whole international community. It proves the importance of similar efforts in other areas of disarmament.

Yet, since 1971, the General Assembly has at each of its regular sessions adopted resolutions calling for "priority" negotiations which would lead to early agreement on a prohibition of all *chemical* weapons. In 1972, Eastern European members submitted a separate draft convention on the prohibition of the development, production and stockpiling of chemical weapons and on their destruction. In recent years, discussions concerning a ban on all chemical warfare have centered on questions related to the verification of compliance with the obligations undertaken by the parties to the future agreement. The scope of a comprehensive convention would, from its inception, extend to all chemical weapons which the parties wished to prohibit, from the stage of their development up to their use, including the means of delivery. Once again, it is political will that is lacking. Here, clear-cut *unilateral repudiation by Britain* would break the deadlock in the Geneva-based Committee on Disarmament. But Britain sits on U.S. coattails!

Where do we stand as regards a *potential* chemical arms race? The United States and the Soviet Union have tens of thousands of tons of lethal nerve gas, contained in millions of artillery shells and other weapons. But the U.S. and U.S.S.R. have been observing a self-imposed moratorium on production of *new* chemical weapons. There is no evidence that the U.S. or Soviet Union have added new chemical weapons in a decade. In fact, according to the Washington Center for Defense Information, since 1976 the U.S. and U.S.S.R. have been negotiating a treaty to stop development and *eliminate* stockpiles of chemical weapons. U.S. production of *new* nerve gas weapons (binary) will undermine prospects for a total ban on chemical weapons.

In spite of many rumors that were set afloat in 1981 about "Yellow Rain," there is no credible evidence that lethal chemical weapons have been used in Afghanistan or elsewhere by the Soviets. Yet the U.S. Army and Air Force have five-year plans for chemical defensive measures, totalling nearly $2 million, which will add substantially to the budget for several years. Worse, construction of new chemical weapons in the U.S. and U.S.S.R. could lead to their development by other countries, as well as by terrorist groups. Since there is no logic in "balancing" nerve gas deaths against each other, and "deterrence" makes no sense, a unilateral decision to *stop production* at once and destroy all stockpiles could and should be taken immediately in London and Washington. Two reasons why there is so much dragging of feet over stopping chemical war preparations are that they are cheap to make and difficult to destroy. Moscow then has no option but to sign the treaty that they have helped to draft. The need for protecting troops and civilians against gas and chemical warfare will automatically disappear. One more step will have been taken to restore some sanity to our earth!

As the worst horrors of science fiction have long been outmoded by what the Pentagon and Kremlin backroom boys have on their drawing-boards, it is no longer a secret that both the United States and the Soviet Union are exploring laser and particle-beam weapons. In fact, in developing these new weapons, the two countries could set off a new phase of the arms race. Laser weapons make a difference in military calculations. Their deployment would force adversaries to develop countermeasures or to increase numbers of offensive weapons in order to deal with the improved defensive capability of the laser systems. But this would be a "new generation" of weapons. Who will stop this madness?

The Pentagon has publicly acknowledged that it is studying the possibility of particle-beam weapons, whose high-energy beams of electrons, protons or neutrons would be directed to inflict damage, in order to ensure, they claim: (1) ballistic missiles defense, directed beams being used to hit incoming missiles; (2) satellite-borne anti-satellite killers, being launched in space to attack enemy satellites; and (3) ship-borne and aircraft-borne anti-missile weapons.

Fortunately, the same report says that the first feasibility demonstrations of laser weapons will not take place until well into the 1980s. Meantime Soviet negotiators, working with U.S. representatives to seek a common position on radiological weapons, have raised the issue of particle-beam weapons. The Russians urge a ban on their development as weapons that would "affect biological targets as weapons of mass-destruction." And the West? A clear answer is needed.

It is difficult to accept the cold fact that the U.S. Senate has voted 52–38 to start building a factory to produce a new generation of nerve gas and other poisonous chemical weapons. The House approved the same $3.15 million project by a voice vote of 337–22. "Will this facet of the chemical arms race be deterred," asked *The Churchman* (November 1980), "by the suit brought by more than a hundred attorneys from all fifty states filed against seven chemical companies on behalf of 4,200 Vietnam War veterans exposed to the toxic defoliant Agent Orange? Or the fact that researchers have found leukemia among 3,200 soldiers exposed to radiation during a 1957 Nevada nuclear bomb test? Even though it may be absurd to term this a 'Christian nation,' at least it should have a conscience."

(2) From napalm to radiation

Skin is easily damaged by heat, the degree of damage depending upon the amount of heat. Burn injuries differ from the wounds commonly caused by conventional weapons in the difficulty of their medical treatment. Where medical resources are modest, casualties from napalm have little chance of receiving medical aid. In recent wars—such as the Americans in Vietnam and the Israelis in Lebanon—napalm weapons appear to have produced an exceptionally high proportion of deaths compared with other weapons. Napalm injuries may be intensely painful. Recovery is slow, and the patient remains in great pain. Napalm and white phosphorus burns are likely to leave a victim disfigured for the rest of his life.

Flame-throwers used in World War I have today become weapons of mass-destruction. In fact, incendiary bomb attacks on cities such as Dresden, conducted during World War II, proved almost as destructive as the atomic bombs dropped on Hiroshima and Nagasaki.

Most human beings have an instinctive fear of fire, and the psychological effects of incendiary weapons are commonly listed among their "attractions" to the military mind. During mass-fires, large numbers of people become trapped by great walls of flame, offering no possibility of escape. And the use of napalm or white phosphorus, which clings to surfaces and to fleeing people while burning, increases the overall psychological impact. With a general breakdown of communications and public services, the result would be panic. Survival procedures become totally ineffective. A 1980 Geneva Conference (described later) sought to limit these war atrocities by a legal world agreement, now widely signed.

Destruction of houses and shelters results in a hostile environment and exposure to the weather, thus increasing overall suffering and loss of life. This situation is likely to be *worse in the developing countries*, for not only will fewer medical resources be available, but widespread malnutrition, chronic anemias and other deficiencies will increase rapidly on exposure. It is the Third World which will suffer without remedy if the great powers imagine (as some living generals do) that "their side" could win a conventional war.

But what now of the neutron bomb? This controversial nuclear weapon kills by neutron radiation while minimizing property destruction. *It is being promoted as a battlefield weapon that could make nuclear war more "thinkable."* Widespread public opposition in Europe, however, did delay the U.S. adoption of the neutron bomb. If opposition grows in the U.S., as it is growing in Europe, the new President may be forced to stop the bomb being produced. But, in the fall of 1981, he yielded to the specter of an imagined tank invasion from Eastern Europe (though no destination was disclosed) and he set the production schedules running at half-cock—all for an eventuality that some Kremlin-watchers would categorize as being the height of absurdity in any foreseeable military calendar in the 1980s.

Officially known as an "enhanced radiation weapon," it is, in fact, a small "low yield" nuclear bomb. Its special shielding mechanism reduces the blast effect, but increases the release of radiation energy in the form of neutrons. The blast and heat from the explosion destroy *everything* within 300 yards, and the *neutron radiation* would kill most people within a mile radius.

It has the same effect on humans as DDT on insects. Neutrons attack the central nervous system, causing immediate nausea, diarrhea, and convulsions. Depending on the dose, some victims die within hours. For others, death comes 60 to 90 days later with respiratory failure, delirium, or coma. Those not killed would be prone to leukemia or other cancers in later years. Russia, however, has proscribed this weapon.

In the event of a genuine invasion in Europe or elsewhere, the bomb is alleged to discombobulate advancing troops and tanks, while leaving bridges, power plants and other important structures intact. But by introducing this *new* weapon, NATO would send the wrong message to other nations. It contradicts the goals of non-proliferation and "zero nuclear weapons." On the contrary, the neutron bomb lowers the threshold of nuclear war, since military commanders might be more likely to use it than bigger nuclear weapons.

Funds for the neutron bomb were included in the U.S. Department of Energy's 1979 budget. Total cost of production could run as high as $1.5 billion, if the President gives the full go-ahead. Will he? One short answer was given by Daniel Ellsberg at a recent Rocky Flats, Colorado, anti-nuclear demonstration. He said: "The neutron bomb is the match to the nuclear oven in which mankind will perish. These demonstrations prove that some of humanity will not go quietly to the crematorium!" This time, holocaust was preventable. But will it be? The American *people* must decide.

Radiological weapons would utilize radioactive material to cause vast damage or injury. The potential for such weapons was recognized in fact more than three decades ago. Yet at that time, the amount of highly radioactive material in existence was small. In succeeding years, the accumulation of radioactive material has increased at an accelerating rate and now exists at facilities in more than 50 countries.

The banning of radiological weapons has most fortunately been making progress on the governmental level. The U.S. and the U.S.S.R. submitted jointly to the Geneva-based Committee on Disarmament in July 1979 a proposed agreement *prohibiting* radiological weapons. The U.S. and the U.S.S.R. urged that the Committee give their initiative prompt consideration, so that a draft treaty text could be developed. As proposed by the two parties, the treaty would prohibit the development, production, stockpiling, acquisition, or possession of radiological weapons.

Nuclear explosive weapons, alas!, which invariably produce radiation along with their other destructive effects, constitute a category of weapons of mass destruction separate from radiological weapons and so would be *excluded* from coverage by provisions of any radiological weapon treaty. However, we can at least end this section on a note of hopeful achievement for Geneva's new Committee on Disarmament.

To that slight record of progress we can add a yet more solid agreement on drafting a convention on specifically inhumane weapons, which has been the first international arms-regulation agreement that has been negotiated at a United Nations Conference. It provides new rules for the protection of *civilians* from attacks by means of incendiary weapons, landmines, booby-traps and fragments that cannot readily be detected in the human body.

To give it its full title, "The Convention on Prohibitions or Restrictions on the Use of Certain Conventional Weapons which may be Deemed to be Excessively Injurious or to have Indiscriminate Effects" was concluded at Geneva on 10 October 1980.

Signatures (including the Communist countries) are steadily coming in, though the U.S.A. is still awaited. The immense highly technical work and long expert negotiations, which covered several years in producing this key humanitarian convention, owed much of its success to the teamwork of the secretariat of the conference, under the resolute administration of Amada Segarra of Ecuador—thus emphasizing, once again, how much the world community owes to the quiet and unassuming services of its own civil servants. In the present case, the titles of the three new protocols, which form the essence of the convention, relate to some of the grim topics dealt with earlier in this chapter, namely: Protocol I on Non-Detectable Fragments; Protocol II on Prohibitions or Restrictions on the Use of Mines, Booby-Traps, and other Devices; and Protocol III on Prohibition or Restrictions on the Use of Incendiary Weapons.

(3) Tankology: machines replace people

If neutron weapons are being advocated as the essential means for stopping Russian tanks sweeping through central Europe, then tanks must be pretty formidable gadgets! They certainly are. They are more than formidable. They represent a new and permanent element in "conventional" war. When the Israeli armor careered through southern Lebanon in March 1978, only 18 *soldiers* were killed; though there were many Lebanese deaths (most of the Palestine exiles in Lebanon having escaped), while nearly a quarter of a million homeless Lebanese civilians fled north to safety, as refugees.

The reason for the extremely low death rate of the invading soldiers, in contrast to the under-protected people whom they attacked, was due to the fact—the TV evidence was clear about this—that the Israelis were all boxed up in machines. The latest design of American tanks—their armor vastly improved since the disastrous Yom Kippur War—and other armored vehicles rolled unmolested across the Lebanese fields and countryside, as the American-made planes swooped down from the skies. There was not a foot-soldier to be seen.

If this goes on (and the military men expect it to) the old concept of cannon fodder going over the top will become meaningless, except for television replays. In fact, as these new fighting leviathans get more computerized, they will move along the ground and across lakes and rivers, like the Cruise missiles move over the ground. They won't need any drivers or gunners at all. They will be so full of electronics that there won't be room—or need—for mere men inside.

Tanks started in a very modest way. In fact, Julius Caesar knew how useful chariots with cutting edges could be in overwhelming the enemy. British munitions chief Lloyd George took up the tank business seriously at the beginning of World War I, when the tank became a major weapon against German machine guns.

Since then the tank has become a forward weapon of assault. Its weight, speed and destructive power have made it the spearhead of advance against the enemy. But one other change has taken place since Lloyd George pleaded for his pioneer tanks.

This change is so fundamental that it should be set out in capitals, thus: ALL MODERN WAR WEAPONS ARE OFFENSIVE.

There are no "defensive" weapons any more. They are only called defensive to console the consciences of worried people "back home." Every weapon—from the proposed neutron bomb to the leviathan tank—is a weapon of *attack*. This is because defense has disappeared entirely. It has been replaced by deterrence, and deterrence *means* attack, or it means nothing. The trouble now is that "deterrence" is no longer deterring. So where are we? War Ministries were later renamed Ministries of Defense. Should we not now call them Ministries of Pretense?

The Middle East War in October 1973 demonstrated the vulnerability of the tank. Both Arabs and Israelis suffered substantial losses of tanks, totalling about 2,000. *Anti-tank* missile technology had by then overcome the best protective countermeasures available. A half-million dollar tank can be destroyed by a very inexpensive, *man-carried* antitank weapon such as the $4,000 TOW missile. These developments prompted Colonel Edward B. Atkinson in *Army* magazine to write a tantalizing article entitled: "Is the Soviet Army Obsolete?" The Soviet Union seems reliant, however, on tanks and tank-dependent tactics that stem nostalgically from World War II. Major-General Howard H. Cooksey, U.S. Army Acting-Deputy Chief of Staff for Research and Development, recently observed that "certainly in the Mideast war, the Israelis found out the hard way that *blitzkrieg* tactics will not work."

Tank modifications are going on the whole time, on both sides of a split Europe. Commenting on the NATO enigma, the U.S. journal *Science* states that the battle tank is still the principal weapon of a modern army: "Far from driving the tank into extinction, technological developments such as the anti-tank missile have only hastened its rate of evolution. For the past 15 years, however, the United States has stumbled from one fiasco to another in its attempts to design a new main battle tank, but seems at last to have a winner" (*Science*, 14 July 1978).

Science goes on to say that both the failure and success of the tank development program are integrally related to the central crisis of the NATO alliance, i.e. the lack of cooperation in designing, developing and producing new weapons. Through failure to standardize, NATO allies at present field 31 different

Battle tanks	Weight	Speed	Range	Gun	Crew
T-55	35.7 t	31 mph	250 m	100 mm	4
M60	45.5 t	30 mph	310 m	105 mm	4
T-62	36.6 t	30 mph	250 m	115 mm	4
Leopard	39.5 t	40 mph	375 m	105 mm	4
Heavy Tanks					
T-10	48.2 t	22 mph	135 m	122 mm	4
Chieftain	53.0 t	30 mph	310 m	120 mm	4

Table 2   Tanks: Soviet—NATO Comparison Chart

anti-tank weapons and seven different tanks! Such diversity causes a formidable logistics problem. It is, therefore, a principal factor in this paradox that the backward economies of the Warsaw Pact can out-produce advanced NATO economics in tanks by a ratio of 4 to 1. The article concludes:

> Though everyone agrees on the importance of NATO standardization, the commonly proposed remedies often seem worse than the disease. European countries, already fretful that they buy $8 of military equipment from the United States for every one dollar's worth that they sell, view calls for standardization as another pressure to "buy American."

Of course, the element of imprecision that has been constantly stressed in this book applies particularly to tanks *in action*. "The Army's latest anti-tank missile was defeated by its worst enemy yesterday—the European weather," reported *The Times* Defense Correspondent on 28 January 1981. "But officers defended its ability to penetrate Russian armor, if not the swirling fog which forced the cancellation of its first public demonstration on Salisbury Plain."

Anthony Sampson describes in graphic detail in *The Arms Bazaar* how the Middle East has been turned into a veritable cesspool of every type and make of weaponry, poured in by the arms merchants of East and West, so that no-one knows who is killing whom and with what. The outbreak of a war of prestige, greed and superstition between Iraq and Iran in the summer of 1980 presented a further illustration of the utterly divergent methods of *dealing* with conflict in this volatile area. Where wiser men would fear to tread, NATO (i.e. the Pen-

	Tanks	Towed Artillery	Combat Ships	Sub-marines	Combat Aircraft	Heli-copters	Missiles
U.S.	3,560	785	150	22	1,053	460	10,035
France	440	80	32	2	275	265	520
UK	1,105	5	93	3	105	45	640
Subtotal	5,105	870	275	27	1,433	770	11,195
USSR	5,220	2,550	41	6	1,565	380	3,950
Total	**10,325**	**3,420**	**316**	**33**	**2,998**	**1,150**	**15,145**

Table 3   Major weapons exported by the Big Four, 1971–75 (including deliveries to developing countries, Australia, New Zealand, Japan and South Africa).
Source: U.S. Arms Control and Disarmament Agency.

tagon) at once rushed in with battleships and planes. The then U.S. Secretary of State, Edmund Muskie, said on 14 October:

> We have organized and are developing a rapid deployment force which will be available for dispatch worldwide on short notice . . . This effort includes programs to improve the reach, mobility and strength of our airplanes and to procure new, fast sealift ships.

Acting for the U.N. and the world community, on the other hand, Mr. Olof Palme, former Prime Minister of Sweden, followed the Iran-Iraq situation carefully *on the spot* in an endeavor to find points of agreement. Within a week, agreement in principle was reached on the evacuation of commercial ships trapped in the Shatt-al-Arab waterway, thus constituting the first Iranian-Iraqi compromise—"the first ray of hope," Palme called it. The first phase of his mission was "to listen, learn and clarify the positions of the two parties," and to establish a basis for the next four steps: namely a ceasefire, withdrawal, frontier delineation and non-interference. Civilization advances through the U.N.'s third-party procedures and conciliatory methods—while warmongers simply send in more weapons. Unfortunately, Palme could get no further concessions; but in April 1982 a ceasefire was under active negotiation.

III
War Games for Real

As the arms race speeds up, under the daily diet of flamboyant speeches, TV and radio bulletins, emotional editorials, and flashy war books, more and more normal people find it increasingly difficult to distinguish truth from falsehood, fact from fiction. In this chapter we enter a realm of stark military fantasy which even ten years ago would have been considered by most normal people as the product of a criminal lunatic. And if this same nightmare had presented itself to the American, British, Russian and other delegates who fashioned the U.N. Charter at San Francisco in 1945, with a world in ruins around them, they would not have believed a word of it. Thirty-five years have turned Hiroshima into a sort of love token, instead of a monument of lasting shame.

However that may be, we now move from present reality, with all its untidiness, into a land of ominous make-believe when a retired English general gives a preview of the third world war, timed to take place in 1985. Unfortunately, he does not stand alone, though he is not in very good company. For Richard Nixon, whom top U.S. historians have called "the only criminal who occupied the U.S. Presidency," has presented us in his 1980 book, *The Real War*, with a call to a new moral crusade: "In the war we are fighting—World War III—there is no substitute for victory and a strategy for victory." Not surprisingly, again the new American President finds himself warmly embraced by a small but politically dangerous elite who label themselves as the Moral Majority.

(1) The Hackett Game

True to well-recognized rules that retired generals remain experts at re-fighting their previous war, General Sir John Hackett has produced a terrifying dream-scenario of the next war in his *The Third World War, August 1985* (1978). Not unnaturally his blood-bath, timed for the crucial year 1985, has to begin, according to tradition, in Poland. That is one reason Poland's labor troubles in the winter of 1980–81 received top priority from the defense correspondents and the Kremlin-watchers. And the December 1981 declaration of martial law was viewed in Washington as fabricated in Moscow. But we are back with Hackett in the *blitzkrieg* era once more.

World War III is actually sparked in 1985, however, by the ubiquitous U.S. marines landing in Fiume to win Yugoslavia back from the Russians who, at long last, had got tired of much-revered Tito's neutrality. So they—the Russians—attempted a Prague Spring on the soft under-belly of Europe. But the Yanks got there first this time. General Hackett never anticipated, of course, that the Russians would choose 1980 for Afghanistan. But suppose the Yanks had got *there* first? Where would we be today?

And the cause of all this? By August 1985, the Soviet Union faces mounting disaffection among its many national minorities. A good point to start. After 40 years—a whole generation at peace—the leopard is suddenly changing his spots and thinks that a European war would be an improvement on détente. The technological gap and the balance of nuclear terror is all the time growing in the Americans' favor, notes Hackett; but the Russians have ground superiority in conventional arms. With the Russian (mistaken) confidence that the Americans will not dare to risk mutual nuclear suicide, the Soviet conventional war machine slides into action on 4 August 1985. A tank invasion of Western Europe is aimed, somewhat vaguely, at the destruction of the Atlantic Alliance. (This was, of course, in ignorance of what the European peace movement would have done to it by 1985.) What this argument does—though General Hackett does not appreciate what he is doing—is to blow the whole "deterrence" dogma sky-high.

They quickly come a cropper, however, thanks to the Western lead in electronics. The forces of the Alliance outwit those of the WAPO from scratch. That is the grim story as told by General Sir John Hackett, former Deputy Chief of the General Staff and Commander of NATO's Northern Army Group in Europe. True to the best Hollywood routines, the good guys will beat the bad guys in the end, and quickly—for, unlike World Wars I and II, it lasted only the *expected* few weeks! And Russia had already changed its spots from red to pink by 1986. Sixty years of Bolshevism had gone into reverse and in only twelve months! History has never been reversed so quickly before.

But it is a tough game while it lasts. Nevertheless, all the NATO rules are faithfully kept. The nukes don't go into the fray until the battle is on the home ground. Birmingham is eliminated; so, too, is Minsk. (Genetic after-effects of radiation do not even get into the Appendix.) And then the world settles down to democracy. Nine end pages out of 360 are on "The Beginning of the Future." But, after the children have put their toys away, survival, what? Silence. We might ask: was all this trouble really necessary?

The Hackett scenario is an ostensibly blatant write-up in favor of an expanded NATO, *here and now*. But it is also a cynical invitation to despair. It is a subtle piece of *War* propaganda that follows the smooth Goebbels technique of inevitable destiny. For it all looks so easy. Hackett sets up row after row of WAPO aunt sallies, so that he can knock them down like ninepins. He changes the "unlikely" into the "inevitable" with unerring skill. How can we contradict so honorable a gentleman?

1985 is an appropriate date to choose, because by then the hackneyed Orwellian legend "1984"—another Utopia-in-reverse nightmare (written in 1949)—will have run out of steam and need revving up. But it is all very strange that, since the carefully limited "nuclear exchange"—Birmingham *v.* Minsk (like Mr. Reagan's concept of "limited nuclear war" in Europe)—could be so successfully manipulated ahead of time, with only a couple of million charred and shrivelled corpses left behind, but that no one had thought of arranging to stop the "exchange" *before* it began! If Hot Line wars can nowadays be so efficiently stage-managed by a prescient general staff on both sides, why cannot their superb cooperation be enlisted in the preventative cooling-off process *instead*?

One does not have to be a dyed-in-the-wool communist to see that to launch a Hitlerian *blitzkrieg* in central Europe would be an act of blind idiocy for the Soviet military hierarchy, quite apart from reprisals the West would immediately take. The Kremlin might consist of a lot of inhuman and amoral men— at least, Ronald Reagan says they are—but it is surely not a ship of fools intent on their own and their country's suicide.

The point is not as to whether Czechoslovakia, Hungary, Afghanistan (see map on pages 6–7) and other cases of Soviet adventurism can be construed, as they can, as evidence of Russian greed or malevolence, but whether such consolidation of Soviet-controlled territory on the European continent 25 years ago assumes or provides a rational argument for supposing that, after thirty-five years of peaceful coexistence, the Soviet government *intends* and *plans* a Hitlerite invasion of the Western countries. Professional soldiers and NATO propagandists, like General Sir John Hackett, have built imaginary scenarios on this pure supposition and guesswork. But their actual writings and official pronouncements contain not a shred of hard evidence that the Russians or their leaders plan to put into operation the programs of aggression that these Western authorities translate as being Soviet intentions. Hackett's *The Third World War* stands on the best-seller shelves of the London and New York bookstores under the categorization of "fiction." That is where it belongs.

The case against this type of wish-fulfilment war game can be condensed into three short, blunt sentences:

(1) Nobody *wants* it—neither Easterners nor Westerners, except a few crackpots;

(2) The best minds in the U.S. and U.S.S.R. are working against military confrontations at a thousand growing points of agreement and cooperation, though both countries are plagued by their unrepentant hawks;

(3) For nearly four decades a whole new system of planetary peace management—where U.S. and U.S.S.R. sit side by side at the U.N.—has been building up a structure of alternative options focused on give-and-take and on common interests.

All of these compelling moves are conveniently omitted

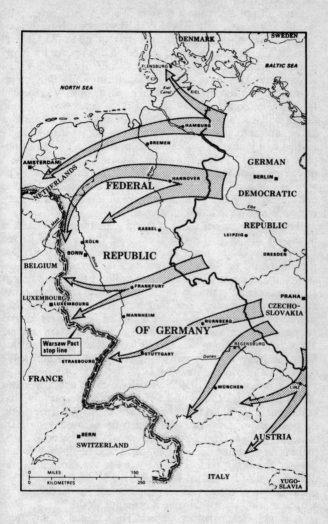

Map 2 The Soviet Plan to attack Western Europe in General
Hackett's *Third World War, August 1985*

from the Hackett game, simply because, if they were included, his stacked deck would collapse.

To sum up. We cannot re-fight World War II, even with its allies switched, with World War III weapons. Nonetheless, the plan does warn us what the generals are up to. As General Hackett's book gets around it will be an eye-opener for many ordinary citizens on how sinister a web of illusions NATO's advance thinkers have spun around them while they slept. Translated into Russian, it is bound to put them wise as to what to *avoid*, if taken seriously at all. But no doubt Soviet comic books will seize on it first. Russian humor always needs a grave subject to work on, as when Nikita Khrushchev jokingly replied to a journalist's question about America's superior nuclear capacity: "Yes, I know what Kennedy claims, and he's quite right. But I'm not complaining ... We're satisfied to be able to finish off the United States first time round. Once is quite enough. What good does it do to annihilate a country twice? We're not a bloodthirsty people."

The tragedy of our times is that a wide range of excellent books on life in the Soviet Union and the struggles of the Russian peoples to build a viable and peaceful society are shouldered off the library shelves by a deliberately touted casuistry that accepts the slaughter of millions of human beings as an acceptable option in world relationships. Perhaps times are changing? Possibly one long-term result of the new European peace movement will be a revival in what are known as "peace studies" (see Chapter VIII) and also Russian studies. There is nothing unpatriotic about looking at tough problems from the other man's point of view, and so help him solve them. That is why we have the U.N.

A recipient of the 1959 Nobel Peace Prize and a member of the British delegation to the U.N. Special Session on Disarmament in 1978, Lord Noel-Baker still thinks that there might be peace *now*, if we can deal decisively with our own warmongers. When Lord Noel-Baker speaks on the arms race, there is no doubting the spirit and sharpness of a man who has devoted the better part of his 92 years to the cause of world disarmament: "It's all the fault of those bloody hawks. If we could get rid of them, and get people to realize the dangers of a nuclear war, we would have a beautiful world."

It is not clear whether General Hackett had at any time consulted the weighty signatories of the U.N. experts' report (cited above), who take quite a different view of what would happen if so-called "tactical" weapons were let loose over European cities. They say:

> In certain quarters it is still military doctrine that any disparity in the conventional strength of opposing forces could be redressed by using nuclear weapons in the zone of battle. Carefully conducted and dispassionate theoretical studies of the use of nuclear weapons in field warfare, including analyses of an extensive series of "war games" relating to the European theater, have led to the clear conclusion that this military doctrine could lead to the use of hundreds, and not of tens, of so-called tactical nuclear weapons in the battlefields ... It can be firmly stated that, were nuclear weapons to be used in this way, they could lead to the devastation of the whole battle zone.
>
> *Military planners have no past experience on which to call for any guide as to how military operations could proceed in circumstances such as these.* When such levels of physical destruction are reached, one might well ask what would determine the course of a nuclear battle? Would it be the number of enemy casualties? Would it be the violent psychological reaction, fear and terror, to the horror of widespread instantaneous destruction? Would the chaos immediately bring all military operations to a halt?

The ominous fall-out of the Hackett plan is already reaching grotesque proportions. As war talk spreads, local authorities in England are being swamped by householders begging to know how to "protect" themselves. Advice on how best to survive a nuclear attack has been published by a British organization called Civil Aid. Mr. Robin Meads, vice-chairman of Civil Aid, told a London press conference that after a nuclear attack hungry people would have to take what they could get: "If you saw a frog running about, you would have to wash it to get rid of active dust, cook it and eat it." His pamphlet admits that food for 14 days, batteries, candles and other essentials are not available in sufficient quantities for a last-minute rush by the whole British population. "So reasonable steps must be taken in advance. Coal, coke, wood and fir-cones will produce heat, but many houses have no fireplaces, and so paraffin, methylated spirits and bottled gas seem the only substitute for normal electricity or piped gas." The pamphlet wisely counsels: "A hay-box used for slow cooking will save a large proportion of heat." This advice is remarkably similar to the British Government's own *Protect and Survive* booklet; but how to preserve that hay-box in 2,000 degrees of nuclear heat is omitted from both.

Professor Gilbert Murray, Greek scholar and humanist, and for many years the Chairman of the League of Nations Union in pre-war Britain, used to say solemnly to us neophytes who worked with him, that war was not caused by bad men. It was a conflict between good men and good men, because only good men could defend its horrors and imbecilities; they did so in the name of some ideal beyond themselves.

No one can deny the sacrifice and self-abnegation that past wars have brought to millions and millions of individuals—a sacrifice and self-abnegation that other men, smaller men, have exploited and corrupted for lesser ends. So war has been given, because of these higher ideals, a glamor and social status that later evaluations have proved to be exaggerated and spurious. Modern anthropologists include it among cultural acquisitions that are neither necessary nor permanent. War is now obsolete as a human institution, because of its intrinsic *in*humanity. It is *against* human nature and has made of mankind an endangered species. On a still-standing wall in Nagasaki is the *shadow* of a woman with a baby in her arms. Just a shadow. There were no remains of the two bodies to be found, although we know they were there when the bomb fell.

However tolerable for past centuries, the depersonalization of modern war, with its endless range of death techniques and mutilation machines, has taken the goodness out of war. We should have learnt this long ago. Even an old warrior like Winston Churchill, in *My Early Life*, wrote:

War, which used to be cruel • and magnificent, has now become cruel and squalid . . . Instead of a small number of well-trained professionals championing their country's cause with ancient weapons and a beautiful intricacy of archaic maneuver, sustained at every moment by the applause of their nation, we now have entire populations, including even women and children, pitted against one another in brutish mutual extermination, and only a set of blear-eyed clerks left to add up the butcher's bill. From the moment Democracy was admitted to, or rather forced itself upon the battlefield, War has ceased to be a gentleman's game. To Hell with it!

The *coup-de-grâce* against Hackett's B *v.* M War Game (Birmingham *v.* Minsk) was surely delivered by the late Earl Mountbatten in a speech at Strasbourg on 11 May 1979:

> Next month I enter my eightieth year. I am one of the few survivors of the First World War who rose to high command in the Second and I know how impossible it is to pursue military operations in accordance with fixed plans and agreements . . . When I was Chief of the British Defence Staff I made my views known. I have heard the arguments against this view, but I have never found them convincing. So I repeat in all sincerity as a military man that I can see no use for any nuclear weapons which would not end in escalation, with consequences that no-one can conceive.

(2) Would a continental war really work?

In answer to this question, which the "build-up" strategists never bother to ask, the following capsule arguments have been put forward by the Center for Defense Information (Washington, D.C.) and are backed by defense analysts all round the globe:

> The possibility of a conventional non-nuclear war in Europe is slim.
>
> Any military conflict in Europe between East and West forces would quickly escalate to nuclear weapons.
>
> The neutron weapon is irrelevant to the defense of Western Europe.
>
> The Warsaw Pact cannot conduct a surprise attack against NATO forces without prior warning.
>
> NATO military efforts should be directed at *avoiding* war in Europe rather than fighting a war in Europe.

For over thirty years (i.e. since NATO began) the U.S.A. has pretended to "protect" Europe from the Russians. This is sometimes referred to by MPs, Senators, and press correspondents as the "nuclear umbrella!" For those thirty or more years Russia has stayed put behind the same buffer states that she consolidated as her agreed "defense" zone at the end of World War II. These lines were actually confirmed in the Helsinki agreements.

This stabilization agreement in 1975 brought a degree of security to *both* sides. It should have been followed up by mutual withdrawal, but the hawks are never satisfied. Somehow, something extra has always been needed by the Pentagon planners to tilt the alleged balance their way. The 1980 review conference in Madrid did, however, plan the foundation for an all-European nuclear-free zone and an all-European security plan; but both U.S. and U.S.S.R. spent the whole of 1981 squabbling over details, while the other thirty-three "Helsinki" members looked on in despair. The new 1981–82 movements for a "nuclear-free Europe" may, perhaps, break this deadlock by rejecting the NATO subservience to Washington policies.

Seven thousand or more so-called "tactical" nukes—i.e. 7,000 super-Hiroshimas—still don't do the trick, even though the Russians have fewer of them. Something more reassuring had therefore to be put on the ground level. So the neutron weapon suddenly sprang in 1978 into the Western headlines as a ground-floor killer and opened a Pandora's Box of agonizing argument. Fortunately, public opinion—at last—had something to say. A worldwide revulsion stopped this new abomination in its tracks. For one thing, the neutron case rested on two very doubtful assumptions, namely: (1) that a war started in Europe could remain conventional; and (2) that nuclear war with tactical nuclear weapons could be limited to Europe.

That is the Hackett line. But neither proposition makes sense. NATO and WAPO would fight a conventional war only as long as each could foresee itself winning. But, if neither could expect to win such a war quickly—a reasonable assumption—the losing side would have to resort to nuclear weapons in desperation. Former U.S. Secretary of Defense Harold Brown once told the House Armed Services Committee: "Any Soviet planner must consider that a successful Soviet massive conventional attack would trigger first tactical, then strategic nuclear weapons used against them." This is the "flexible response" doctrine, supported by the compliant British defense establishment.

The essential question is how any responsible Soviet leader would *respond* to the NATO employment of even *one* such weapon. This is the Birmingham *versus* Minsk gambit. But a noted Soviet military writer, Marshal Sokolovskii, has stated: "Once the military movements on land and sea have *started* they are no longer subject to the desires and plans of diplomacy, but rather to their own laws."

Because of the fallacious "balance" doctrine that has dominated every arms race, once war begins the momentum of military operations and the imperatives of survival and victory must take over. Political control will cease to exist. An enemy's battle intentions are always uncertain. Field commanders, unable to communicate quickly with their political leaders, will have recalled Montgomery's advice. The use of tactical nuclear weapons, after the first decision had been made, would be delegated to hardpressed combat commanders fighting for their existence.

The conditions initiating a nuclear war, however "limited" its initial intentions, could not be later controlled by an act of will. This is because the political will would itself *be lacking in the first place to prevent the war*. The uncertainty and fear surrounding what defense ministers and newspaper columnists glibly call a "nuclear exchange" could only result in the nuclear disaster that both U.S. and Soviet Union political leadership have sought to avoid.

It is important to get things into stark perspective. NATO's original strategy did not begin with all these off-beat imponderables. The U.S. *started* the race with the monopoly of the A-bomb and, then, the H-bomb. They relied on them for "national defense," not their allies. This was long before the Russians began to catch up with them. It was Secretary of State John Foster Dulles who, with evangelistic fervor, invented the era of "massive retaliation." This relied on the dominant *threat* of U.S. strategic bombers and nuclear retaliation to deter any threats to West European security. Anybody who had lived in the United States (like the author) during this sad period of the alleged "world Communist conspiracy" and McCarthyism, will recall the psychology of inducted fear that prevailed of a (non-existent) imminent Communist takeover of America! The umbrella fantasy followed for Europe.

However, the Russians were not concerned with American defense. But with Russian defense. So, as the Moscow planners strengthened *their* nuclear capability, "massive retaliation" lost its relevance as a deterrent. Mutual retaliation would guarantee a nuclear war which no one would win. Thus, after prolonged debate in NATO councils, the Alliance adopted in December 1967, the more costly strategy of "flexible response," which theoretically provided *multiple* war-fighting options, if conflict did begin.*

---

*The author has analyzed the early history of NATO and its lamentable failings in his book *The End of an Illusion*, Bobbs-Merrill, 1968.

	NATO		Warsaw Pact	
	delivery systems	nuclear weapons	delivery systems	nuclear weapons
Nuclear land mines	–	300	–	–
Heavy artillery	900	3,000	–	–
Surface-to-surface missiles	1,000	1,000	1,000	1,000
Surface-to-air missiles	500	500	–	–
Tactical aircraft	2,000	3,900	2,350	2,500
Total	4,400	8,700	3,350	3,500

Table 4   Tactical nuclear weapons and delivery systems currently deployed in Europe (estimates rounded).
Source: Center for Defense Information estimate

This new flexible response strategy assumed that the U.S. and its European allies could *contain* a Soviet attack initially without nuclear weapons, but it also assumed that nuclear weapons would be used if we could not stop "Soviet aggression." The irrelevance of all this to the Afghanistan situation is now evident. The United States has even proposed that, with increasing numbers of non-nuclear forces, there would be "no need" to use nuclear weapons at all in Europe.

To sum up this rake's progress, the very flexibility of flexible response has naturally diminished the credibility of its deterrent objective. Yet it has succeeded in nurturing a continuing debate within the Alliance, which continues to undermine NATO's unity. This became obvious at the end of 1979 when the Netherlands Government—and public opinion—refused to play with the 572 Pentagon missiles. The revolt continues, supported by mass public opinion across the European continent.

But the revolt is not only on one side of the ocean. When the U.S. Senate recently approved a $3.8 billion military construction bill, it refused to authorize any of the combat-construction projects for Europe, as sought by the Carter administration. Senator John Stennis, chairman of the Armed Services Committee, pointed out that much of the $375 million in combat-related "construction requested for NATO is an Alliance responsibility that should not be unilaterally funded by the United States." So the divided Allies were being pressured to dig deeper into their own pockets, to pay for the American arms imports in 1981–82, at the very moment when their peoples were getting out from under the tattered umbrella. To protect whom? Yet one thing that the NATO strategy of flexible response has done is to intensify the conventional arms build-up on *both* sides. So back to Square One.

The bad joke of all this nuclear shadow-boxing is that the Soviet Union itself, as far as we know, has never accepted the concept of conventional war in Europe. The Soviet Union continues to reject the idea that a major war in Europe could *remain* non-nuclear. They have at least commonsense on their side. In so far as they consider nuclear warfare inevitable in such a war, can they not be expected to employ nuclear weapons at the outset—rather than leave the choice to NATO? Even a U.S. deputy secretary of defense, Mr. Morton Halperin, has said: "The NATO doctrine is to fight with conventional arms until we are losing, then to fight with nuclear tacticals until we are losing, and then to blow up the world."

One Soviet military commentator has actually stated: "It has been proved that under present-day conditions local or limited wars would be nothing but the prelude to a general missile-nuclear war." Although the Soviet Union has now placed renewed emphasis on its conventional forces, as a response to the recent change in NATO's own emphasis on conventional forces, Soviet leaders continue to recognize that nuclear weapons would definitely be used in a major war (somehow) confined to Europe. Soviet Marshal Sokolovskii announced bluntly: "The basic means for armed combat in land theaters in a future world war will be the nuclear weapons." This is precisely the late Earl Mountbatten's conviction.

Nonetheless, despite the likelihood of any WAPO aggression quickly escalating into a full-scale nuclear conflict, NATO has been encouraging the costly military build-up on both sides, thus increasing the tension that could precipitate such a war. In 1977 the U.S. spent $46 billion—over 40 percent of its military budget—for the "defense" of Europe. The Allies contributed upwards of $60 billion. As stated above, because of the worsening economic crisis in the U.S. and the decline of the dollar, Congressmen in 1978 and 1979 were pleading with NATO allies to pay more for America's gift-horses. Hence, the cost of the 572 "upgraded" nuclears in the 1980s now falls on the Europeans. Since its inception 33 years ago, NATO has continually strengthened its conventional forces. Yet for these

Ground Forces	
Main battle tanks	886
Other armored vehicles	4,014
Artillery pieces	453
Anti-tank weapon systems	22,736
Naval Forces	
Destroyers/escorts	21
Attack submarines	9
Fast patrol boats	29
Minelayers/minesweepers	19
Air Forces/Air Defense	
Combat aircraft	331
Helicopters	277
Anti-aircraft guided missile systems	745
Anti-aircraft guns	997

Table 5 New weapons added by European NATO Forces, 1976–78 (excluding increases in U.S. weapons positioned in Europe).
Source: U.S. Department of Defense

33 years its military leaders have maintained that these forces were still "not adequate." Adequate for what? Does *anybody* know?

The authoritative Jane's annual military review in London, *All the World's Aircraft*, said in 1980 that there is "steadily mounting concern" that a strict balance of military might, "on which the guarantee of continued peace has depended" (*sic*), no longer exists. And in the 1981 edition, Jane's came out more boldly and stated that *the nuclear deterrent that has kept the peace of the world for 36 years is dead*, killed by the crumbling cohesion of both the Eastern and Western alliances. The aviation expert of Jane's said in a report: "With the cohesion of both NATO and the Warsaw Pact alliances crumbling, and the vast popular antiwar movements gaining strength, a massive and urgent reduction of nuclear weapons is clearly essential."

This obsolete war game was given away when U.S. General Bernard Rogers, Allied Supreme Commander, himself admitted that the Soviet Union and the Warsaw Pact countries "have *caught up* with NATO in military strength and . . . if we can't catch up again with the strength of the Soviet bloc, the gap will only increase and become so great that we'll never catch up at all." (Associated Press, 17 December 1980)

We might recall that in late 1978 a veritable barrage of propaganda burst out in press and political speeches on "the Russian threat." This pushed the totals higher still. As Tennyson wrote: "Is there any peace in ever climbing up the ever-climbing wave?"

Suddenly, however, from out of the blue in early 1980, the "threat" shifted to Afghanistan (which shares a thousand kilometers of frontier with the U.S.S.R.). The imminent invasion of Europe silently dropped out of the editorials and the Persian Gulf springs back into world history. The causes of World War III had shifted to a side street in Teheran.

Yet the respondent Soviet doctrine comprised five elements:

(1) Participating countries should agree "not to set up foreign bases in the Persian Gulf area and the adjacent islands."

(2) They should not deploy nuclear weapons there.

(3) They should "not use or threaten to use force against the countries of the Persian Gulf area and not interfere in their internal affairs."

(4) They should not try to bring the Gulf States "into military groupings."

(5) They should agree "not to raise obstacles or pose threats to normal trade exchanges and the use of the sea lanes linking the states of that area with other countries of the world."

How did the West react to this firm Moscow pronouncement? We might note a popular British journal's comment:

When a "new" doctrine of peace is propounded by a superpower, it is right to treat it with caution even cynicism. But to reject it out of hand is imprudent and could prove self-damaging. The Western press chose to mock Soviet President Brezhnev's call for non-intervention in the Gulf region. Addressing the Indian parliament, he invited world powers to join with the U.S.S.R. in a pledge to forswear military and naval intervention in the Gulf area. Earlier he attacked the West for its decision "to whip up the arms race rather than to limit it." (*South* editorial, February 1981, London).

Admittedly, the timing of the proposal was neither opportune nor propitious. With the Soviet forces deeply involved in Afghanistan, "a doctrine of peace and security" which would guarantee "full respect to the independence, sovereignty, territorial integrity and non-aligned status of the countries in the region was hardly likely to command much respect. But why was it ignored?

Meanwhile, former Secretary of Defense Harold Brown had been constantly enhancing the *readiness* of U.S. home forces to provide *rapid reinforcement* to NATO. Combat units in Europe and selected divisions in the U.S. were to be manned at 100 percent to improve *combat readiness*, he declared. (This was before the Afghanistan defection.) Stocks of replacement weapons and ammunition in Europe reached their highest levels in the history of the Alliance.

Yet there is still not enough to go around. For, with the Iranian revolution in 1979, the next stage was to plan mobile units of 100,000 men destined for the Gulf region. Some Americans, however, recognized that the Gulf states might have different political and military needs from the U.S. What is good for General Motors is not always good for OPEC. The "security" framework proposed by President Carter would have comprised separate relations with each country in the region, not a uniform alliance. CENTO, the ugly sister of NATO in the Middle East, had long ago faded away like a bad dream. But the hotly disputed AWACS and other "deals" are still in the works—to put NATO into the Gulf.

However, in January 1980, Kuwait's Foreign Minister Sabah al-Ahmed called on the Arab world to devise a strategy confronting *both* Washington and Moscow. (In February 1981 an all-Arab conference issued a stronger remonstrance.) He said that the Israeli occupation of the West Bank was backed by the United States and was "no less serious" than the Soviet intervention in Afghanistan. *The great powers were gambling at the expense of small countries around the Gulf.* Nor was he alone. The United Arab Emirates complained that the United States was using the Soviet action in Afghanistan as an *excuse* to expand it military presence in the Gulf. So what next? Will our World War III planners amend the NATO treaty so as to stretch the American umbrella now as far as Pakistan?

Six Gulf nations—Saudi Arabia, Kuwait, the United Arab Emirates, Bahrain, Oman and Qatar—have meantime agreed to form a Council for Gulf Co-operation to pool their resources and safeguard *stability* in the region. On the other hand, the U.S. intruders would not seem to be doing so well. According to a Washington dispatch (18 December 1980), U.S. early-warning planes cruise high over the Gulf above the U.S. frigates which patrol the Gulf's waters. They seem to be coordinated; but, in fact, they do not even communicate directly with each other! The radar plane reports to the Air Force in Europe, and the frigate to the Navy in Honolulu, halfway around the world in the other direction.

"Once when F-14s rose to challenge a U.S. presidential jet over the Gulf, its Air Force pilot believed that the fighters were Iranian. The planes actually were American and had come from U.S. carriers. But the pilot's confusion was understandable. Neither the Navy nor the Air Force knew that the other had planes in the area, and neither knew the radio frequencies necessary to talk to the other" (The *Los Angeles Times* reported). Nor has the last been heard of the Libyan planes shot down in another Gulf incident (the one called Sidra) off the Mediterranean coast of Libya in the summer of 1981. Was that also a NATO operation?

Reverting to Europe, NATO spending is higher today than at any time in the past decade. In 1971–76, NATO allies in Europe showed a real increase of 11 percent in military spending. Together, the U.S. and its NATO allies spent over a 100 *billion* dollars in 1977 for military forces in Europe alone. Now the United States has insisted on an arms budget expansion of at least three percent annual "real growth," that is, three percent over and above inflation. But are we getting our money's worth? This is not merely climbing up the ever-climbing wave, it is sending a financial helicopter above it. And we know how unpredictable helicopters are!

Admiral Gene R. LaRocque, U.S. Navy (Ret.), redoubtable Director of the Center for Defense Information in Washington, states that "conventional war of any duration would be virtually impossible in Europe today." The question has been asked, however: "Could the Soviets penetrate NATO defenses quickly and achieve their objectives before Allied decisions have been made to use nuclear weapons in their defense?" He replies that the success of such a Soviet blitzkrieg would depend on two factors: (1) their ability to carry out a surprise attack and, then, (2) quickly penetrate NATO defenses, seizing key objectives in Western Europe.

Against the "uncertainty" (i.e. military guesswork) of these backroom strategists, one has to set the megalomania of some of Washington's political bosses, who were so thrown off course by the Iranian challenge. In an address to the International Platform Association in Washington on 2 August 1979, Mr. Zbigniew Brzezinski, President Carter's hawkish adviser for national security, lumped together the Middle and the Far East as being on a par with Western Europe—an America First policy that President Reagan's Cabinet fully approves:

> The American military power must be in a position to protect our essential interests abroad, including the three vital strategic zones beyond our Hemisphere: Western Europe, the Near and the Far East. This means we must assure that we have the reach and the means to project our power where it is needed, and to do so in the appropriate form and level of intensity. In this task we consult [*sic*] our allies and friends in every realm, co-operate with them and react on their wishes. *But we remain the leader and must bear the burdens of that role.* [our italics]

Much has been said and written about the Soviet capability for a "massive surprise attack" against Western Europe, yet that possibility is more conjecture than fact. But endless repetition transforms conjecture into reality. Russian intentions in the Gulf areas are even more vague and "uncertain." Mr. Brezhnev himself rejected in January 1981 Western allegations that Russia was a threat to the Gulf. He called on the United States, China, Japan and other countries to join Moscow in renouncing force, military bases and nuclear weapons. But a U.S. spokesman said it was ironic that Mr. Brezhnev should propose such a peace policy with more than 80,000 Soviet troops in Afghanistan. So X = 0. Stalemate again!

Historically, this kind of attack has rarely occurred. Admiral Sir Peter Hill-Norton has called such a surprise attack scenario "nonsense." Even General Alexander Haig, a NATO hawk and now Secretary of State, once remarked: "The NATO agreed-on 48 hours warning of an impending attack is the absolute bottom we can expect." (The term "agreed-on" might well worry the fastidious.) And he noted it was more realistic to expect a warning period of eight days to two weeks. Other strategists have looked at this fantastic adventure from the point of view of available roads, railway lines, and canteens to feed the advancing troops; and they put the minimum at 20 days. An army still marches on its stomach. The canteens must keep up with the tanks.

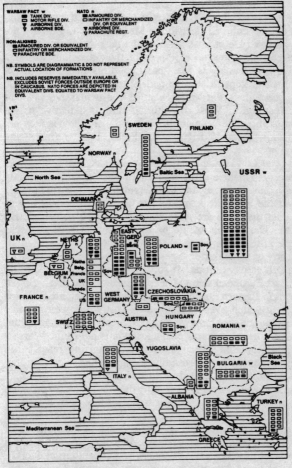

Map 3   NATO/Warsaw Pact Forces in Europe.
Greece's membership of NATO is in the balance

Former Secretary of Defense James Schlesinger has himself criticized the "Pearl Harbor complex" in the United States. He has asserted that the "total list of potential indicators of a Soviet attack in Europe is several hundred items." This point was enforced by General Haig, again, who said that 50 to 60 percent of the Soviet submarine force is located in the Kola Peninsula; they would have to be put to sea, moving out seven to 14 days *before* a general attack. The Soviet Union would have to augment its outnumbered fleet in the Mediterranean, too, and activate its Civil Defense system. Soviet tanks and armored personnel carriers show no readiness of their divisions to move quickly. Some analysts fear that two-thirds of Soviet heavy equipment is kept in storage and is unready for the surprise attack. One does not know whether those massive rows of tanks, featured in Western editorials, are as defective in operation as those unfortunate helicopters—or whether they are really showpieces to frighten the Poles, East Germans and Rumanians.

Admiral La Rocque states that weaknesses within the Warsaw Pact also make a surprise attack on Western Europe highly unlikely. The 26 Soviet and East German divisions are not able to cover the 300-mile length of the German frontier. Most of these Pact divisions are maintained at only 50 percent active strength. The Soviets would be forced to wait several weeks for *their* allies to mobilize. And would they?

Do any of these buffer states *want* to lose their own security and march across Europe? If so, *why*? The political reliability of the East European states is deeply questionable. Eight Soviet divisions in Eastern Europe, 25 percent of the total, are assigned to keeping watch over their allies. A costly war would create serious political problems in Poland, Czechoslovakia, and Hungary. And for what purpose? Yugoslavia is not in the Warsaw Pact, and Rumania's head of state is organizing mass peace and disarmament demonstrations alongside the West Europeans. And Poland? Is it ready to march west?

The moment has come to revamp the whole NATO program in Europe. How much cold-war brainwashing does it need to take the "Russian threat" seriously? We have taken time to analyze this Western-made specter because of the millions of reams of newsprint that have been devoted throughout the 1960s and 1970s to feed NATO's egotism and expanding budgets.

This analysis does not answer every doubting Thomas, but

it does show that the Soviet juggernaut is more myth than reality. NATO planners discount the real problems facing even the élite Soviet divisions. As U.S. General Davison has argued: "the [Warsaw] Pact forces are not ten feet tall. They have some major disadvantages which permit us to place them in a more realistic perspective." This is not the same story (for reasons we need not examine) of Soviet tanks and planes moving in January 1980 smoothly across their own southern border and finding a "WELCOME" message already displayed at the Kabul airport by the pro-communist Afghanistan Government. There is a legal aphorism: "Analogy is no argument." But the public is fed on analogies all the time. Politicians thrive on them. A year or more will pass before the miscalculations and stupidities of the Afghan invasion are seen in their historical and geographical perspective. In the meantime, the damage will have been done, all round.

Yet, since the comparison has been often made concerning the Soviet mini-invasion of communist Czechoslovakia in 1968, thousands of vehicles and equipment had to be requisitioned from farms and factories in the Soviet Union. Soviet field armies must also operate in Europe within 80 to 90 miles of their own railheads; but their railheads are vulnerable to air attack and are more difficult to repair than roads. The ability of Soviet forces to conduct even the most limited operations would depend on the adequacy of vehicle maintenance. But need we go on to stress the obvious? And all this happened— however deplorable—*within* the Warsaw Pact area fourteen years ago, while NATO looked on helplessly and the United States forces were themselves invading in the jungles of Vietnam.

Admiral La Rocque proposes, instead of NATO's shadow-boxing, a "War Avoidance" campaign. His proposals, as a military man, strike an air of common sense. They are extremely important and are worth setting down in his own terms:

The adoption of a "war avoidance" strategy would not mean that conventional forces no longer have an important role to play. In Europe, however, the existence of nuclear weapons in large numbers on both sides has made conventional forces less important than they were in the past two world wars ... *The U.S. must rid itself of the presumptuous delusion that only the presence of large American ground forces in Europe stands in the way of aggression and political domination of the continent by the Soviet Union.* Europe is not ours to lose.

He insists that a "war avoidance" strategy would face positively what is in fact the situation in Europe today. To continue the self-delusion that a war in Europe would *not* quickly escalate into a nuclear war or to downplay the catastrophic dangers of such a war is a far more hazardous alternative.

At last, however, we are beginning to see the light at the end of the tunnel—*war avoidance*! Is there a better place to stop the arms race? *Security will grow as we put the arms race into reverse*. That is the crucial turning point for decency and humanity. But have the U.S. and the U.K. Government set up study groups of disarmament experts and peace researchers working on *war avoidance*? If not, why not? Why not Royal Commissions and Congressional Committees on War Avoidance? Why not government programs on war avoidance? Who is stopping us—the Russians or ourselves?

(3) Who wants a Blitzkrieg anyway?

Something the Western military hawks forget or never knew (since they were probably not then born) is that Lenin's Russia came near to complete extinction from 1918 to 1922. The Bolsheviks were fighting not only the "whites," but the *six invading armies* of the West. The young half-baked Republic was attacked from four seas—the White Sea, Baltic Sea, Black Sea and Caspian Sea; from north and south, east and west, British tommies and American doughboys, Poles and Czechs, Finns and Germans, pressed in on Moscow and Leningrad from all directions. They were thrown back. The October 1917 Revolution had won. Not all revolutions are pretty things to outsiders, but they mean a great deal to the people who suffered and died to bring them about.

"Never again!" The common people of the Soviet Union have echoed this cry for 60 years. You can't expect them to change that cry now, surrounded by a worldwide line-up of "capitalist" weaponry and NATO strategy. Whatever the form of government, and however much the West hates it, for all the Russians *security comes first*.

Yet it nearly did "happen again." In 1941 Hitler's tanks suddenly swept through from devastated Poland. They ravaged

Russia right up to the very suburbs, again, of Moscow and Leningrad, leaving behind them a third of Mother Russia gutted and blackened—with *twenty million* Soviet citizens dead from shells, bombs, or starvation. These are living facts. No Russian today forgets them. Should we?

The story of Russia's bloody victory and incredible sacrifices and final recovery against Nazi Germany should be too well known to need repeating. But "never again!" swells louder today throughout the land. It doesn't need Kremlin propaganda to stimulate it. Yet is is not loud enough for the war-hawks of the West to hear. On the contrary, the same (illegally) over-armed and divided Germany—or, at least, two-thirds of it in the West—is now equipped with countless missile sites mathematically aimed to destroy all of Russia's major cities. In the 1980s, as we have seen, West Germany will receive *most* of the 572 new warheads from Washington—unless the West Germans, like the British, decide to send them back.

Most of the Soviet people are convinced that their preoccupation with defense is well founded. The compulsion to provide security at any cost has nearly always overridden everything else. President John F. Kennedy recognized this on 10 June 1963:

> No nation in the history of battle ever suffered more than the Soviet Union suffered in the course of the Second World War. At least 20 million lost their lives. Countless millions of homes and farms were burned or sacked. A third of the nation's territory, including nearly two thirds of its industrial base, was turned into a wasteland—a loss equivalent to the devastation of this country east of Chicago.

The Russian people in the 20th century have suffered the horror of war on a scale that perhaps no other country has experienced. What Soviet leaders believe to be adequate defense forces will be likely to differ from what others think. But their own people are behind them, in spite of occasional dissidents on individual human-rights issues.

Viewed through Soviet eyes and in historical context, much of their military effort is aimed at overcoming their imagined vulnerabilities and matching American, NATO, as well as Chinese capabilities. Soviet fears of military dangers can be greater than those of Americans. Thus:

The Russian obsession with national defense has deep historical roots and permeates Soviet society. It creates dangers of over-reaction to past weaknesses and could cause them to go beyond the basic requirements of defense (Admiral Gene R. La Rocque).

How would *you* look at all this, if you were on the other side of the missile curtain—a normal average Soviet citizen? Forget about communism, but would you—as a Russian—want to throw away 35 years of coexistence by a sudden—massive and suicidal thrust into Western Europe? If so, where would you be *going*? (No one ever tells us that.) To Portugal or Spain or the mid-Atlantic? Where would such a crash program *finish*? What would happen afterwards? Has Western leadership not tried to answer these basic Soviet questions?

The Soviet Union is a country whose history has instilled in its national spirit an understandable deep-seated *fear* of foreign threats. Within one generation, as shown above, Russian territory has been occupied by foreign military forces for three extended periods. Neither Britain nor the U.S.A. knows this experience. Efforts to deal with contemporary issues today are merged with the memories of the carnage and appalling destruction of World War II. Unlike the U.S. self-induced pathological fear of "communism," these are facts, as they appear to the normal Soviet citizen.

The persistence of the "siege" mentality, accentuated nowadays by the cold war, and the deep-rooted nationalism of many Russians, exert a powerful influence on all Soviet policy. Dissidents face this apprehension in the Soviet courts. The Kremlin can't give them an inch. Most of the Soviet people are convinced that their preoccupation with defense is well-founded. The compulsion to provide security at any cost has nearly always overridden everything else. A workable disarmament plan is the best gift the West can give to the *people* of Russia.

Perhaps the greatest contrast between American and Soviet military matters is in the degree of secretiveness that surrounds Soviet military affairs. This policy of secrecy in military matters dates far back into Russian history. In the 20th century it has been reinforced by the bitter experience of World Wars I and II. Technical information on military forces is not freely available, not even to the military. Officials in the Soviet Foreign Ministry have little or no access to data on Soviet military force levels. They probably know more about Western military developments than about their own. Excessive military secrecy stimulates suspicion and mistrust—and not only in Russia! This was encapsulated in an amusing remark by U.S. Deputy Defense Secretary Roswell Gilpatric back in 1962: "The Soviets are forced to work hard to match efforts that they *know* we are making to match efforts that we *think* they are making!"

Where *are* the Soviet plans and time-tables for defending "the Motherland" by launching a Hackett-type mutual destruction on the West—except in terms of territorial self-defense? The Soviet Union itself announces no such plan either to its own people (who obviously must be got ready for it) or to the world at large. All is conjecture. Quite the reverse. All Soviet propaganda is focused time and time again on all-round cuts in armed forces and destruction of nuclear stock-piles. The 250,000,000 Soviet citizens would have to make a quick change of view to accept such a 48-hour *initiative*, however it was dressed up by the Kremlin. But it all falls on deaf ears in the West. The Russians are coming! The race must go on to beat them.

In October 1979 Brezhnev, in a surprise speech, offered as a *starter* to withdraw 1,000 tanks and 20,000 troops. Was this (genuine or phony) taken in the West as a "war avoidance" gesture? Every type of cold-war dialectic filled the editorial columns as to Brezhnev's motives and why the 572 upgraded warheads were the only valid form of Western response. In March 1982, he proposed an itemized "freeze." Same result!

The cold-war columnists and politicos did not bother to set this latest effort to implement "détente" within the context of Soviet *long-term disarmament policy*. For example, when Nikita Khrushchev took over from Stalin in 1955, he proposed in July that year to dissolve both NATO and the newly formed Warsaw Treaty in favor of an *all-European system of security* to include all states. During the negotiations for a partial nuclear test-ban treaty in 1963 (see Appendix (A)) Krushchev tried again to get a non-aggression treaty between NATO and the "Warsaw" nations. Since his ouster in 1965, the United Nations agendas have carried year by year Soviet proposals (even if some are phony) to limit or halt the arms race, which the West automatically pigeonholes or side-steps. That has been happening too in Geneva at the (barely reported) sessions of the new U.N. Disarmament Committee. Both Russia and China are there. This should be the forum where the West should take the lead in pressing for drastic arms cuts. But are we?

Are we in the West to believe that Kremlin leaders today are planning to destroy the fruits and stability (in their opinion) of 60 years of communist growth and consolidation by "taking over Europe?" Can it be that the hard-line generals and political advisers and parrot-like news-media are on the wrong track, always turning the remotely "possible" into the quite "probable?" Are we misled by our own bellifists into running the wrong war by the wrong people for the wrong reasons? Who wants a *blitzkrieg*, but the arms profiteers and a handful of military egos—they exist on both sides—who love to play war games for a living?

(4) Revving up the Cold War

It may be objected that the foregoing analysis puts too much blame on the United States and its policy-makers. There is a reason for this. Anyone who (like this author) has spent half an adult lifetime moving across the United States will know how tragically the cold-war mentality has blighted and corrupted both the Republic's domestic and foreign affairs ever since Harry Truman gave the signal to release the atomic bomb on Japan. The Hiroshima curse has lain like an evil omen on the conscience of the American people ever since. Underneath all the impassioned condemnation of the Soviets, millions of Americans ever since World War II have been unconsciously *expecting* the Russians to come and take them over!

This may sound absurd. And it was. But it is difficult for the average Britisher, brought up in a society where this obsessive fear does not exist, to bridge the psychological gap separating our two countries. Children were practicing regular drills in lying flat under their school-desks in California in the 1950s, as instructed by the local authorities. The noonday air-raid sirens whined their depressing warning regularly in New York and other cities year after year through the 1960s. Directions pointing to (quite inadequate) "fall-out" and air-raid shelters still clutter up hotel staircases and school corridors. "The Communist World Conspiracy"—no details were ever spelled out for the common folk—became an article of faith with countless after-dinner speakers and Jackson-type senators, until the dominoes of the Vietnam War took its place.

Two months after his retirement in 1949, former Secretary of Defense James V. Forrestall had become so convinced of the communist "threat" that when a fire-engine disturbed his sleep he ran out in his pajamas, screaming that the Russians were coming. He committed suicide by jumping from the sixteenth floor. But before his mental illness was diagnosed, many Defense Department officials and the usual run of journalists accepted his anti-Soviet hallucinations for real, *whilst he was still in office*. The Russians are (rightly) blamed for their outrageous practice of imprisoning dissidents in psychiatric hospitals. But how many statesmen, who are now seriously planning *real* war games, could pass a simple psychological test? We come back to this question of motivation later.

Once more, practically every newscast—whatever the subject—has been for years loaded with the sickly spell of "communist" misdoings. This was triggered in 1979 by the discovery of Soviet "build-up." But no comparative figures ever appeared in print to support this, until Mr. Reagan began his so-called "zero" campaign. The comparative charts in this book prove the opposite. When such figures *are* given, they are selected to suit the local scenario: i.e. three times more Russian than NATO tanks in Poland. Why not? NATO doesn't live there. But Poland's border is all along with Russia's.

Every American newspaper presents as American folklore the hysterical outpourings of dutiful editors and faithful columnists ferreting through every topic, no matter how remote—chess games, whale fishing, scholastic and athletic achievements—to prove to a susceptible audience that the Soviet Union *is* the "enemy," an enemy to be out-maneuvered and, somehow, eliminated. The timing of some of these scares is highly significant. As mentioned earlier, the "news" of the escape of alleged toxic chemicals in a mid-Siberian town came on the final day of the Geneva Conference convened to put a stop to biochemical warfare. Then the rumor, having done its hate-Russia work, slowly dies out.

The recent emphasis by the former United States President on human rights has actually worsened this already dangerous estrangement of two great countries. The ridiculous precedent of Senator Jackson's failing to swap American grain for Russian Jews (80 percent of whom do not go to Israel) was followed in the summer of 1978 by the massing of newspaper protests at a series of (to us) outrageous but (to the Russians) routine trials under Soviet internal law of leading Russian dissidents—a brave but very tiny segment of Soviet citizens.

But we can recall that this new onslaught was unexpectedly sandbagged by an unscripted interview in a French newspaper by Mr. Andrew Young, then United States Ambassador at the

United Nations. From out of the blue he said that he did not know what can happen to dissidents, because "after all, in *our* prisons, too, there are hundreds, perhaps thousands of people whom I would describe as political prisoners. Ten years ago, I myself was standing trial in Atlanta for having organized a protest movement. Three years later, I was a Representative for Georgia. It is true that things do not change as quickly in the Soviet Union, *but they do change* all the same" (our italics).

When put on the official carpet for his truthfulness in telling what everybody knows, he explained that one *could not compare the American and Soviet systems:* "I do not agree with this opposition between systems. Take the United States. Present-day American society has nothing in common with that before Franklin Roosevelt. In the thirties and forties, the trade union movement touched off a radical revolution in American life, without which we could certainly not produce today nine million cars a year. In the fifties, there was the revolution of civic and racial rights; today it is the women who intervene more and more in our economy. And this constant evolution is the rule everywhere."

Then he astutely added: "I think the present Soviet dissidents might well prove the salvation of the Soviet Union. They are a natural development of Soviet society, but its leaders have not yet understood it." Ambassador Young added that he had no fears of a third world war breaking out. "Our relations with the Soviet Union are much too good," he said, "and at all levels, *save publicly*." Will this new America redeem the old in time?

Russia is one or more decades behind the West. This has always been true of Russian social history. It is surely time that Andy Young's insight was shared by all seekers after peace. It has long been the experience of this author that there are vast numbers of Andy Youngs in America, but few of them are able to make their way to the top in politics.

Dr. Yuri Novikov is a Russian psychiatrist who worked for six years in the Serbsky Institute, where many well-known political dissidents have been incarcerated. A defector himself to London, he told *The Times* (17 July 1978) that he saw the misuse of psychiatry as a logical development of Russian history and the present system:

For centuries Russians have been discouraged from pluralistic thinking. The methods of the KGB are the same as those of the nineteenth-century security services. Of course, strictly speaking, it is not *thinking* differently that is punished, but *acting* differently, which is why the KGB is always looking for concrete acts, such as currency offenses, to pin on dissidents. But forcing people to act differently from the way they think leads to neurosis.

If the West considers itself superior in its attitude towards its own rebels and minorities, then that superiority could best be displayed on the *international* level in terms of the U.N. Charter's first requirement: "To practice tolerance and live together in peace with one another as good neighbors."

But note how the human rights issue has been turned inside out as a weapon to embarrass Moscow. That peace is a human *right* and disarmament is an essential step toward it has never crossed the minds of our "linkage" specialists who, faced with a choice of two evils, choose both. Among these missing links we find the hard-core U.S. Senate, who shy away from SALT II, and the foremost of the U.K. journalistic hawks, Lord Chalfont, who expressly cuts SALT down to fit his own theories about how the Soviet Union should handle human rights issues:

> And to those who still insist that agreements with the Soviet Union should be pursued irrespective of that country's domestic political arrangements, it is important to put one simple question: what guarantee is there that a country which cynically ignores an international undertaking on human rights, signed by its own head of state, will have any greater regard for a treaty on nuclear weapons? (*The Times*, 17 July 1978).

These Western "peace" dissidents will do all in their power to block any step, however slight and however reasonable, to establish good relations with the Soviet Union, particularly in the vital area of disarmament. What is their effect on the doves and hawks in the Kremlin? The hard-liners of the Kremlin's military complex must thank their lucky stars for the Jacksons and Chalfonts. As is well known, the former President's initiative to promote world human rights has been exploited in America as a further weapon against the Russians.

Whatever views are entertained by citizens of the West about the internal politics of the Soviet Union, and the alleged "build-up" of its conventional arms on the territory of Eastern Europe, it must be admitted that the United States has always led the nuclear race, which is the crux of the arms race. The U.S. has consistently been the pacemaker and proud of the fact. It produced the *first* atomic bomb in 1945 (1949 for the Soviets); the *first* intercontinental bomber in 1948 (1954); the *first* nuclear-powered strategic submarines in 1960 (1968); the *first* MIRVed missiles in 1970 (1975). Now the *first* modern Cruise missile. The Russians later led the way with ICBMs and antiballistic missile systems, but the U.S. quickly caught up. Every major advance by one side has been answered by the other side.

Why not be the *first to stop*? A reversal of the arms race can begin the same way. There is no mystery about unilateral disarmament. It is rearmament the other way round.

Testifying before the Senate Foreign Relations Sub-Committee, General Alexander Haig's naïve self-confidence was revealed as he laid down what he described as the guidelines of the Reagan Administration's policy in these terms:

> The United States can shape events and form a consensus among like-minded people, which will enable the allies to deal with the fundamental problems. These include the management of Soviet power, establishing an orderly international economic climate, the economic and political maturation of developing nations and achieving a reasonable standard of international civility (*The Times*, 10 January 1981).

The "management of Soviet power?" *But how*? Could the true answer be found in a remarkable admission (our italics) made by Secretary Haig before the Senate Foreign Affairs Committee in November 1981:

> From the end of World War II until the 1970s, U.S. defense and foreign policy were underpinned by *the reality of U.S. nuclear superiority*. Indeed, it probably would not be too much to say that *we took nuclear superiority for granted* and were not fully conscious of the ways in which it shaped our thinking and our strategy.

"The management of Soviet power," however, might have had a slight chance of success in the early 1950s, when the United States was unquestionably the earth's strongest nation and Ronald Reagan merely a revered Hollywood idol.

There is another dimension, too. Richard J. Barnet, Founder of the Institute for Policy Studies, Washington, D.C., has rightly called "deterrence" a massive hostage system to which "most Americans are unwitting prisoners." And he concludes:

Security is fundamentally a spiritual and psychological problem. What we trust defines who we are as a nation. To develop the spiritual, psychological and economic resources for survival and growth, we will have to put our trust in something other than weapons stockpiles . . . The only ways to stop the arms race is for both sides to communicate to each other a clear intention to stop.

In similar terms, His Holiness John Paul II, on 2 June 1980, addressed scientists at the Headquarters of UNESCO:

I, child of humanity and Bishop of Rome, address myself directly to you, men of science, to you assembled here who are the highest authorities in all the domains of modern science. And, through you, I address myself to your colleagues and friends in all countries and on all the continents. I appeal to you in the name of this dreadful threat which hangs over mankind, and, at the same time, in the name of the future and the welfare of humanity throughout the world. I beseech you: let us do our utmost to institute and respect the primacy of ethics in all the spheres of science. Let us strive, above all, to preserve the family of man from the terrible prospect of nuclear war!

IV
Holocaust as Big Business

The whole shady business of arms sales abroad is polluted with fraud and corruption. *The New York Times* (21 November 1981) reports that Frank E. Terpil, a fugitive former U.S. intelligence agent, had been accused of selling arms to various authoritarian governments and terrorists. He was indicted by a U.S. grand jury on charges that he conspired to sell guns, ammunition, and coding devices in 1979 to the now-deposed regime of President Idi Amin of Uganda. There were others also charged in the indictment with conspiring to obtain false U.S. passports and other travel documents for a former high official of Iran under the Shah of Iran.

The truth is: No foreign weapons sales are respectable and safe from abuse. The duplicity of "foreign aid" to the impoverished peoples of the Third World becomes transparent when the Western trading consortia and their faithful camp-followers in the Kremlin tot up their annual investments in the Bloody Traffic (see figures below). What they do not reveal is that these contraband exports (for they are forbidden under U.N. Charter principles) do not go to raise the food or health standards of needy peoples, but to assist their military élites to consolidate their national power and to wage their foreign wars.

As a case in point, the British Army Equipment Exhibition, chief purpose of which was to boost the sales of arms to foreign countries, particularly the Third World, took place while the U.N. Special Disarmament Assembly was in session in New York. The *Observer* summed up the ambivalence of the British position, which has not radically changed since then:

> Britain's cross-purposes are well defined. In a carefully written speech at the U.N. two weeks ago, which was much praised by other delegates, Mr. Callaghan spoke of Britain's central role in disarmament, and stressed that the suppliers of arms had a special responsibility to practice restraint. Yet only two weeks later teams of British salesmen are shouting their wares at an arms fair, to sell still more guns, tanks and ammunition to customers abroad. Where exactly does the special responsibility lie?

But vigorously protesting against the arms fair was the Campaign Against the Arms Trade—a British federation of Churchmen, Liberals and pacifists—who had chosen "Death Sales Week" as the slogan of their demonstration.

It does not follow, however, that this nation of shopkeepers is doing too well out of the arms business abroad. While the Ministry of Defense was equipping an "arms sales" ship to visit four countries in 1978, the Royal Institute of International Affairs came out with a study dealing with the whole function of the British arms industry, which was employing 275,000 people on work worth some $6 billion a year. *About a quarter of this is for export.*

British arms sales *cannot be justified on budgetary grounds*, but must be judged by the extent to which they sustain British technological capacity. But this, too, is limited because the bulk of British sales are in trainer planes, helicopters and patrol boats, rather than high-technology products such as advanced combat aircraft. In any case, the Services dislike being turned into a sales promotion organization and expect their equipment to be designed to meet British requirements, rather than those of potential customers.

In the case of the Shah of Iran's orders for a new mark of Chieftain tank, British servicemen saw another country getting equipment that would not be available to the BAOR for at least five years. (It may shock a new generation of readers to know that Britain still has an Army on the Rhine.)

Turning to the United States, Seymour Melman, Professor of Industrial Engineering at Columbia University, wrote in the *New York Times*:

> For Government managers, the armed forces and a military economy have been mainstays for empire-building at home and Pax Americana abroad; for corporate managers, a military economy assures risk-free profit . . . Fundamentalist religiosity is often permeated with worship of the nation-state, a form of idolatry.

On 5 March 1980, sellers and buyers met at the first international exhibition of military wares held in Asia. Malaysia's national stadium, the country's largest indoor sports arena, was crammed with rifles, machine guns, rocket launchers, ammunition for these weapons, the electronic and optical accoutrements of the latest in sophisticated war gear and scale models of tanks, planes, ships and the other vehicles of warfare.

Hughes Aircraft Co. had invited all comers to a multi-media presentation of "a combination of hardware, mockups, and graphics to describe some of the 1,500 programs and products that have made the company a free world leader in the design, development and production of electronic systems for defense" (*New York Times*, 6 March 1980).

The exposition had been put together by Kiver Communications, a Chicago concern with outposts in Britain, Japan and Singapore that is headed by an American, Milton Kiver, and specializes in trade shows. Although strictly commercial in character, politics had not been avoided. Singapore had been chosen originally, but turned down the request. China wanted to send a large delegation of arms experts but could not obtain Malaysian visas for them. Israel and South Africa wanted to exhibit, but were refused because Malaysia recognizes neither nation. Most of the 230 exhibitors were Western European, with France, Britain and Italy most strongly represented.

Why are not the exuberant Japanese exporters mentioned in this list? In 1967 Japan's Ministry of Commerce and Industry promulgated a strict regulation against exportation of "finished" war materials for sale. But, according to a special report in *Le Monde* (10 April 1980), American armaments and planes are being produced under license in Japan and negotiations are now proceeding with the United States for the joint production of missiles. A confidential letter, moreover, has been published in the Japanese journal *Mainichi* envisaging a clandestine Japanese cooperation with NATO, especially Germany. *Le Monde* also reported that a private-enterprise plan to export equipment for uranium enrichment to Pakistan had been nipped in the bud by British Secret Service intervention.

Pentagon pressure on Tokyo to act as NATO's cat's-paw in the West Pacific is featured at several points in this narrative, for reasons that Map 1 should make obvious. Fortunately for world peace, Premier Zenko Suzuki insists that his government would continue to hold military spending below one percent of gross national product over the next few years despite U.S. pressure for an increase. Replying to questions in the Japanese parliament's Administrative Reform Committee, Mr. Suzuki said: "We have no intention at the moment of changing the policy of maintaining defense spending below the one-percent level." He added that a five-year program was being prepared on the basis of this policy.

(1) Traders in death

The international arms trade is one of the most alarming factors contributing to the growing militarization of the world. In fact, the world-wide spread of the most modern weapons through the arms trade may be as dangerous to world security as is the U.S.-Soviet arms race itself. The arms trade with Third World countries has caused the most concern because it represents an extension of the conflict between East and West into North and South and because the weapons supplied to these countries have been extensively *used*. Nearly all of the wars that have been fought since 1945 have been fought in the Third World, and the bulk of their weapons have been supplied by the main industrialized countries, with the U.S. and U.S.S.R. well in the lead.

The modern arms trade does not stop at the harbors and airports of the importing country: it goes deep inside the nation and imports technicians and massive investment capital as well. This new peril has been described by Michael Klare, of the U.S. Institute for Policy Studies, as a big step up in the transfer of conventional arms, which will actually increase the danger of nuclear war:

The increasing sophistication of weapons permits deeper penetration of enemy territory, making more civilian targets vulnerable sooner, thus increasing the likelihood of quick escalation to nuclear conflagration. The chances that the nuclear powers will be drawn into a local conflict increase as more and more of their technicians operate at critical nerve centers to service the weaponry increase.

The following figures of the value of exports of armaments in one recent year give some idea of the value of this trade as it grows toward the *hundred billion dollar* mark in 1982:

Country	$ million
U.S.	38,257
U.S.S.R.	22,053
France	3,819
U.K.	2,832
China	2,163
FRG	1,958
Czechoslovakia	1,391
Canada	1,273
Poland	1,141
Italy	1,093
Others	3,090
Total	79,070

Source: Arms Control and Disarmament Agency, 1978

Mr. Klare cited the notorious Iranian arms transactions as an example of this invasion of American carpetbaggers. For each billion dollars spent by Iran for arms, 40 percent went for weaponry and 60 percent for technical services. The F-14 Tomcat, for example, would require one Iranian pilot and 20 *American* computer technicians to service the plane for 24 hours, for each hour logged in the air.

The Iranian revolution caught many of these unfortunate Americans off base. "In the hectic arms trade with Iran in the 1970s," states the *Washington Post* (26 January 1980), "the broad security interests of the U.S. Government were confused—and sometimes overwhelmed—by the personal financial interests of American weapons merchants who swarmed to Teheran. The Shah, Mohammed Reza Pahlavi, complained that he sometimes was unable to tell whether various weapons systems were promoted to further U.S. policy or to generate profits for U.S. defense contractors and fees for their representatives."

The unlamented Shah was reported to have said: "You Americans pretend to be so righteous . . . But it's hard for me to believe that your MAAG officers (the military advisory group at the U.S. Embassy) haven't already been hired by American companies and aren't under their influence . . . Are they giving me real advice or just promoting companies?" This throws a lurid light on what happened to the U.S. Embassy when the revolution swept the Shah away.

Documents, contracts and interviews between U.S. and Iranian officials, military men and businessmen have since portrayed a booming arms trade, hard-sell techniques, questionable payments and possible conflicts of interest, all of which raised the cost of the weapons to the Iranian Government. As one example of the cheating surrounding this arms trade, according to one report, the U.S. Justice Department's criminal division was investigating the business activities of a Secretary of Defense's personal adviser in Iran from 1973 to 1975. When the Russians went into Iran's neighbor in 1980, they knew exactly what had been going on next-door. But did anybody else?

Reverting to Mr. Klare, he also warned of a new dimension to proliferation: "By 1985, 30 to 40 nations will have the capacity to produce sophisticated military equipment." At present, the developed countries are primary suppliers. For instance, U.S. arms sales between 1973 and 1975 "jumped from 1 billion to 12 billion dollars a year." This pace continued with the end of the Vietnam War in 1975 and the consequent loss of the domestic market for arms. Moreover, with the poor balance of payments due to spiraling oil prices, the U.S. has actively sought foreign arms markets, especially in the Middle East, as shown above. The aforementioned *Le Monde* revelations underline America's anxiety to "assist" China to obtain the Mitsubishi T-74 tank. Happily, the Japanese are not so gullible. They are resisting.

Another arms analyst, Anthony Sampson, author of *The Arms Bazaar* (1978), takes the British Government especially to task. He says: "The language of the British arms salesmen is as zealous as that of any highpowered huckster, with an added element of military confidence."

In January 1981, Mrs. Thatcher asked Mr. John Nott, Minister of Defense, to help ease the financial squeeze by increasing export sales of British military technology. She feels Britain has not profited sufficiently from its technological leadership in military research and development.

It is, of course, easy to pass the blame on to Third World countries. They resent, as an infringement of their new-found sovereignty, any attempt by arms suppliers to control their imports, and will always threaten to buy from the Soviet bloc. This moral issue has to be faced, for the figures on our charts show that the West is leading the Russians *far ahead* in this disgraceful abrogation of the United Nations Charter. Hamstrung though Britain is by being shackled to the NATO warchariot, there is still one path to integrity and freedom along which the British people can resolutely lead the whole United Nations and that is to abandon and renounce *unilaterally* this "bloody traffic" as a crime against mankind.

The word "unilateral" seems to frighten the supporters of a continuing arms race. But all decisions by a responsible democratic government *must* be unilateral. Unilateral action does not apply only to rejecting megamurder weapons, nor does it undermine multilateral action under U.N. agreements. Quite the reverse. Unilateral action is an essential first step in all disarmament programs. It is where genuine disarmament starts. That is why the new European peace movements are a stimulus to, and not a distraction from, the mainstream proposals pressed by the U.N. majorities for general and complete disarmament all round.

(2) Profiteers proliferate

While in the last ten years the total world military expenditure has greatly increased, its distribution for various regions has been changing. For example, whereas in 1967 NATO and the WAPO spent 81 percent of the total military expenditure and the Third World (excluding China) spent about 6 percent, these amounts had grown by 1977 to 71 percent and 14 percent respectively. Figure 6 shows changes in the military expenditure of various regions over the same ten-year period. It can be seen that the greatest changes have occurred in the Middle Eastern countries and Africa. In fact, between 1971 and 1976 military expenditure in the Middle East region increased threefold, for the reasons explained in later chapters. Africa con-

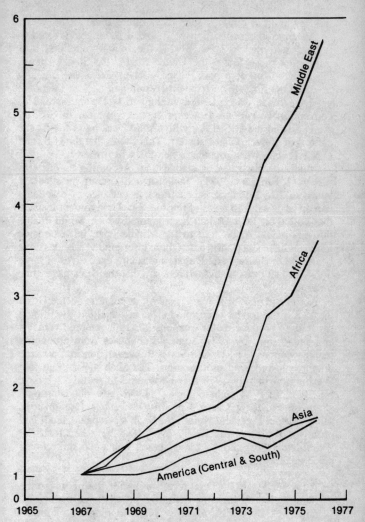

Fig. 6   Changes in military expenditure (at 1973 prices and exchange rates) of various regions since 1967. The 1967 military expenditure values of each region were taken as a unity.
Source: SIPRI Yearbook 1978

tinues to spend a considerable amount of its resources on the military and has doubled such expenditure *since 1973*.

An enormous proportion of financial resources devoted to military activities is spent by the four major suppliers. It is ironic that these four—the United States, the Soviet Union, the United Kingdom and France—have been spasmodically involved in efforts to curb the proliferation of nuclear weapons, yet have made no concerted attempt to tackle the spread of conventional weapons. However, a start was made in 1977 by the U.S. and the U.S.S.R., with a joint working group on the control of conventional transfers. This shows that the U.S. and U.S.S.R. can work together when the will is there!

Much of this traffic is clandestine. According to *The Observer* (1 February 1981), Swedish anti-aircraft missiles are being sold to Middle East countries in defiance of Sweden's ban on arms sales to areas of tension. The Government insisted that no export licenses had been granted which would enable this equipment to be sold to the Middle East, but extensive inquiries have since shown that these laser-guided missiles have been sold to Bahrain and Dubai, and senior executives of large non-Swedish arms manufacturers say that the deals have gone through.

At the end of World War II, only four countries—the U.S., the U.K., the Soviet Union and Canada—had any significant capacity to produce major weapons (aircraft, armored vehicles and ships); but, by 1977, some 48 countries were producing major weapons. The United States, however, ran into a fierce dilemma in blocking proliferation. The Shah of Iran had told Washington in July 1978 that he wanted to spend $2 billion for 70 more F-14 fighter planes. His request put additional strain on President Carter's promise to *reduce* foreign arms sales. Former President Nixon, the Shah's personal friend, had promised the Shah practically everything he asked for! The *Washington Post* report, cited above, contained this choice piece of reporting:

A former MAAG official recalls a session during which the Shah leafed through the definitive international manual on naval vessels, *Jane's Fighting Ships*, tapping the multimillion-dollar vessels he wanted. "It was as if he was going through a Sears, Roebuck catalogue," the U.S. official said. However, the Shah was displeased with the huge arms commissions in which some of his top generals and members of his family participated, albeit secretly.

President Carter had declared publicly that his policy was "to reduce the level of arms sales in each succeeding year . . . We are determined to bring a downward trend in the sale of weapons throughout the world." But the Shah had considerable political leverage because of his influence over oil policies. Also, the United States wanted the money badly from Iran to help offset its growing unfavorable trade balance. That is one reason why Carter continued to back this runaway horse long after the race was over! In the end it was Carter who went over the sticks.

Another example is even more farcical. The United States recently agreed to let Israel sell some 50 KFIR fighter-bomber aircraft to *Taiwan*, equipped with American engines. A sale of between 50 and 60 KFIR aircraft to Taiwan, at a cost of some $500 million, had been in the pipeline since President Ford *rejected* an Israeli request for a similar deal three years before. But what sort of an impact will the sale of KFIR aircraft to Taiwan have on the Americans' new love-match with China? Reagan is already caught between the devil and the deep blue sea over these rival foreign arms deals. His inclination is always to say "Yes."

And this maniacal trade is not merely quantitative. It is also qualitative. The immediate result of the qualitative race is the creation of an endless number of weapon "systems." One viable alternative to stopping new weapons development honestly is to sell a portion of them to other countries, who really do not need them or cannot handle them. (One African country had to build special roads to accommodate the heavy tanks it had bought.) This is where the arms *trade* directly contributes to the arms *race*, and this is another area in which *unilateral* action is urgently needed, as with the slave trade a century or more ago. One country ought to lead.

The arms trade is intensified by financing the development costs of new weapons systems, on the one hand, thus speeding up obsolescence of existing weapons, on the other. The weapon that is purchased today pays for the development of its superior tomorrow, thereby contributing to its own uselessness. Moreover, specialized armaments are changing so fast that even the superpowers cannot afford to procure more than a limited number of units from each system. The arms race has recently

145

become, therefore, more a scramble for variety than a race for quantity. To the basic task of killing *people* has been added the new task of killing *weapons*! But whether killing people or weapons, someone is making a lot of money out of this foul trade.

Another important by-product of this technological arms binge is that major domestic arms production is impossible except for a few industrialized states. This leaves the great majority of developing countries in the awkward position of dependence on the rich man's arms trade for their biggest "security" needs. Dependence on foreign weapons and technology leads almost always to political dependence. Iran, America's onetime pampered ally in the Persian Gulf, provided a horrible example. There were over a thousand Americans working on or in the Shah's new military air fleet alone. And more and more would have had to go there soon after, along with the other sophisticated equipment that he ordered. All this was going on behind a thousand-mile frontier with the Soviet Union. What were the Russians thinking? Look again at Map 1.

The Iran revolution was a shocker to everybody, Russians included. When in January 1980, the Russian tanks swept into the country next door—Afghanistan—President Carter made speeches about what happened in Prague in 1968. We all read about this glib comparison in all the newspapers, too. But the 1968 and 1980 events could not have been more disparate. Carter did not happen to remember so clearly what had happened in Iran in the 1970s. This *lapsus memoriae* does not justify what happened in Afghanistan, of course, but it warns us that ducks and drakes can live so close together that it is difficult to distinguish between them. The war-hawks in Washington were busy building up their potentials in the Persian Gulf *before* Russia sent troops to Afghanistan under the convenient terms of the Afghan/U.S.S.R. Treaty of Friendship.

In January 1981, the recovery of the 52 imprisoned diplomatic staff was proclaimed as a victory, when in fact it was another serious defeat which Iran had inflicted on American foreign policy. The defeat was not really the illegal seizure of the Embassy in November 1979; it was the collapse of the Shah's regime, which was the favorite child of U.S. military posture. Jimmy Carter sat on the ruins of his ideals. Yet time may show that by his patience, restraint and self-control, President Carter averted war. History may vindicate him as a far greater man than the Neanderthals who destroyed him.

* * *

To appreciate the destructiveness of modern weapons one does not need to wait for their deployment in combat. They perform their destructive functions during peacetime by diverting human, material, and financial resources from urgent economic and social tasks (see next chapter) into these extravagant and criminal devices for destroying life on this planet. For that reason alone, our repudiation of the arms race must be clear, absolute and unequivocal.

The Brandt Commission in February 1980, in its unusually frank report on international development, was convinced that "more arms are not making mankind safer, only poorer." Total military expenditure was approaching $500 billion a year, of which more than half is spent by the United States and Russia. The next highest spender is Britain. Annual spending on official development aid is only $20,000m. "If only a fraction of the money, manpower and research at present devoted to military uses were diverted to development, the future prospects of the Third World would look entirely different," they concluded. The problem lies not in knowledge, therefore, but in action—in what is called *conversion*.

It is because short-term political leaders make short-term political judgments, while "off-the-cuff" TV judgments are no judgments at all, that the ordinary public are trapped in a snake-pit of fear and ignorance, aware of their peril, but not knowing where to turn to escape. For this reason, the later pages of this book call for an intensive world campaign in disarmament and peace education of a fundamental character.

(3) Overselling the Third World

Since 1945, nearly all the wars fought in odd corners of the world have been in the Third World, and their weapons and equipment come from us. The Third World is rapidly being transformed into a battleground, where local disputes over boundaries are being turned into proxy wars of East *v.* West. *Three-quarters of the international arms trade is now with the Third World*. It is fast on the increase. The number of aircraft, missiles, armored vehicles and warships supplied to the Third World in the last six years is equal to that sent in the previous twenty.

Jonathan Power (*IHT*, 15 June 1978) draws attention to another comparison: "The West, during the period of 1970–76 provided 60 percent of sub-Saharan African arms imports: the Russians only 30 percent and the Chinese 10 percent. These

147

sales are increasing at the rate of 12 percent a year, far above the rate of economic growth of even the fastest-growing developing countries. Africa itself is increasing purchases at the rate of 20 percent annually."

Since the Third World patterns its armies on those of industrialized states, these costs will continue to escalate. Weapon systems are becoming more intricate, and more expensive—and obsolescence sets in quicker as every year goes by. Long-range surface-to-air missiles were sold to one developing nation in 1958; but to 27 in 1975. Supersonic aircraft went to one developing nation in 1957; but to 43 in 1975. Seventy percent of U.S. arms exports go to the Middle East. Rather than accept the repeated U.N. solutions to establish stable frontiers for Israel along the 1967 lines in agreement with the Arabs, the Reagan administration is now suggesting a U.S. military base in Palestine. The 1981 AWACS sales pile on the agony and add fuel to the expected blaze.

Sales of new weapons to Iran and Saudi Arabia started with President Nixon and were continued by his successors. This colossal lethal input into a future World War III battlefield on the southern borders of Russia has been justified not only on grounds of "national security" but by an impoverished United States (as stated above) in search of petrodollars. The biggest scandal of all is Saudi Arabia's defense expenditure of $2000 *per capita*—the highest on earth! One of Lockheed's executives said they were *expecting* military conscription there when the Prince Sultan suddenly announced it (*IHT Special Supplement*, February 1980).

According to the Stockholm Peace Research Institute, the United States is the largest arms salesman to the Third World, with 38 percent of the world's total. Britain and France, however, are providing another 18 percent. Yet selling conventional killers is a cruel way of winning friends and influencing people. Governments find, however, that it is "quicker and easier to administer an arms program" than one of economic aid, as evidenced by the Brandt Commission.

This is the old question of priorities. Priorities of what? Human needs or inhuman profits? The Russians also seem to prefer it that way, but with less hypocrisy. In Africa, the Soviet Union spends about three times more on guns than butter. Its incursion into Afghanistan is running up further bills, and even losing its bread as well as the butter, since the U.S. reduced grain sales. The 96 non-aligned nations meeting in New Delhi

148

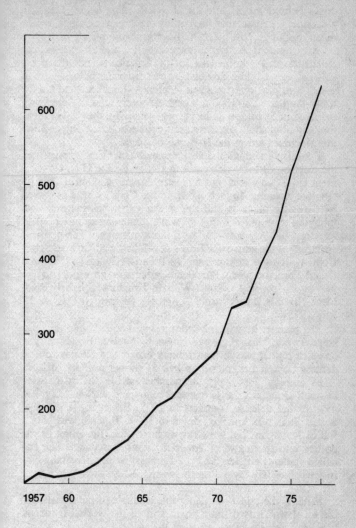

Fig. 7 Rate of increase of military expenditure in the Third World, 1959–77 (constant 1973 prices, 1957 = 100). *Source*: SIPRI data

on 11 February 1981 told the U.S.S.R. to *go home*. This was a stronger argument than boycotting the Olympic Games, which meant nothing! Will the 1982 boycott mean more?

Back home in America, however, all is a close secret about the death trade. It feeds a lot of Americans, but the press concentrates on "the Soviets." Apart from the notorious twin giants who run America's war machine—Lockheed and Northrop—there are also Exxon, General Motors, and ITT currently involved in 58 *billion* dollars global sales. But they never mention anything about overseas arms contracts. Even Singer Sewing Machines are in the H-Bomb business.

For this vast conglomerate empire, which virtually pressures the election of local delegates to Congress, the U.S. Government is just an agent, not a master. So "arms control" has no tangible meaning. In fact, the Northrop Corp., whose proposed F-18 fighter plane is still under challenge, has increased its lobbying team in Washington, while remaining solidly hooked into the "old boy network" of military officers. "The political spectrum of the aerospace firm's new lobby team now stretches from a Georgia connection, Joel Paris (Georgia's National Guard Director when President Carter was governor) to the new-style, low-key lobbyist William Timmons, formerly President Nixon's liaison with Congress" (*Washington Post*, 18 July 1978).

The manner by which Northrop is still hooked into the "old boy network," however, was shown by a recent Pentagon rundown of retired and former military officers on the payrolls of defense contractors. Northrop had 61 former military officers in its employ, just triple the number on the payroll of McDonnell-Douglas, the aerospace contractor that actually got most of the defense contracts in 1977. Before the U.S.-supported Shah was knocked down in 1979, Teheran was chock full of Pentagon "old boys" as we have seen, funneling petrodollars into the maws of American arms merchants. The so-called students outside the U.S. Embassy were understandably furious, but they locked up the wrong Americans.

What is the effect of this terrible example of industrializing the local warlords of the "poor" half of the world? It means two basic things. First, it means this:

The blunt fact is that the developing countries are contributing *proportionately* more to the rise in spending on arms than the super-powers. Their share rose from 6 per cent in 1966 to 15 percent in 1976, and there is no sign of a let-up. Admittedly they are aided and abetted by the salesmen and governments of the developed world, including those of Britain. The point is simply that everyone contributes to the problem, so that everyone must contribute to its remedy (*The Times*, London, 3 July 1978).

The other basic fact—overlooked by the champions of "free enterprise"—is that the undernourished and underhoused half of mankind is being despoiled of its natural resources and turned into a market for mutual destruction, so that the West's military hierarchy can continue to live in opulence at their expense. So where do we start? With the sellers? Or with the buyers? With the rich? Or with the poor?

Yet this depressing story of military plutocracy is not without the stirrings of conscience. Several British voluntary agencies and peace-groups, for instance—Campaign Against the Arms Trade, International Voluntary Service, Oxfam, Pax Christi, Volunteer Action and War on Want—have formed the Committee on Poverty and the Arms Trade (COPAT) and have opposed successive British Governments for their involvement in arms sales to the world's poorest nations.

They point out that these arms sales are shown to retard or even reverse the process of development. A tragic cycle of poverty-repression-militarization is created. Scarce foreign exchange is wasted, land is taken out of food production to produce exports to gain more foreign currency. The peasantry are dispossessed, becoming workers on starvation wages. Such societies become increasingly dependent on an alien, expensive and unproductive technology. COPAT agencies are urging that the British Government work with management and trade unions to convert the British arms industry to socially valuable production.

In a later chapter we pursue further this assertion of a public conscience among the peace and disarmament groups in the United States who are advancing specific proposals for dismantling the war machine. Meanwhile, Britain has begun by proposing that the 1982 U.N. Special Session set up a Disarmament Authority (which might be structured along the lines of the proposed Sea Bed Authority) or a U.N. Disarmament Agency, with a fully equipped staff and mandate, like the WHO and ILO, dealing with world health and labor problems. Again, the expansion of the present U.N. Disarmament Commission with adequate technical staff to assist governments to switch their arms budgets to development is awaited. Could there be a better use of that eight thousand million pounds—plus its equivalent in dollars and rubles?

These immediate and unilateral measures to relinquish Britain's share in this nefarious traffic must be viewed in the global context. Lord Noel-Baker, President of the World Disarmament Campaign, has stated:

> I think the only acceptable objective now is the fulfillment of the policy of the Final Document of the Special Session of 1978, i.e. general and complete disarmament of all nations by progressive stages down to the level at which governments only retain the forces and weapons they need to maintain internal order and to make a manpower contribution of the resources so released to world development, i.e. to welfare and social justice for all nations and particularly for the Third World. This was agreed to by 149 governments in 1978 with no reservation or dissent. It was remitted to the Geneva Committee and the New York Commission as the policy to be prepared "simultaneously" with any lesser measures and to be ready for the Second Special Session in 1982.

V

Wasted Billions

Of the 122 million children born in 1979, the International Year of the Child, one in every ten is now dead. (1980 and 1981 told a similar tragic story.) Almost all of those 12 million infants died on the knife of poverty: a poverty so absolute that the bare necessities of life are beyond its reach; a poverty so stubborn that a trebling of world output has failed to loosen its grip on one fifth of the world's people; a poverty so unnecessary that it mocks any pretensions to planetary civilization.

Turning to the rich countries themselves, we have already seen that armaments are a contributory cause of inflation in any economy, i.e. they drive up consumer prices, simply because consumers can't consume armaments, but they have to pay for them. So let us now look at some facts and figures.

We can start with the "wobbly dollar." In the summer of 1978 it exchanged for one and a half to an English pound from four dollars to the pound before NATO appeared. This is not cause and effect, of course; but one reality is that the countries of Western Europe have relatively gained in wealth since the end of World War II, while the U.S. share of world economic power has proportionally declined.

European nations have undertaken, until recently, relatively few military responsibilities *outside* their continent and none has felt powerful enough to play a world role nor serve as full accessory to U.S. military adventures, though the U.S. Congress has been constantly pressuring its NATO allies to "share" the heavy U.S. burden in Europe. So "Europe" is expected to pay for the 572 extra-special warheads that the Pentagon is clamping on it for the 1980s.

Asks Gaston Thorn, the President of the European Community: "In studying in detail all the various aspects of relations between the European Community and the United States, the question that must be asked is this: What kind of wind is now buffeting us? Is it a wind of isolationism? Or is it one which portends greater unity between the two principal partners in the Western world?" The answer is that it is the war wind of an out-of-control arms race that has done as much to separate our two democratic societies as it has to split Europe itself farther apart. (The 1929 recession began in Wall Street!)

Flora Lewis of *The New York Times* (21 November 1981) gives a summary of the "American Image" abroad with a pregnant paragraph:

The gap between what other people think about the United States and what Americans seem to think those people think has widened substantially in recent months.

The powerful United States, which came out of World War II with flying colors, i.e. having gained in production, trade, and investments *from* that war, has since 1945 poured its wealth, manpower and resources into the still unfinished struggle in divided Korea and the unspeakable costs and miscalculations in Southeast Asia, as well as into escalating European "defense"—always chasing the will-o'-the-wisp of communism, thereby hardening the latter's appeal to weaker nations. It is a strange irony that, today, the mighty dollar cannot look the resurgent yen in the face, since—among other reasons—Japan is bound by treaty to limit its military commitments to virtually domestic safety purposes.

Consequently, U.S. "toughness" and insensitiveness in seeking to impose military solutions on its "allies" is isolating the American people from other "free" peoples. As a case in point, Mr. Ichio Asukata, the leader of the Socialist Party, Japan's main opposition group, protested in the parliament that the government had increased expenditure on defense by 7.6 percent this year because the United States was urging its Asian ally to take a greater responsibility for the security of the area. He said: "Welfare has been sacrificed because the government has embarked on a plan to build up the defense force in violation of the terms of Japan's constitution. At present international tension is being intensified and it is at this moment that Japan should be making an effort *to break out of the vicious circle of the arms race*." Calling on the government to create a nuclear-free zone in Asia and the Pacific, Mr. Asukata told Mr. Zenko Suzuki: "If you, Mr. Prime Minister, say you will abide by the terms of our peace constitution, then you should stop building up our defense forces and take a clear stand that Japan is nonaligned and neutral." (*The Times*, London, 29 January 1981.)

A further new factor is the U.S. *dependence* on the developing world. Since the 1960s a hopeful phase of Third World thinking has persuaded many Americans to say "We need a less militaristic approach in U.S. foreign policy." We quote here Professor Glenn A. McLain, a former consultant on International and Balkan Affairs, U.S. Department of State, who has said: "As rich as America is in natural resources, we now import over two-thirds of our needs in six major minerals: bauxite, chromium, cobalt, magnesium, nickel and tin. Naturally, these, like our needs in oil resources, are essential to the creative business and military planners in the United States." And he adds:

All of these minerals are found in the countries of the Third World. These and others used by America in international trade in 1976 alone amounted to $28.5 billions. These important economic facts highlight the continuing importance of the Third World in future strategic planning by American government, business and military leaders (*The Churchman*, October 1979).

Economics is a treacherous subject. But in spite of the Western governments' attempts to switch the blame on the oil crisis and much else *outside* their control, some facts cannot be contradicted. The first is that the arms race has pushed up the price of practically every item in your food basket. You can't buy a nuclear submarine; but your tax money has to buy it! In the unemotional language of a detailed documented report produced for the information of all governments by the United Nations research staff, we read the following warning:

> High military expenditures sustained over a long period of time are likely to aggravate upward pressures on the price level in several ways. First, military expenditures are inherently inflationary in that purchasing power and effective demand is created without an offsetting increase in immediately consumable output or in productive capacity to meet future consumption requirements. This excess demand creates an upward pressure on prices throughout the economy...
>
> Second, there are reasons to believe that the arms industry offers less resistance to increases in the cost of labor and of the other factors of production than do most other industries, partly because of its highly capital- and technology-intensive character and partly because cost increases in this sector can more readily be passed on to the consumer [i.e., the taxpayer]... Finally, and more generally, the division of substantial capital away from the civilian sector impedes the long-term growth of productivity and thereby renders the economy more vulnerable to inflationary pressures.*

(1) Budgeting for Armageddon

In 1970 the nations of the world were spending $200 billion a year on armaments. The total had by 1978 doubled to $400 billion. It is now exceeding $550 billion—that is at a rate of more than *a billion dollars a day*! The size of regular armed forces increased to 23 million in 1978, 2 million more than in 1970 and 7 million more than in 1960. It is still growing and costing mankind more and more in diverted economic investment. We are in 1982 keeping 25 million armed and equipped men for killing other men, yet they cannot "defend" us. NATO's decision to *increase* present spending of 3 percent *over inflation* is the act of a drunken driver going full speed along the edge of a precipice.

Admiral (retired) Gene La Rocque said in October 1981:

Economic and Social Consequences of the Arms Race and of Military Expenditures, U.N., New York, 1978 (updated to 1982).

Surely, we need to buy whatever weapons are necessary to defend the United States, but spending $1.5 *trillion* in the next five years will distort our society and decrease our security. This means we will spend *$34 million every hour* for the next five years. It will cost a total of more than *$10,800* for every taxpayer in America. Here are the facts:

(1) The U.S. and its NATO allies have *outspent* the Soviet/Warsaw Pact military forces for many years—$215 billion to $175 billion in one year alone.

(2) This year the Pentagon says the cost for 47 weapons systems will be $50 billion higher than its *estimate* for the same weapons a year ago.

(3) Now we are building 110 new warships. The massive U.S. Navy exceeds the Soviets in warship tonnage and out-numbers the Soviets in aircraft carriers by 13 to 1.

(4) We have 347 strategic bombers to the Soviet's 156. One hundred of the Soviet bombers are still propeller-driven.

(5) We have always had more strategic nuclear weapons than the Soviets. Today we can explode more than 9,000 nuclear weapons on the Soviet Union, while they can explode 7,000 on us.

(6) The United States will build 17,000 new nuclear weapons in the 1980s, as we move forward with current plans for the MX, Cruise, Trident, Pershing II, and other missile systems.

Washington in 1980 passed funds for another nuclear-powered carrier and a $119.3 billion defense appropriations bill that was described as the largest money measure ever put before Congress. Three of the Navy's fleet of thirteen carriers are nuclear-powered; a fourth nuclear carrier is under construction. Supporters of nuclear-powered carriers argued that they are needed to "offset" growing Soviet naval strength. The usual refrain. And the Russians are catching up, for they have the most to lose. This race between the U.S. and U.S.S.R. navies is one of the newest and most dangerous phases of the arms race. Such vessels are extremely mobile targets, Senators have said, yet equivalent to overseas bases, of which the U.S. already has *hundreds* across the globe.

Opponents of more nuclear-powered carriers argued that they are "sitting ducks" in a nuclear age. They cost up to three times as much as conventional carriers. "Does anybody think that the building of a new nuclear carrier will deter war with the Soviet Union?" asked Representative George Mahon, former chairman of the House Appropiations Committee, who opposed the new carrier. But "We need a platform from which to project our power," Rep. Richard White said (repeat: "*project our power*"!), noting that the number of U.S. military bases abroad had shrunk from more than 100 to fewer than 30 in recent years. The Senator must have missed some fifty countries. There were 26 bases in Turkey alone, but in May 1980 the Turks insisted on joint control over the keys.

Turkey is a military dictatorship, so it is being courted. Greece is now in the doghouse. It got rid of its military dictatorship. And its vicious colonels' regime was thrown out of the Council of Europe because of its record of murders, tortures, and oppression. Melina Mercouri is now a minister in Andreas Papandreou's socialist government, which is quietly slipping out of NATO and forgetting the Pentagon's 1983 weapons. Was not Greece the birthplace of freedom and democracy anyway? Pentagon dictators need to apply.

The major industrial nations are now exporting military weapons worth $8 billion a year to the poor developing countries, as we saw above—three times as much as in 1970 and four times as much as in 1960. Why so continuous a growth? Since the 1970s, the United States and the Soviet Union have increased their *stockpiles* of nuclear warheads from 8,000 to 14,000. (We say "stockpiles" because all of this is totally useless junk, and must remain so—of no *economic* value.) Other nuclear powers, Britain, France, China, India (and probably Israel) have another 500 deliverable nuclear weapons. This is before the 572 extra begin to arrive. And all sensible people in all countries without exception are hoping that they *will never be used*. So why not stop stockpiling them NOW?

Over three decades, a large military establishment has become a permanent fixture in the economies of most of the major powers. Millions of people, in and out of uniform, are employed in the dubious business of preparing for World War III, *without any belief in it*! This is quite a new psychological situation for military leaders themselves to face. In many countries all over the world, the arms race has become a substitute way of life. In addition, to those directly involved in producing, maintaining and operating the instruments of war, millions of civilians are being told that they owe their economic security to the arms race.

Many cities in close proximity to arsenals, airfields, weapons manufacturing plants and other military bases do, of course, derive a major part of their livelihood from military spending. Yet the inability of the United States to maintain full employment in peace-time is well known. West Germany, with a much more modest military budget, however, has suffered less inflation and unemployment than the United States in recent years. Japanese military expenditures are less than one percent of the gross national product, and its economy is at maximum strength, even after the impact of quadrupled oil prices on a nation *totally dependent on imported oil*.

As stated above, Article 9 of the Japanese Constitution of 1946 renounces war and military forces forever. But "we're pushing them—against all their own instincts—back into a military posture," said an American in Tokyo. And Hobart Rowen commented in *The Washington Post*: "The Japanese would rather lead any invasion with computers, integrated circuits, automobiles and robots, than with guns, aircraft or missiles." (Japan's commitment to the peace race we return to in our Conclusion.)

What these facts make clear is that high military expenditures compel a nation to spend a great deal of its resources in profitless, dangerous and ruinously expensive armaments and to do so at the expense of the long-term economic well-being of its citizens. According to the U.S. economist, Arthur F. Burns, a war economy may appear to bring full employment, but it can never bring prosperity: "To the extent that we allocate labor, materials and capital to national defense, we cannot satisfy our desires for other things."

On 24 July 1978 the U.S. Arms Control and Disarmament Agency reported that the nations of the world are spending more than $750,000 *a minute* for military purposes. The (then) $400 billion total was two and a half times the amount the world spent on public health. The United States and the Soviet Union accounted for two-thirds of the weapons exported to other nations, *with the Middle East the biggest customer*. The United States exported 39 percent of the arms sold abroad and the Soviet Union 28 percent. The fighting in Africa is manifested in the Agency's report by sharp increases in weapons imports by countries there. African military expenditures climbed from $1.4 billion in 1967 to $5.9 billion in 1976. It still climbs.

"In the fiscal year just ended," said *The Washington Post* (7 October 1978), "the United States sold $13.6 billion worth of weapons and military services abroad—a record that a President who campaigned fervently against such transactions is hardly inclined to boast about."

President Reagan does not need to boast. The hawks are always pushing him on for still more! "I know from experience," once said a certain frank and astute politician, "that the leaders of the armed forces can be very persistent in claiming their share, when it comes time to allocate funds. Every commander has all sorts of very convincing arguments why he should get more than anyone else. Unfortunately there's a tendency for people who run the armed forces to be greedy and self-seeking. They're always ready to throw in your face the slogan: 'If you try to economize on the country's defenses today, you'll pay in blood when war breaks out tomorrow'" (quoted from *Khrushchev Remembers*, 1970).

According to Paul Warnke, a very enlightened former head of the Arms Control Agency, though his own influence on the U.S. war budget was minimal, his last report was done "to stimulate informed attention" to the growing arms trade and the "scarce resources" it was consuming. The following items summarize his findings:

(1) One tax dollar in six now goes to promote the arms race;

(2) The average family pays more in taxes to support the arms race than to educate their children;

(3) Nuclear bomb inventories of the two superpowers, already sufficient to destroy every city in the world seven times over, are growing at the rate of three nuclear bombs a day;

(4) Developing nations now have one soldier for 250 inhabitants; one doctor for 3,700;

(5) Modern technology makes it possible to deliver a bomb across the world in minutes; women in rural areas of Asia and Africa walk several hours a day for the family's water supply;

(6) Developing nations use five times more foreign exchange for arms imports than for agricultural machinery;

(7) U.N. peacekeeping forces around the world spend $135 million yearly; national military forces *3,000 times as much*.

Nevertheless, in Washington a group of former national

security officials has called for a $260 billion increase in military spending over the next six years "to restore the nation's capacity to deter and contain Soviet expansion." The Committee on the Present Danger asserts that "for more than 10 years this country has neither provided adequately for the common defense nor protected its economic stability." The group presented a plan for bolstering the Administration's program for military spending by $260 billion through fiscal year 1985. It was this type of well-heeled pressure group that undermined Carter's best intentions. In the light of the foregoing figures, this hard-core Committee is evidently determined to turn the present danger into a future disaster.

(2) What to do with arms money

Professor Seymour Melman of Columbia University, a long-time authority on the U.S. military economy, has said:

> Since 1951, the military budget has exceeded the total net profit of all corporations every year. The net profits of all corporations are understood as a potential capital fund. The military budget comprises a sum of money large enough and of a composition of skilled manpower and materials to be understood as a capital fund. *So the largest capital fund in the U.S. since 1951 has been the military budget* [our italics].

Another critical variable is technology. And for the last quarter century, every year, the U.S. Government has dominated research and development. Federal governmental expenditures have ranged from 66 to 80 percent for military and related enterprises. These are the only expenditures that the new President has no intention of cutting in the next fiscal year.

The importance of capital and technology is that they dominate production. Without productive capability a community cannot live. In order to live, a community must produce. But this cannot be taken for granted in the face of an intensive war economy, because the elementary resources for production, that is, capital and technology and the presence of manpower, are pre-empted. There *has* to be a deleterious effect. Precisely, that is now taking place in America. *Her vast war industry is bringing America nothing but trouble*.

James Treires, Staff Economist in the Washington Center

for Defense Information, has stated: "It must be made clear that the requirements of peace will guide economic policies toward full employment and stable prosperity. Men and women who now produce aircraft, bombs and tanks can just as easily produce subway cars, homes and solar heaters. But these simple economic facts do not translate easily into effective programs. Political struggles, ideological abstractions, and entrenched interests may greatly complicate the transition." America awaits a "New Deal" program of conversion from war to peace production. But who will bring it?

In each nation, in fact, a different set of *government* actions will be required to ease the transition from the frantic arms race of today to a more relaxed international climate, in which meeting the material and spiritual needs of its citizens will become the dominant theme. Despite the variability in national cultures and economic circumstances, a few basic principles should, according to James Treires, guide government policy:

(1) Full employment should be guaranteed by the central government. It is now accepted in the United States that support of the jobs and economic security of the defense sector is a legitimate concern of the Federal Government. It is time now to demand the *same right* for workers in private employment;

(2) Income distribution must be a major concern of governments. Extreme inequalities are a threat to the long-term stability of any government;

(3) Responsibility for major decisions about the allocation of capital investment must be assumed by all democratic governments, acting in concert with private economic interests;

(4) As disarmament education sweeps over ever-wider areas of the globe, the earth's citizens will learn to demand of their elected leaders what every human being wants most—peace and security, not merely to endure but to enjoy life—so that the energies now consumed in the arms race may be diverted to the public good.

Ruth Leger Sivard, the pioneer American researcher in this field, seeking for alternatives, says: "For a poverty-scarred world, the vista of economic and social opportunities that disarmament can offer is dazzling. What would $400 billion a year, or even a fraction of it, if turned away from death and destruction, do to succor and enrich the lives of all people on earth? The potential is so vast as to seem beyond comprehension."

In fact, at today's rate of military spending, a fraction no larger than five percent of that budget could translate into food and shelter for millions of people; it could mean hospitals and schools where there are none; cleaner air and water; children saved from crippling malnutrition, blindness, preventable disease; the poorest one-third of humanity able for the first time to live with hope of normal, productive lives.

Mrs. Sivard points out, however, that before the world can enjoy those benefits, we must find more effective ways to move toward the disarmament goal, and she suggests "the mutual example approach," as it is called, which endeavors to *lower* the opposing threat rather than racing endlessly to exceed it. "Mutual example reverses the arms race by using the same procedures that created it: action, observation, reaction. In the build-up of arms, *unilateral* decisions are the normal method and they can be made quickly. They are based on a continuous observation of the moves made by the opposing parties. If the same procedures can be used for the de-escalation of arms, there is hope that a turning point can be reached." This is the WAR AVOIDANCE policy we are advocating in this book. This is where a genuine Committee on the Present Danger could get to work on *real* safety. But will it?

A glance back in history, Mrs. Sivard says, gives some cause for encouragement. A mutual example was tried in the 1960s of restraint by the two superpowers. "Mutual example" was a Soviet term, but it was the U.S. which, in secret conversations with the U.S.S.R. in 1963, first raised the matter of informal budgetary restraint. This approach was followed up, still in secret, in 1964, until ruptured abruptly by the American entry into the Vietnam War in 1965. Mutual restraint between the two superpowers can be reflected in what has since been known as "détente," encouraging stability in their military expenditure.

Again, we meet with the term "unilateral." Perhaps it is in the economics area that the "unilateral" approach to disarmament will prove most feasible and acceptable. However, the militarists have spread the illusion that, for *their* particular country, it means giving in to the Russians, appeasement, or some other form of opprobrious weakness. But it is not only the Russians who are looking for a breakthrough in the East/West defense dilemma. Mr. Eric Heffer, British MP, states: "In East Europe today the pressures for peace and greater democracy are increasing." And he draws attention to the movement for a nuclear-free zone in Europe, backed by scientists, economists, academics and trade unionists from all over Europe; and he asserts that such a movement, initiated by the West, "is bound to help to relax tension, and the arguments advanced by the Soviet Union for repressive measures because of military dangers will diminish" (*The Times*, 5 May 1980).

(3) Would disarmament cause unemployment?

The truth is leaking out on both sides of the Atlantic that, instead of giving jobs, the arms business has the unhappy knack of losing jobs. Admiral Gene R. La Rocque of the Center for Defense Information, has asked the question: "Is military spending good for the economy?" and he answered his own question in the following laconic fashion:

(1) Twenty-five years of heavy emphasis on military programs have created a strong pro-military constituency as concerned about jobs and income as national defense.

(2) Military spending as an economic stimulant is wasteful and inefficient. As a job-creator, it is among the least effective kinds of federal spending.

(3) American manufacturers are losing efficiency and competitiveness in world markets because of diversion of talent, research effort and capital to the arms industry.

(4) The U.S. still relies heavily on wasteful military pump-priming to generate jobs and increase the gross national product.

(5) *Large Pentagon budgets are a major contributor to the continuing huge federal deficits.*

This attitude would, at first blush, seem to ignore what many ordinary people are thinking. For example, when public opinion pollster Samuel Lubell interviewed voters around the country, he heard comments like these: "It's a hell of a thing to say, but our economy needs a war;" "Defense spending should be increased to make more jobs for people;" "If this country didn't have a war, the economy would come apart."

However, Admiral La Rocque has stuck to his guns and has insisted: "The idea that military spending can produce prosperity is widely accepted, but difficult to prove. Simple logic tells us that workers, facilities and materials used for military purposes could otherwise have been employed to produce more goods and services for American consumers."

The American economist, Arthur F. Burns, once Chairman of the Federal Reserve Board, explains this thus: "The civilian goods and services that are currently *forgone* on account of expenditures on national defense are, therefore, the current *real cost* of the defense establishment." But there is little doubt, unfortunately, that high unemployment generates more enthusiasm for military spending. Senator William Proxmire has said: "At a time when we have a large number of people unemployed, that economic argument is probably the most effective argument of all. I think that we would have been able to kill the B-1 plane in the Senate last year, if it hadn't been for the economic argument."

In recent years, the Pentagon and its contractors have responded to public criticism of their excessive costs and gross waste by aggressive publicity extolling the economic benefits of military spending. Firms, employees, communities and legislators who benefit from particular projects are being persuaded of their *dependence* on local military spending and of what a cut in the military budget could mean to them. It is the losers—taxpayers and industries in other areas—who foot the bills, *but have no comparable public relations effort to tell the public about their losses*.

Against this attitude, one energetic American non-governmental organization, the Coalition for a New Foreign and Military Policy (Washington), reports that military spending at a rate of $78 billion a year is responsible for the *un*employment of some 907,000 Americans. And every additional billion dollars of Pentagon spending causes the loss of 11,600 jobs in the United States. Why is this? This is because one of the most persistent myths of modern times is that military spending is good for the economy.

This myth is alleged to have begun in 1941. The facts seemed clear: the U.S. then had a Depression, the worst in modern history. Millions were unemployed. Then, war was declared, and 11,000,000 men joined the armed forces. Millions of people went to work in war plants. And the Depression ended. Hence, the conclusion drawn by most Americans was simple: "World War II ended the Depression, therefore military spending creates employment and is good for the economy."

No one explained that it was not the war that ended the Depression, but the enormous sums spent by the Federal Gov-

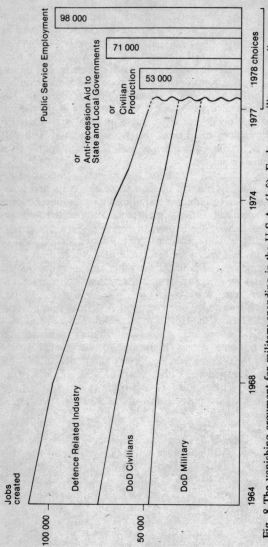

Fig. 8 The vanishing argument for military spending in the U.S.A. (*left*). Each year military spending creates fewer jobs, e.g. only 45,800 in 1977, but (*right*) up to twice as many could be created by investment in areas shown.

Source: U.S. Center for Defense Information, based on data from the Department of Defense, Congressional Budget Office and Bureau of Labor Statistics

ernment on hiring soldiers and on buying war materials. Sums of this magnitude spent on *anything* would have ended the Depression. "We could have rebuilt the railroad system, upgraded our supply of housing, and built desperately needed new schools and hospitals."

In a booklet entitled *Prosperity Without Guns*, Dr. B. G. Lall of the New York State School of Industrial and Labor Relations at Cornell University, analyzes the economic impact of reductions in defense spending in the United States. Betty Lall says that:

> This booklet has been written to make the public more familiar with the evidence that reductions in military expenditures need not have negative economic effects, if *properly planned in advance*. In fact, while some communities, labor, and businesses may experience temporary difficulties due to conversion, the evidence is that within a few years the net impact on the economy can be positive.

She points out that many Americans are unaware of the work of already established federal agencies that have been helping communities faced with plant or base shutdowns. Many also are unfamiliar with studies which demonstrate that dollar for dollar, "most non-military spending generates more jobs than military spending." Though economic changes resulting from arms control or disarmament cannot occur overnight, for arms control and disarmament agreements take time to negotiate, this transfer time could be used to prepare for the expected changes. Thus the necessary adjustments would not be difficult and benefits would soon be felt by all sectors of the population.

Dr. Lall explains that during the conversion process many workers in the arms industries would have to make readjustments, so that things cannot be left to chance. But plans are needed to arouse business, labor, management, government, and communities to contract cutbacks so that the temporary hardships for the most vulnerable can be mitigated.

On the financial side, she explains that the largest single item in the federal budget, which comes out of general tax revenues, is defense. For the fiscal year 1978 $116.4 billion or *nearly 25 percent of the total budget* was allocated to military spending. This military budget included expenditures for military research and development (R & D) and absorbed over half of all government funds spent on R & D. As a result, it

167

is estimated that *almost half* of the nation's scientific and engineering talent devotes its efforts to military affairs.

But substantial cuts in military spending would not only affect employment directly related to the military. There would be a "ripple effect" within a community where defense plants are located, so that construction, retail, and service employment would be affected. Firms doing subcontracting could also be affected when defense contracts are cut, and could direct their energies to *permanent* markets.

Studies of workers in U.S. military industries laid off in the past have shown, however, that such workers receive higher pay than their counterparts in civilian employment. This has become a problem in taking civilian jobs, with substantial pay cuts. Conversely, communities, faced by the closing of military-oriented plants, strive to preserve jobs and maintain economic activity generally. Most communities have not anticipated, at this point of general arms build-ups, a loss of military contracts, nor planned how they would replace jobs and business lost. But those that *have* planned have been able to overcome adverse effects much more rapidly than others. The average lag between the time of lay-offs in private plants and recovery of employment in the community appears to be about five years.

Since broad government economic programs are not likely to be very helpful to specific communities in the short run, disarmament planning must therefore involve local communities afflicted with cutbacks. A regional rather than a single town or city approach is frequently the best way of tackling the problem in the United States. Several towns within a county might work together. A financing mechanism might be provided by the pooling of resources of local banks and savings and loan associations and might involve a loan from a government development agency.

Turning to the United Kingdom, it is of special interest in conversion of war to peace industry to notice how national policy is related to local trade union initiative. Dr. Mary Kaldor, Fellow of Sussex University, takes a more fundamentalist position and believes that the government can only act as an investor and reverse the direction of existing policies, if current organizational structures are changed along these lines:

(1) nationalization of some sectors of the defense industry, including the profitable civilian sectors, such as offshore engineering;

(2) workers' participation in the nationalized industries, in order to generate ideas for alternative products and shift the central direction of government policymaking;

(3) planning agreements with all private armaments companies, in order to ensure that capacity is freed from armaments production and that profits from armaments are invested in suitable projects in Britain rather than abroad.

It is when we come to the reality of staff sackings and redundancies, however, that recent British experience has something concrete to offer. Two areas involved in armaments manufacture can be briefly surveyed here as pointers to the broad canvas that conversion will have to cover when governments begin to take seriously their pledge of general and complete disarmament. A report by a Labour Party Defence Study Group in 1977 (*Sense about Defence*) gives this example among many:

> An ASW Cruiser is being built by the Vickers Shipbuilding Group at Barrow-in-Furness. The group employs around 13,000 workers and has an annual output of £64 million [$130 million]. The cruiser takes up about a fifth of Barrow's shipbuilding capacity. Over its lifetime it will involve 7,000 to 8,000 man years of work. A further 28,000 to 32,000 man years will be taken up in the supplying industries— steel, marine equipment, etc.

This report looks at two aspects of the problem—technical and political—and it makes specific recommendations of relevance to defense conversion in the U.S.A. It shows that the conversion potential of the resources engaged in the production of the ASW Cruiser is fairly typical of other naval shipyards. The problem of warship conversion is not so different from the problem of *finding* work for surplus capacity in shipbuilding generally. But does the Government's commitment to world peace express itself in *specific replanning programs*, or is that left to somebody else? Disarmament is the negative side of conversion. It is the positive side we must think about first.

Vickers Limited is the largest armaments company in Britain, producing the whole range of armaments from small arms to ASW Cruisers and the multi-role combat aircraft. But the shipbuilding process, and the skills and facilities available at Barrow, are commensurate with any kind of large-scale labor-intensive construction which involves heavy metal fabrication and complex logistical problems of supply, storage and scheduling. The possible types of conversion may be broadly divided into three: merchant shipbuilding, alternative land-based manufacturing, and new sea-based technologies.

From the factory floor level, a scheme that has become known in Britain as the Lucas Aerospace "Corporate Plan" is described by its promoters as "a positive alternative to recession and redundancies." The experience of the Lucas aerospace shop stewards' committee has become some kind of touchstone. What is remarkable about the Lucas combine is that instead of resisting redundancies, caused by spasmodic cuts in government defense expenditure, the workforce has suggested the development of *alternative socially useful products* which the market needs and to which the engineers' skills could adapt. The workers' collective ideas have been put into a corporate plan. The technical implications of the plan are being widely discussed in Britain. Both the Transport and General Workers' Union and the Labour Party have made the plan central to their own arguments for the feasibility of defense cuts.

The instigators of this plan use as an example the fact that there are 6,000 kidney failures in Britain every year: 1,000 patients receive transplants, 2,000 are kept ticking over, the other 3,000 go into decline and death. The shortage of kidney machines at Birmingham Hospital, for instance, means that you go into decline if you are under 15 or over 45. The combine wants to produce more and better machines, so a medical team, including practitioners, a bio-engineer and a kidney specialist, has been set up to help them. Moreover, the combine is confronting the Department of Health with needy patients and the information that Lucas Company has the products and the skills to build these machines. Not only would this be real job creation, it might shock the Government out of their lethargy over conversion. Is not this more sensible than the Birmingham-for-Minsk horror in an ex-general's nightmare?

Mike George, Research Fellow at the North East London Polytechnic Centre for Alternative Industrial and Technological Systems, says:

In our so-called advanced country, we still have millions of sub-standard houses, we lack cheap, efficient heating systems, we are desperately short of some types of medical equipment: but Lucas aerospace workers who could be making these goods are to be thrown onto the dole queue. These workers are demonstrating that a cut in arms production need not result in mass unemployment—it could result in lower unemployment; it could also mean that we start to produce for social need instead of mass annihilation.

The two newly established U.N. Centres for Disarmament (in New York and Geneva) should now be authorized and staffed to prepare detailed studies on conversion programs to assist member states to meet their U.N. obligations and promises. Under the U.N. Special Session on Disarmament in 1978 some dozen inter-governmental expert groups were set up to deal with technical aspects of international arms reduction; but there is no standing U.N. body yet established to advise governments on this basic issue of *conversion*—i.e., how to put the arms race into reverse. This is the next major step for the United Nations to take, though each national plan must be a unilateral program in itself.

No one can pretend that the "other side" is blind to these benefits. For example, Mr. Ernest De Maio, Permanent Representative of the World Federation of Trade Unions, says: "Ending the arms race means peace, tax cuts, more jobs, higher living standards and lifting the psychological trauma of impending disaster. Continuing the arms race fulfills the death wish of a moribund socio-economic order and the probability of ending the human race. There are no viable alternatives to peaceful co-existence."

Meanwhile, private groups all over the world are springing into action to pressure their governments (see Appendix (B)) to switch from warfare to welfare. One example is the "Transarm for Survival" campaign in Belgium. It is within this framework that Belgian groups are demanding the blocking of the (military) National Defense Budget and the reallocation of the funds thus acquired for the realization of three complementary objectives:

(1) the reconversion of the arms industry for socially useful purposes;

(2) the investment of funds in the research and implementation of Nonviolent Civilian Defense;

(3) the expansion of development projects, put forward and conducted by the Non-governmental Organizations.

171

"Contrary to Pentagon claims, more jobs are generated with civilian production than with military. Moving $10 billion out of military procurement into industries which would help our national security by making us energy independent, will add 34,000 more jobs to the economy."

This conclusion emerges from Marion Anderson's research study, *Converting the Work Force* (1980). This detailed occupational analysis, examining both direct and indirect job effects, shows that transferring funds from U.S. military procurement to civilian procurement will generate 3,400 *more* jobs per billion dollars spent. She states: "For three decades, military procurement has been an unstable part of the American economy. Management and workers alike have worried whether they were going to get their next contract and what they would do if they did not. Investing in solar-power production, gasohol production, railway construction, fishing vessel construction, professional services and education will both enhance our national security and provide jobs for a job-hungry nation."*

*The arguments for arms conversion, as summarized above, have been greatly expanded by the author in a 1982 book entitled *Dismantling the Arms Race* (Logan Page Ltd., and Hamlyn Paperbacks, London.)

VI
Down with Imperialism!

Before all the old empires have quite disappeared, the new empires are pushing their way to the front of the arms race, prodded on and often paid for by the old empires. The new empires come in all shapes and sizes: Russia in Afghanistan, Israel in Golan, Morocco in Western Sahara, U.S. in the Persian Gulf—to name a few. But they all aim for the same thing: someone else's territory, his minerals or oil wells. These new-style smash-and-grab episodes or strategic "deployments" fill up a lot of hot newspaper and TV space. Africa is the main target. And the big power interlopers all claim that they are in Africa (or the Middle East or Asia) "by invitation" and insist on being left alone to share the benefits with the private enterprises or military czars back home. That is why the neo-colonies are getting their guns so easily.

The Russians and Cubans are latecomers. But they are now sending in their limited task forces to train rebel forces, while the U.S. trains dictators, standby forces at home, as well as "exiles" from Cuba, Nicaragua, *ad lib*. Flash-points of World War III are being multiplied in Africa and the Middle East and

Central America. They may unexpectedly start off well-laid fuses, so must be watched. We can look at only a few different examples of these smoldering fuses here; but there are many others. It is part of the East-West war game to spread the "Cubans in Angola" story and overlook the contraband Western oil flowing to South Africa to feed its tank forces fighting the legal Angolan government from across its illegal border with Namibia.

The sheer irony and patent contradictions of some of the *sauve-qui-peut* scrambles toward the Indian Ocean (declared a zone of peace by peoples who live around it) became obvious in March 1980 after the Iran and Afghanistan upsets. U.S. officials then began inspecting installations at Berbera, in the Horn of Africa, which had been developed and *actually used* by the Soviet Navy before Somalia put them out in 1977. Meantime, Kenya (next door), being enticed by the same Washington handouts to supply port facilities at Mombasa, has since expressed great apprehension that this build-up of Somalia's militarism will threaten attacks on Kenya as well as Ethiopia. In March 1981, Mogadiscio was explaining that it had no quarrel with Kenya. Nevertheless, the Pentagon takeover of the northern shoreline has the makings of another Vietnam, with U.S. troops and equipment flowing in.

(1) France invades Zaire

The Organization of African Unity (OAU), though not unified on much else, responded unanimously in Khartoum in July 1978 to oppose French paratroopers dropping on Zaire. OAU adopted a resolution condemning *all* foreign military bases, alliances and pacts in Africa, yet affirming the right of each OAU country to act as it sees fit. It called on member states to "put an end as soon as possible" to any engagement that runs counter to nonalignment. This is a warning to Americans, Russians, Frenchmen and the rest; certainly to South Africans. The British had (wisely) already got out and later set an example in decolonization in Zimbabwe in 1980, well worthy of emulation by others elsewhere. De-imperialism had worked.

France, however, is the only outside power to *admit* having bases in Africa. It has military "facilities" in Chad, Gabon, Senegal and the Ivory Coast, as well as in tiny Djibouti and the Comoros Islands. By mid-1980, however, the French presence in Chad had become very thin, and we will pass over the demise of Bokassa's Central African Empire, subsidized by

France. Mauritania depended on French warplanes and tanks to wrest the Saharan phosphate away from the Polisarians; but got out of Western Sahara in 1979 while the going was good. But Morocco is still using French planes and machines to fight the Polisario; she also used U.S. military planes in June 1978 for an air-lift to bolster Zaire's hold on Katanga's copper mines.

Algeria, Morocco's neighbor, cannot accept what Morocco is doing either in Western Sahara or in Zaire. Fortunately OAU has so far held the ring and kept the peace between them. Morocco will probably soon follow Mauritania and call for quits IF (and it is a big "if") the United States and France cut off the extra arms. But will they? In October 1979, the Carter Administration reversed its earlier policy towards Morocco and decided to supply King Hassan with new weapons for his campaign against the Polisario, who are still strongly resisting in Western Sahara. The decision produced a prolonged debate between the White House and the State Department. The Moroccans will now be supplied with the DV-10 armed reconnaissance aircraft and the Cobra helicopter gunships they requested more than a year before. The U.S. then wisely held off, but is now back in the snakepit again.

This shift of policy happily drew Congressional hostility. The chairman of the House Foreign Affairs Subcommittee on Africa said that he would oppose the sale: "Morocco has been a friend," he said, "but friendship does not oblige us to support a war that cannot be won and a course that is not just." Senator George McGovern held a similar position in the Senate and expressed his opposition to bolstering this illegal and abortive Moroccan annexation of Western Sahara, which the World Court in an advisory opinion unanimously condemned, recommending a U.N.-conducted plebiscite. Why not support the U.N. position? The Africans themselves do.

Meanwhile, Cuba has maintained an estimated 20,000 soldiers in Angola, but OAU did not regard this as a "base," since it is agreed that the Cubans *will be sent home* as soon as the South African troops stop backing the few remaining Portuguese anti-government rebels there. Castro's independence is proverbial and he first shipped Cubans in two old tubs across the Atlantic without Russia's knowledge, so it is said, to get the Portuguese out of Angola, and nearly succeeded! The OAU could not swallow the Washington line that "Africa was swarming with Russians." They said they had met Western colonialists, but not Russian ones.

The whole matter of neo-colonialism and military intervention came to a head when France sent paratroopers and (foreign) "legionaries" to put down the Shaba province rebellion in June 1979, only to fall out with Belgium who (having been ousted from the Congo colony herself in 1963) preferred negotiating a settlement with the rebels. The old imperialists are still quarreling with each other.

But the new military imperialisms are very expensive, and the Africans are paying a high price for them. The U.N. Charter stresses the importance of regional arrangements for dealing with the maintenance of international peace and security. In keeping with this provision, the Charter of the OAU foresees the dangers of intra-African conflicts, so provides for peaceful settlement through an OAU Commission of Mediation, Conciliation and Arbitration. Solutions to many delicate issues have already been found through this machinery. But there is no "news value" in settling disputes. We give too little credit to the way Africans are settling their own disputes without either Western or Soviet help. The Western news media are grossly defective about peace, but they resent UNESCO's proposals for widening their coverage of the Third World.

It is essential for outside Powers to keep away from the unfortunate surge of conflicts continuing in the Horn of Africa. This has already resulted in vast numbers of casualties and made a million people homeless, especially in the province of Ogaden (Ethiopia). Its long-term solution requires a peaceful settlement consistent with the principles of the Charters of both the OAU and the United Nations, not more imported weaponry and more U.S. bases.

Addressing a recent meeting of the OAU in Khartoum, former Secretary-General Kurt Waldheim warned: "We cannot overlook questions about outside intervention in disputes that are essentially intra-African." Many African leaders are apprehensive lest their continent become the arena for power bloc confrontations. "These disputes must be dealt with *inside the framework of international law*. It is only the strict observance of this rule of law, as defined by the United Nations," he said, "which will ensure peace and progress in Africa."

(2) The Turks grab Cyprus

The dilemma in Cyprus is not a simple exercise of devolution of powers from an existing central government to its component parts, a compromise between the conflicting demands of two national communities. During recent history, some Greek Cypriots looked upon Cyprus as a Greek land destined to be united with Greece; while some Turkish Cypriots looked upon the island as an old Turkish land and they adamantly refused to be "colonized" by Greece. Both these nationalistic viewpoints are irrelevant to the present need for a settlement. The problem of keeping the peace, therefore, as presented to the United Nations, has been very much like Solomon's "baby." In fact, it is much more complicated, since the military dictatorship in Turkey now *insist* on cutting the baby in two!

Through the centuries, the two national communities have cherished their own "national" aspirations. So it was almost inevitable that the two communities would come into violent collision. But in 1960 the two communities accepted a compromise and worked out (when "decolonized" by Britain) a republican constitution. The two national communities then agreed, by texts signed in London, to forgo past aims in lieu of a "partnership Republic." Under agreed terms of cooperation they shared the legislative, executive, judicial and other functions.

Since Greece and Turkey—both members of NATO—have quite a number of "private" grievances to settle against each other, their open conflict in Cyprus contains volatile material indeed. Hence, the crucial importance of the U.N.'s peacekeeping role. The function of the United Nations peacekeeping force in Cyprus (UNFICYP) was originally defined by the Security Council on 4 March 1964 as follows: "in the interest of preserving international peace and security, to use its best efforts to prevent a recurrence of fighting and, as necessary, to contribute to the maintenance and restoration of law and order and a return to normal conditions."

However, in 1974 the Turkish army invaded Cyprus and took over the northeastern provinces with great savagery, expelling 200,000 Greek Cypriots. Hence, the Security Council condemned this long-premeditated aggression and enlarged the authority of the Force, stating "that in existing circumstances the presence of the United Nations peacekeeping force in Cyprus is *essential* not only to help maintain quiet in the island but also to facilitate the continued search for a peaceful settlement."

This military occupation by the Turkish army presents a pattern of oppression and injustice similar to that of the illegal Israeli occupation areas in Palestine, as we shall explain below.

These cases of deliberate military occupation of someone else's territory are the most difficult cases the U.N. has to resolve. They are a threat to world peace and a gross violation of the rights of all peoples to return to their homes.

In supervising the ceasefire lines between the Cyprus National Guard and the Turkish invaders and also the area between those lines, UNFICYP has continued to prevent a recurrence of fighting by persuading both parties to refrain from violations of the cease-fire by shooting, by forward movement, or by construction of new defensive positions. UNFICYP also continues to provide security for many farmers, shepherds and other civilians of *both* communities living or working in the area between the lines. As the Turks won't permit it to operate in territory under their control, UNFICYP continues to discharge its functions with regard to the security, welfare and well-being of the Greek Cypriots and also for Turks living in the northern part of the island.

Maj.-Gen. James Joseph Quinn, of Ireland, is UNFICYP's present Commander. The strength of the Force is merely 2,500 men. It is now composed of military contingents from Austria, Canada, Denmark, Finland, Ireland, Sweden and the United Kingdom, and also civilian police from Australia and Sweden. The Secretary-General continues to keep the strength of the Force under careful review. So far, proposals submitted to the Secretary-General by the Turkish side have insisted on retaining a third of the island under Turkish control. Needless to add, the President of Cyprus, Spyros Kyprianou has termed them quite "unacceptable." Shaky Turkish governments follow each other: so it is the army that rules! NATO is silent and helpless.

The Cypriot Government has reluctantly agreed in principle to a compromise that Cyprus become a federated yet *unified* state; but not until the borders between the two parts reflect more justly the fact that the Greek Cypriots outnumber the original Turkish population by *four to one*, and not until the bulk of the Cypriot refugees are allowed to return to their homes and shops and farms. Peacekeeping has never been more demanding than in Cyprus, yet UNFICYP cannot advertise its day-to-day successes, while it is stopping a major shooting war from *beginning* in the dangerous eastern end of the Mediterranean. And again, a *political* settlement through the U.N. is the only feasible solution.

The new Greek Prime Minister, Andreas Papandreou, has

firm views on NATO's negative role and also on Turkey's militant role in the Eastern Mediterranean. Soon his leadership at the United Nations is expected to wake up the consciences of the Western governments to act through the U.N.

(3) Does Israel prefer territory to peace?

This was how the inveterate Ben Gurion, first Prime Minister of Israel, put it just before he died: "Israel must choose between territory and peace." But, so far, the changing and unstable political leadership of Israel has sought to shelve that crucial decision—unless driven to do so by war, as in 1973 with Egypt. Every conceivable emotional plea and dialectical argument has been used to evade or delay a decision, *on which the peace of Israel itself ultimately depends*. The single exception to this non-acceptance of the U.N.'s repeated solutions to ensure Israel's security—at the same time providing justice for the displaced Palestinians—occurred as a result of the disastrous Yom Kippur War in 1973. Egypt then recovered some—with more to follow—of her lost territory in Sinai. It would seem that only war will get back what war lost! And now Israel's open support for the so-called "Christians" in South Lebanon may again bring war with Syria one day soon. Added to which, the claim put forward in December 1981 to annex illegally and by force the Syrian territory called Golan, occupied by Israel since 1967, is an act of imperialism which has been condemned unanimously by the U.N. Security Council and the whole European Community.

So let us look behind the current scene from a historical perspective. Most people simply refuse to face what the Middle East conflict is all about. To "solve" the Palestine problem, in short, would require quite a different public attitude and a fundamental shift in political policies toward what used to be the "Holy Land," in its total Middle East setting. Western political leaders, in office for only a handful of years, have attempted no long-term solutions. They have, therefore, only supported their own national interests, based on some kind of short-term military "balance." It hasn't worked and never will. They think of "defense" and "strategy." But that has not only failed to solve the long-term problem of peaceful settlement, either for the Jews or the Arabs; it has also produced a potential flash-point of World War III, and everybody knows it. This unsolved problem has become a curse and menace to the whole

U.N. system and the rule of law in the world, while three million people suffer brutal military occupation or exile away from their former homes, farms, and workplaces.

One consequence of this failure to deal with the long-term issues surrounding peace in the Middle East has been that the tiny but hopeful nation of Israel has become a threatened garrison state, with a GNP arms budget that is the highest in the world, even though it receives approximately half of the arms export trade of the U.S.A. Obviously, all this is grossly wrong. It cannot last because of its inner contradictions and manifest injustice. It is a problem that can only be solved, or understood, by standing back from it. That is why the U.N. approach is so important.

The late Hugh Gaitskell, in his Godkin lecture at Harvard in 1957 on "Co-existence and the United Nations," said: "Professional politicians, when they have been in the job for any length of time, are not well fitted for really deep thinking, partly because they have no time for it and partly because the very practice of their art involves them in continual simplifications. If the expert is a man who knows more and more about less and less, the politician is a man who knows less and less about more and more."

Our short-term political leaders in the West have ignored two crucial trends that have happened in the Middle East during the present generation, though Western historical scholarship has explained it all over and over again for those who have time to listen. Firstly, there has been the continuing revolt of the Arab peoples since the end of the *First* World War—depressed and divided as they were after 500 years of Ottoman hegemony. This "surge of Islam," as it has been described, has already redrawn the world's political map. Consequently, the West now faces the political, economic, and spiritual emergence of a vast Arab-Moslem nationhood stretching from the northwest coast of Africa, across the borderlands of India and China to Indonesia. To exploit this vast developing area as an open market for mass weapons and strategic ploys is an act of political folly which defies moderate language.

This is the matrix within which the peace and security of nearly 500 million people have to be determined. The U.S.A. was trapped (in more ways than one) in this new situation without knowing what it was all about. Most unfortunately and tragically of all for Israel, she was engrafted as a Western and anti-Moslem state (for reasons we need not examine here) at the most "strategic" corner—from the point of view of military rivalry—of this immense Arab-Moslem land mass.

This small Western enclave, so recently planted there by external events in Europe, can only survive as a *de facto* and *de jure* sovereign state—as Israel should—by the closest possible cooperation with the U.N., which assured its birth and gave it authenticity under international law. But that essential cooperation has been consistently rejected by Israel's militant and ex-terrorist leaders, who still see themselves living in the days of David and Goliath, but equipped with cluster bombs, napalm, and KFIR fighter-bombers. For reasons too dubious to be examined here, the U.S. government has, since the 1967 Security Council Resolution 242 was passed unanimously, consistently resisted, opposed or vetoed United Nations common action in implementation of the balanced long-term security plan embodied in that resolution.

How different, however, is the picture drawn by some Western scholars, who are nonetheless ardent promoters of Israel's security and survival. Arthur Koestler, for example, in his closely researched historical survey, *The Thirteenth Tribe*, strongly defends the *right* of modern Israel to exist, as all democratic people do. But he points out: "That right is not based on the hypothetical origins of the Jewish people, nor on the mythological covenant of Abraham with God; it is based on international law—i.e., on the United Nations' decision in 1947 to partition Palestine, once a Turkish province, then a British Mandated Territory, into an Arab and a Jewish State." And he concludes:

Whatever the Israeli citizens' racial origins, and whatever illusions they entertain about them, their State exists *de jure* and *de facto*, and cannot be undone, except by genocide ...one may add, as a matter of historical fact, that the partition of Palestine was the result of a century of peaceful Jewish immigration and pioneering effort, which provide the ethical justification for the State's legal existence.

For this reason—as we have stressed before—the peace of the Middle East and Israel's security and survival can never be assured in military victories over her neighbors, least of all by nuclear "defense;" but only by an open acceptance of the U.N.'s role, which gives Israel its legal validity and a constitutional basis of statehood within the family of nations.

The occupied territories are *not* a safeguard of Israel's integrity or security, but a curse on its existence as a lawful entity, just as they are a violation of the U.N. Charter, the 1949 Geneva Convention and international law. The repudiation of the human rights of nearly three million disenfranchised Palestinians has imposed a badge of shame on Israel's policies and reputation which rankles ever deeper in the world's conscience. The peoples of Palestine must be given the opportunity to turn their great energies to the construction and consolidation of their own Arab state, alongside Israel's, with mutually agreed borders.

As a partial and *ad hoc* endeavor, "Camp David" was marked by three characteristics, which the media have tended to forget: first, that it was the Yom Kippur War that *succeeded* in winning back for the Egyptians their lost territories in Sinai; second, that it left far more difficult issues still to be resolved, namely the restitution of captured lands belonging to other Arab neighbors, Syria and Jordan—to which we can add the freedom of south Lebanon, still under indirect Israeli military control; and third, that the restoration of the Palestinians to their occupied homeland still awaits Israel's acceptance. So there has been *no settlement*. It is significant of this failed Camp David agreement that, as part of the bargain, the U.S. was committed to contribute some 3–4 billion dollars for *more* armaments—i.e. to continue the arms race! That is why a *real* peace settlement is still desperately needed and why the Palestinians must be given back their ancestral lands by peaceful resettlement.

Where, therefore, does there lie a measure of hope, of peace, of security? It lies, as we have said, in the only comprehensive system of world law and peacemaking that we have in existence today. The Charter of the United Nations, of which all the Arab countries and also Israel are signatories, has set down in the plainest terms the basis of that settlement. The finely balanced phrases of Resolution 242 admit of no ambiguity, except by those who are determined to thwart it. Into this chaotic picture of differing religious and rival statehoods, the U.N.—to whose Charter the State of Israel owes its own existence and future security—possesses all the needed machinery of peaceful settlement to safeguard peace in the Middle East. The question is: shall we use it while there is still time?

Here, then, we can summarize the essential decisions of the U.N. General Assembly (December 1979) which in 1980 reaffirmed the hope of peace and survival of *all* the states involved in the Arab-Israeli conflict, comprising three fundamental steps:

(1) a two-stage phased withdrawal (facilitated by minor border adjustments under U.N. control) of the Israeli military occupation of the Arab territories overrun in 1967; (2) a Geneva Conference, with *all* the parties represented (which means the PLO), to define the terms and guarantees of a permanent settlement in the interests of *all* the peoples of Palestine; and (3) the development of Jerusalem, as proposed in the Partition Plan (agreed by the Israelis), under an interim U.N. administrative statute conferring equal rights on all the religious communities, the question of sovereignty being left over until the frontiers of the Arab state can be at last defined, along with Israel's secure borders, under international law and with U.N. approval.

Palestine will always be the home of three great religions. And in Arab Jerusalem the *Via Dolorosa* still reminds us that the victories of the Prince of Peace were not the victories of the imperial legions, but of the humble spirit which knew no enemies.

(4) U.S.S.R. claims earthly satellites

What really happened at the Big Three Conference at Yalta in 1945 has been the subject of many books. Most of these downgrade both the U.S. and U.K. war leaders (Roosevelt and Churchill) as simple dupes, outwitted by the wily U.S.S.R. spokesman. Stalin is usually described as the arch-conspirator who got all his own way in shaping post-war Europe just as he wanted, with everything east of the Elbe included in the new Russian empire.

But there is another view which the Yalta records reveal against a longer backcloth, supported by the documents. This less popular interpretation finds Stalin the somewhat unwilling chairman (as he was) with two old-style empires sitting on each side of him—the British Empire in fast decline and the American Empire putting up big claims, especially in the Pacific. (At Yalta, the U.S.S.R. agreed to declare war—as it did—on the then undefeated Japan, at Roosevelt's strong insistence.) Thoughts about Europe were very different then from what they are today.

The United States had, by that date, already taken over much of the financial padding of the British Empire, while the African colonies were committed to early independence. So

U.S. eyes were more on Korea and Japan and on the "containment" of China. In this game of musical chairs on each side of the chairman the records show that Europe did not get top priority. Stalin had hardly any need to put in his strong claims for an eastern buffer zone. His tanks were, in any case, on their way deep into it, amidst the welcomes of the Poles, Bulgarians and others, who were being "liberated," in deed and in name, from five years of terrible Nazi occupation. The cold war has over-varnished the *facts* of how the old war ended in 1944−5. But the geography has stayed put ever since.

The division of Europe, between West and East—as we view it thirty-five years later—was almost a foregone conclusion at the defeat of Germany. The future of Europe was *not* a big item on the Yalta agenda; *the dismemberment of Germany was*. We forget that! What Roosevelt *ought* to have done, what Churchill *could* have done, is now beside the point. What *is* to the point is the Soviet Union's domination over the governments of Eastern Europe. They were creatures *not* of abstract economic or social theory, but of the chaos and confusion of the World War II aftermath, when the communists knew their minds and what they wanted.

The Helsinki accords finally acknowledged in 1975 this *fait accompli* in Eastern Europe. But attention has more recently been drawn to the question of human rights—which were but a minor product of the Helsinki Final Act, occupying only about two sections of that long, informal but precise agreement.

The Russian tanks that invaded Hungary in 1956 and Czechoslovakia in 1968 were brutal reminders that the Warsaw Pact was *real* politics and that Moscow would take no chances with dissident governments or dissident individuals. Yet it should be recalled that the Pentagon did not rush to defend Budapest in 1956 nor bar the Soviet tanks in the Prague Spring. NATO, the West's guaranteed protector, had nothing at all to say. Any more than it had anything to say, or do, when Turkey invaded Cyprus in 1974. And in 1980 NATO was sidetracked by Carter's desperate effort to handle the Persian Gulf. It proved even more helpless in the Afghanistan intervention. Where is NATO today, except as a recipient of ever more nuclear weapons? Where will it be tomorrow?

Yet the Soviet Union botched their own view of détente in 1980. The supreme folly of the aged and decrepit Kremlin— or at least its ambitious military brass—to invade pro-communist Afghanistan, though in obvious response to the U.S.

conflict with Iran next door, set the dogs of war barking across the Western world. "Russian expansionism" then became the rallying slogan of the cold warriors, who can only think of "containing" Russia by fleets and bases and allies around its periphery. The outreach of containment in this instance meant Pentagon bribes and weaponry for China and Japan. America's World War III planners were in 1981 also urging Japan to violate its own constitution and import the arms race into the North Pacific. But in 1982, the Japanese were more interested in China and Russia as markets and as partners in trade and industry for peace.

Behind the scenes, the Pentagon has quietly urged Japan to build conventional military power "capable of defeating Soviet naval and air forces above, on and below the seas for a distance of 1,000 miles from Japan's shores." But we cannot fail to observe that (as with Europe's security) it is not Japan's defense that really matters, but America's. In fact, some U.S. officials claim that "the Japanese could make a significant contribution to the defense of Northeast Asia if they acquired the naval and air power, the modern equipment and the logistical support to accomplish that mission." And, if a conflict should break out, they say, Japan would clear the skies of Soviet aircraft and bottle up the Soviet surface and submarine fleet based across the Sea of Japan in Vladivostok. Such a Japanese military build-up *would free more U.S. forces* to move from the Western Pacific to the waters around Southeast Asia and especially into the Indian Ocean (*IHT*, 15 January 1981).

As British Admiral of the Fleet Lord Hill-Norton says: "The making of defense policy is now a complicated and difficult matter for the lifetime professionals, and well beyond the grasp of armchair dilettantes" (*The Times*, 9 January 1981). For that reason, to study the *Japanese* search for peace, defense, and détente from Tokyo (as this author did in 1980) yields very different views and approaches than those that seem to dominate NATO headquarters.

In any case, Russia's need of "satellites" as a tangible bastion (in Soviet eyes) between NATO and WAPO, has been by this date accepted by the West as a temporary but inevitable evil. It is a brutal fact of European life: the child of the Second World War. But where the West has a special stake is in shaping its *own* policies, so as not to encourage Russian hawks to clamp down more on Eastern Europe, as they did in Hungary and Czechoslovakia. Tito died unbroken by the Soviet "menace."

The Afghanistan invasion cannot be traded off by arms ship-
ments to Pakistan and China or bases in Somalia. What the
West needs most to do is *relax* tensions by means of what
Admiral La Rocque calls "war avoidance" policies.

The responsibility of the Western States has been made
transparently clear by those Helsinki accords, to which their
signatures are appended, alongside those of the communist
states. This pledge is to fulfill their *own* obligations under the
Final Act, as developed later at Belgrade in 1978 and Madrid
in 1981. Its clauses, *covering peaceful settlements of disputes
and other specific programs of all-European cooperation*, are
now a commitment which rules out deliberate planning of another European war, least of all a confrontation of the United
States and the Soviet Union *in Europe*, as well as striving for
the military hegemony of the Middle East and the Gulf.

The implications of the Helsinki Final Act for peace and
security in Europe are slowly coming to recognition, without
their human rights appeal being overlooked. For one thing, the
accords eased relations between the two Germanies; for another
thing they have promoted economic ties between West Germany and Poland. After two world wars *over their soil*, West
Germans are ultrasensitive to becoming a nuclear battlefield
in the 1980s. So the Helsinki "movement" is becoming something much broader in the 1980s than a sounding-board for
dissidents' petitions. Hence, Chancellor Schmidt's bold initiative for a new West German *Ostpolitik*, and his face-to-face
negotiations in December 1981 with the East German Communist leaders.

In May 1980 some 130 parliamentarians from the 32 countries of CSCE (the Conference on Security and Cooperation in
Europe) gathered in Brussels for an Inter-Parliamentary Conference on European Security. The IPU was founded in 1889
and is a recipient of the Nobel Peace Prize. One purpose of the
May meeting was to propose plans for universal détente and
progress in disarmament measures in Europe in preparation for
the Madrid follow-up conference of the Helsinki accords. So
disarmament *in Europe* for Europe is finding new and powerful
friends at last. The "nuclear umbrella" is already in shreds. It
should be replaced by a nuclear-free peace zone (once called
the Polish Rapacki Plan) covering all the countries of Europe,
dismantling the Iron Curtain mentality, stage by stage. The
many European peace movements have opened a new chapter.

CSCE is, of course, composed of governments; but some progress was made at the Madrid Conference when, in February 1981, the United States government withdrew its opposition to the French proposal to call an *All-European Disarmament Conference*, probably in 1982. Poland, along with Yugoslavia and other East European nations, pressed for positive steps in European disarmament, but the U.S. delegates wanted "confidence-building" measures as a pre-condition. Progress was minimal, but non-governmental groups such as the Bertrand Russell Peace Foundation in London have pressed for a Nuclear Free Zone Pact to supersede NATO and WAPO.

VII
Waging Peace

The greatest success story among modern campaigns was the eradication of smallpox. For the first time in history a disease that had been among the world's worst killers was wiped off the face of the earth by a massive international effort. In 1967, the World Health Organization (WHO) initiated a worldwide campaign to stamp out the disease. Given the shortage of funds and poor coverage of health personnel in developing countries, it was useless to try to vaccinate everyone. The strategy the campaign chose, therefore, was to concentrate resources where they were most needed. Every new case of smallpox was located and tracked down by traveling teams who would ask around in schools, markets and community institutions. Everyone who had come into contact with the reported case would be vaccinated, *creating a human barrier against further transmission.*

Yet the sixth great influenza pandemic of the 20th century could break out at any moment. So a close-knit network of 103 monitoring centers in 73 countries across the world is standing by "permanently on red alert," manned by the World Health

Organization. Why not a World Disarmament Agency (WDA) which, among other functions, would stand by "permanently on red alert" against the far worse pandemic of inter-state war? As WHO has similarly set up a world "flu-watch", *with the cooperation of all governments*, why not a U.N. red-alert system to blazon its advance warnings across the air-waves before a single soldier shifts or war-plane zooms toward an assumed enemy?

The first important step to stamp out the war disease is to excoriate the "1985" mentality, promoted by nostalgic World War II generals and their opposite numbers in the Kremlin. General Hackett's private World War III would be run (as he admits) by "the older men, all with experience of the Second World War." This applies equally to the Russians, who certainly want to get rid of war—but in their own way.

Fortunately, two important things have happened since they all gained their well-earned medals. The first thing is that, by 1985, three-quarters of the earth's population will have been born *after* World War II ended. Are they not entitled to a world of their own? Are they to be buried with the dead of yesterday's wars—with the errors and follies of past wars, however heroic?

The second thing is that for 40 years quite a number of really talented people on this planet have been planning peace. They belong to all nations, all creeds, all social systems. Many small wars have been stopped and more have been prevented by (as Churchill said) jaw-jaw, not war-war. Stopping wars is not news, however; starting wars is. Can you get *stopping* a war on to the TV screen? George Bernard Shaw did it with a play. We need more such plays. The U.N. records are full of conflict prevention and peaceful settlement. But who reads them? It is not NATO, as claimed by the hawks, that has kept Europe's peace for 35 years; but these quiet peacemakers behind the scenes. Not least, the influence of the non-aligned leadership at the U.N. has a high claim to war-prevention. Western news media miss this.

In science and technology, in art and literature, in business deals and administration, in every phase of security and cooperation, Americans and Russians, English, French and Germans must forge ahead with *all* European programs aimed at implementing Helsinki, not forgetting that the U.N. Economic Commission for Europe already has some quarter-century of experience, under its Yugoslav Secretary-General, of bringing East and West together on practical day-by-day peace-making.

Nations are afflicted with the "virile image" of themselves. They must appear in their own view strong and invincible, in order to be convincing to their adversaries. Unfortunately, they appear to other parties to be aggressive, intransigent, unyielding and unwilling. Psychosocial problems among nations have received so far very little attention or study. Yet often these are the critical factors in the achievement or non-achievement of international agreements. The press and other media habitually inflate this pseudo-masculinity. This applies particularly to U.S. views of the Soviet Union, and *vice versa*. It also applies to Israel, fighting back at centuries of persecution and ostracism.

There is no reason, now that we *know* that nuclear war is unworkable, both ways, why the American and Russian *people* should not get to know each other better. In books and plays, films and music, visits and TV performances by satellite, the 1980s could well become a Decade of Toleration. Both countries have much to learn from each other; both countries *need* each other, if their peoples, and the rest of mankind, are to enter the twenty-first century as secure and friendly nations.

The maintenance of international peace and security in a disarming or potentially disarmed world depends on the evolution of effective international institutions in peacemaking and peacekeeping, as laid down in the U.N. Charter, to provide the security which nations are unable any longer to provide for themselves. In the absence of such means, nations will fall back on the illusions that more and more terror will bring more and more peace. This is why we must go beyond merely condemning the arms merchants and their clients. We must work hard on that "moral equivalent to war."

Too little attention is paid in the U.S. and Western press to the proposals put forward by the Soviet Union in the peace and disarmament field. It is important to remember that the U.S.S.R. *has* ratified SALT II, while the U.S. has failed to do so and, under President Reagan, seems very unlikely so to do.

It is most significant that at a meeting of Defense and Foreign Ministers to start planning what was called "a post-Afghanistan strategy for the alliance," one of the officials said: "We need a consensus on the long-term Soviet threat, *otherwise public opinion will not accept the necessary defense measures*, especially outside the traditional Alliance area" (our italics).

So a body of Western Experts is set up to think up and propagate details of the "Russian threat." In his 1981–82 budget proposals to Congress President Reagan put the U.S. Government's money behind his long-standing pledge to "rebuild the nation's defenses" by proposing a $169.5 billion boost in military spending *beyond* levels already planned over the next five years, while proposing across-the-board budget cuts in all other areas of federal spending. To waste this colossal sum on war, he has to exaggerate the "Russian threat" and repeat what his experts are telling him it is.

On 25 September 1980 the U.S.S.R. submitted a memorandum on *Peace, Disarmament and Guarantees of International Security* at the U.N. General Assembly. The proposals included the cessation of the nuclear arms race and renunciation of force in international relations. Specifically, an international convention was proposed, binding participants not to use nuclear weapons in any circumstances; not to produce or store such weapons; and to destroy all stocks within three months. Negotiations were to begin at once toward this plan, and in 1981 the complete and universal prohibition of nuclear weapons tests was to begin. *Again, silence from the West.*

The science of peace has many advocates today. A new doctrine for modern man has been gradually pushing its way between the outmoded rival antagonisms of communism and capitalism. With the help of the Third World and the non-aligned countries, working through the U.N., as we have noted, the beginning of a new type of *world* democracy is slowly emerging. As U.S. representative Mrs. Benton told the U.N.'s Special Session on Disarmament in 1978, the important thing is to bring all these new aspects to the comprehension of the ordinary citizen.

"Fundamental changes in the world often occur without being noticed," says Nobel Peace Prize laureate Sean Mac-Bride. And he continues: "An instance of this has been the important change which has been taking place since the Second World War in the center of gravity of power, *from governments to public opinion*." Two factors have rendered this change inevitable, he states: (1) higher standards of literacy and education, which enabled public opinion to be much better informed on national and international affairs than ever before; and (2) the development of the mass media—printed and audiovisual—which has brought news, information and views instantly to the entire human race. Even people who cannot read are instantly informed of events as they take place throughout the world (*The Times*, 21 March 1980).

Meanwhile, disarmament campaigns across the world, research institutes and even statesmen of the smaller and medium-sized countries—especially in Canada, the Scandinavian and some Asian countries—press for urgent interim measures to block the Big Powers from destroying the planet. Here follow a few of their on-going proposals, as this gargantuan conflict between the warmongers and the peacemakers gathers world-wide momentum.

Henry Thoreau, American naturalist and philosopher, said: "If a man does not keep pace with his companions, it is perhaps because he hears a different drummer. Let him step to the music he hears, however measured or far away." More and more Americans are listening to Europe, not to Russia!

(1) "Ban the Bomb!"
This cry grows ever louder among popular movements in the U.K., the U.S. and U.S.S.R. Four types of bans are *being operated now* under the United Nations disarmament machinery, so this is a good beginning toward a *total* ban. (See details below and Appendix (A).) Nuclear war is genocide—an international crime.

In October 1981, just outside the gates of the Greenham Common USAF base, which is scheduled to host some of the Cruise missiles that NATO has decided to deploy in England, a woman, handsome, fortyish, dressed in a comfortable jumpsuit, was standing on the back of a truck, shouting into a megaphone. "I've never been on a demonstration in my life before," she was saying. "I'm not a political person. But when I read about this march in the newspaper I decided that I had to do *something*. So I dropped everything and came. And I brought my child with me. Because this is about her future." She was one of about 50 women who had walked for seven days the 120 miles from Cardiff to Greenham Common in order to protest about the Government's decision to purchase the American Trident missile system and to accept Cruise missiles on British soil. (*The Observer*, London, 18 Ocotber 1981.)

(1) *Nuclear Test Ban*. This has been debated at the U.N. since 1963, but the United Kingdom, France and the United States still lag behind. Underground testing still continues; while France has continued testing in the atmosphere and in

the oceans, refusing to sign the 1963 Partial Test Ban Treaty. France has so badly damaged parts of the South Pacific atoll of Mururoa with its underground nuclear weapons testing that it may move the tests to another island in French Polynesia. Underground testing has enabled nuclear weapon states to develop new generations of warheads. If it were stopped *it would freeze the nuclear arms race*.

(2) *A Moratorium*. Haven't we already enough nuclear weapons to blow up the planet six times? And more conventional weapons and men under arms than ever before in "peacetime" in human history? Can't we call it a day and *STOP* piling on the agony? Rumania, a Soviet satellite, put this proposal before the 1978 U.N. Special Session on Disarmament, and has been pressing it at the Committee on Disarmament in Geneva ever since:

> All participating states should agree to freeze military expenditure, military forces and armaments at the 1978 level, and beginning as early as 1979, to move on to their gradual reduction. In the first stage, up to 1985, the reduction should be between 10 and 15 percent of the present levels and should cover all components of the armed forces, land, sea and air, and all categories of weapons.

(3) *Nuclear Free Zones*. These are beginning, but the Big Powers (or their satellites) are blocking their extension. Latin America has been declared a nuclear free zone under the 1967 Tlatelolco Treaty. But Argentina and Brazil are reneging. India presses for an Indian Ocean Nuclear Free Treaty. But Britain, U.S. and Russia are each opposed to it. Middle Eastern Arab nations want to keep out nuclear weapons, but the superpowers refuse. In their midst, Israel clings to nuclear "options" to safeguard her illegally occupied territories, supported by U.S. "strategic" agreements. So the struggle for sanity in the world's danger zones goes on.

Conversely, on what is called "NATO's northern flank" and what the Swedes and Danes prefer to call "the Sea of Peace," the Russians are maneuvering six nuclear-equipped submarines in the Baltic. One of them ran aground off Sweden and filled the headlines with ugly rumors in the fall of 1981. Thus, the infamous MAD doctrine has given a bastard birth to MAB. Why? The growth of Soviet military power "is increasingly threatening the security of the northern flank of our defensive alliance," said U.S. Ambassador Komer on 19 January 1981: "The strongest Soviet naval forces are in the Kola Peninsula . . . If the Warsaw Pact concentrates forces against the northern flank of NATO, reinforcements will be necessary, and necessary soon." That is the purpose of the program initiated by the Pentagon for the "storage" of heavy equipment for a 10,000-man U.S. Marine Amphibious Brigade (MAB) which will be "pre-positioned" in central Norway. This new military term "pre-positioned" has a somewhat dubious context.

(4) *Outer Space Treaty*. By this 1967 Treaty, over seventy nations have prohibited the placing of nuclear weapons in orbit. But the Big Powers are now thinking up new devices for destroying satellites *in orbit*. Two-thirds of the "spy" and other satellites now in orbit are under U.S. or U.S.S.R. military control. However, American and Soviet officials have been wisely having preliminary talks on hunter-killer satellites in Bern recently, in order that they may develop a better understanding of each other's views. This is good news. Hunter-killer satellites would be able to destroy or capture other craft in orbit. The talks will continue at a later date. We must press for their conclusion by an extension of the 1967 Treaty, which would also prohibit earth-based *laser* weapons. And watch that new Space Shuttle! The military men have an eye on it.

(2) A World Disarmament Conference?

The convening of this Conference was pressed at the 1978 Special Session on Disarmament. Although both Russia and China and nearly all the small and medium states want it, the U.S. and U.K. so far oppose it. Why? Other nations in NATO are divided: some for, some against. Where do *you* stand?

The 1978 Special Session put off a decision for four years. That means 1982 will be a critical year to prepare for a World Disarmament Treaty to replace the NATO and WAPO pacts! For the liquidation of these rival war alliances is a *sine qua non* of genuine disarmament. But 1982 will witness a fierce struggle between the arms insisters and the war resisters. The contest will be particularly acute in the United States, with the Haigs and hawks in the saddle. And the Russians will have a field-day with propaganda. It is the Pied Pipers that call the tune; but it will be the children who will die.

Meanwhile, in the summer of 1980 another special session of the U.N. General Assembly met in New York to deal with the relations of development to disarmament. These continuing efforts of the U.N. to provide a bridge between the so-called developed nations and the developing world are being frustrated by the insistence of the Big Armed Powers on putting their military strategies first. Mrs. Inga Thorsson's U.N. Report in 1981 on "Arms and Development" is one of the most vital documents of this century.* For the switch must now be made between guns and butter, between swords and plowshares, between nuclear death and reverence for life.

The criminal and self-defeating U.S.S.R. blunder in Afghanistan in January 1980 was worsened by Pentagon threats of widening the battle area to include the whole Middle East and Gulf region. Obviously, there must be found some spot on the planet where reason and sense can be brought to bear on this unilateral thuggery by military empire-builders? The United Nations has been painfully and slowly building the global machinery and psychology—called "political will"—to master this anarchy of irresponsible statesmanship. What is, then, the U.N.'s agreed program for disarmament?

In opening the second Session of the Committee on Disarmament on 5 February 1980, the Secretary-General set out the current U.N. program in the following terms:

The Committee is now called upon to initiate constructive negotiations on a number of important questions. The participation for the first time of the five nuclear-weapon states in this negotiating body should open new opportunities for concrete progress in . . . a comprehensive nuclear test ban, with its direct bearing on the halting of the arms race and the strengthening of the non-proliferation regime, nuclear disarmament, the prohibition of all chemical and radiological weapons, effective arrangements for assuring non-nuclear-weapon states against the use or threat of use of nuclear weapons—all these are subjects which need to be dealt with urgently for reducing the appalling threat to the human community.

The urgency of these steps becomes more strident as war fears spread across Europe—especially in West Germany, which has been twice dismembered within living memory. While, across the frontier, the Soviet Union has told France

*The findings of this report are included in the author's *Dismantling the War Machine*, Logan Page Ltd., and Hamlyn Paperbacks, London.

that it would have to *increase* nuclear arming if Western Europe deployed the 572 new weapons. This message, which accused the U.S. of trying to "Europeanize nuclear war while America digs in across the Atlantic," was delivered in a speech in Paris by Soviet Ambassador Chervonenko. "Soviet arms control specialists are telling U.S. contacts that they are prepared to plunge into another round of the arms race, but would much rather not do so." (*IHT*, 28 June 1980)

In Geneva on Wednesday, 31 March 1982, the United Nations observed, by a solemn ceremony and an impressive exhibition of the contemporary records and documents, the Fiftieth Anniversary of the First Disarmament Conference in 1932. That sad period in the history of the abortive League of Nations (with the U.S. a non-member) was carefully surveyed by leading authorities. But one conclusion emerged with unmistakable clarity: the *failure* of that 1932 conference led directly and inevitably to the Second World War.

A Third World War is *NOT* inevitable, unless our governments make it so *NOW*. There is still time to stop it.

But it is not sufficient merely to oppose the mad policies of governments. The new "peace movements" of Europe, and beyond, have made a surprisingly good start. They must, as soon as possible, move into *positive* peace programs. The West, because of our traditions and opportunities, must make a habit of using the U.N.'s unique offices in the first place—ahead of others—and so help to set up an example to build up the rule of law in this dangerous world. It is when governments and their peoples say "it is *OUR* U.N., we must use it for our security and welfare," that one of the main purposes of the Charter will be achieved. For it states (Art. 2): "All members, in order to ensure to all of them the rights and benefits resulting from membership, shall fulfil in good faith the obligations assumed by them in accordance with the present Charter."

This is how one motivated American citizen (Mr. Walter Hoffman, Chairman of the Campaign for U.N. Reform) argued in a telegram to President Carter in December 1979:

WE URGE YOU TO AVOID UNILATERAL MILITARY ACTION IN THE CURRENT IRANIAN CRISIS UNDER ALL CIRCUMSTANCES. US ARMED INTERVENTION COULD HAVE DISASTROUS CONSEQUENCES AND COULD TRIGGER WORLD WAR III. KEEP WORKING THROUGH UNITED NATIONS SYSTEM IN SPITE OF ITS WEAK-

NESSES. WE COMMEND YOU FOR BRINGING HOSTAGE ISSUE TO
UN SECURITY COUNCIL AND TO INTERNATIONAL COURT OF
JUSTICE. BLOCKADE SHOULD NOT BE IMPOSED UNLESS UN AP-
PROVAL IS OBTAINED. URGE YOU TO ASK FOR UN OBSERVERS
AND UN MEDIATION. ASK UN TO OFFER TO PROVIDE FORUM TO
INVESTIGATE ALLEGATIONS AGAINST THE SHAH IN RETURN
FOR RELEASE OF HOSTAGES. UN IS OUR ONLY HOPE OF BRING-
ING HOSTAGES BACK ALIVE AND MAINTAINING WORLD PEACE.

No one who has read thus far will doubt the magnitude of
the issues facing the world in the 1980s. They will determine
whether some species of Hackett game is to be played out to
its logical conclusion (*sic*), or whether the switch can be made
in time from Doomsday to Development. The 1970s were designated by international agreement as both the Disarmament
Decade and the Development Decade. The fact is that the world
community has so far failed in both directions. Our defense
bills have increased, in real terms, at some 2.5 percent a year
through this decade, which has seen no real disarmament. This
was before the overall 3 percent was imposed by NATO in
1979. In fact, the MAD race has accelerated faster than ever
before, especially in developing countries. There is worse to
come, unless we *STOP*!

It is now accepted by economists that unless there is a
reallocation of resources from defense to development, the
hopes for a new international economic order (NIEO) to save
the starving 500 million children in the poorest countries, are
doomed to frustration. The realization that the NIEO could
succeed only if the arms race could be *reversed* and resources
reallocated to development stimulated the Special Session devoted to Disarmament in 1978. For the first time in world
history, the (then) 149 members of the United Nations considered where the arms race was leading them, and how it could
be halted. The more important stage was scheduled for 1982.
We repeat: "Where do *you* stand?"

> If reduced to a simple denominator, this Report deals with
> peace. War is often thought of in terms of military conflict,
> or even annihilation. But there is a growing awareness that
> an equal danger might be chaos—as a result of mass hun-
> ger, economic disaster, environmental catastrophes, and
> terrorism. So we should not think only of reducing the tra-
> ditional threats to peace, but also of the need for change

(3) Remote-sensing techniques

One of the chronic obstacles to stopping the arms race in the past has been lack of *verification*. What happens if a nation cheats on its promises to disarm? So disarmament agreements have been blocked in two ways. The Americans have said: "We don't trust you; we must have our inspectors go in and see if you are doing what you agree to do." The Russians reply: "We don't trust you either; we won't have your inspectors prowling around our secret installations!"

This is a spurious argument at best. If a mutual bargain to cut down arms on both sides takes so much time and trouble to reach, the possibilities of its breach are remote, because both sides *want* it. The big thing is to get the cuts agreed in the first place. Obviously they will have to benefit all sides. For example, an almost forgotten State Department bulletin reads:

> U.S. participation in SALT is based not on blind trust in the U.S.S.R. but upon an expectation that the Soviets will act in their own best interest. It is in their interest to restrain the nuclear arms race and not to start a nuclear war that would destroy their society. Arms competition is more burdensome for them because they are the poorer country, and more dangerous because they would be at a disadvantage in an all-out race with a competitor of our strength, resources and technology.

In many U.N. discussions, progress has been stalled on "on-site" inspection. Now the argument is beginning to wear thin. Since the days of Gary Powers and his notorious U-2 gamble, there is probably not a nuclear weapon site in either the Soviet Union or continental Europe, or the United States, that has not been photographed—even down to details of postage stamp size. Hence, the "other side" knows where to hit, within a couple of yards, if it can. This revolution in aeronautical science has now made nonsense of the military strategists' theory that they don't know what the other side is doing, though the M-X fantasy may present (temporarily) some extra problems.

Even as far back as the Cuban crisis in 1962, U.S. delegate Adlai Stevenson was able to screen for the information of the

U.N. Security Council large-scale photographs of exactly where Krushchev's missiles were installed (this author was present). Since that date not a spot on the surface of the globe is hidden from the aerial spy's candid camera. What are we waiting for?

Moreover, scientists will soon put an experimental sensing device 1,500 feet under the sea floor to check whether it improves earthquake monitoring, so the U.S. National Science Foundation has announced. This seismic device will be the first ever placed permanently under the sea bottom, and could be the forerunner of a network of *neutral* instruments placed by the U.N. throughout the oceans of the world.

The Swedish Government told the U.N. Special Session in 1978 that the main part of a verification system under a comprehensive Test Ban Treaty should consist of an international exchange of seismological data from a global network of seismological stations. Sweden is therefore participating in the ongoing efforts within the framework of the Committee on Disarmament pursuing this matter in Geneva. "The right of full access by parties to a comprehensive test-ban treaty to relevant data is of vital importance;" and Sweden has backed this up by offering to establish, to operate, and to finance an international seismological data center.

The U.N.'s Expert Group on Seismic Detection (set up by a General Assembly vote of 124 to none) recommended in 1979 the establishment of an international control and monitoring system, consisting of a global network of some 50 seismological stations, as well as arrangements for fast worldwide exchange of data over the global system of the World Meteorological Organization (WMO). The Group called for special data centers, strategically located throughout the world, for use by participating states.

Thus the earth is becoming—overground and underground—an open book, except for the closed minds of a jingoist minority whose dogmas inherited from past wars are so remote from commonsense that no sensing device will break through their mistrust of their fellow-men or their illusions of the virtues of violence.

Dr. John Cox, in *Overkill*, has put this real issue into perspective:

So the main stumbling block in the way of disarmament is simply a lack of willingness to disarm... Aerial photography has proved most useful and the major military powers now have very accurate knowledge of the disposition of each other's forces and weapons, missile accuracy and numbers and many other matters of considerable military importance. These spying techniques could equally well be used to verify disarmament.

Our world pool of knowledge on "monitoring" disarmament increases from day to day. All that is lacking is the *political will* to employ today's technology to advance peace and security instead of activating the "1985" nightmares of yesterday's generals. Peter Jankowitsch of Austria, Chairman of the Outer Space Committee, reminds us that this U.N. project has now entered its third decade of cooperation. "The first two decades begin with the first signals of *Sputnik*—full of the drama which only the exploration of a new dimension of human life can bring," he said. "But the third decade of space cooperation might be the one in which human presence in outer space becomes a permanent feature. We really begin to push forward the frontiers of our planet."

Among the issues now before his Committee is the comprehensive remote-sensing of the earth *from space*. It is true that the communist countries are a little shy of all this disturbing revelation of their alleged earthly secrets and, especially, its threat to "national sovereignty." But the first pioneers of space will surely get used to it, given time. We must be patient with governments, until they catch up with U.N. ideals and procedures.

France presented to the Special Session in 1978 specific proposals for setting up an "international satellite monitoring agency," as a permanent organ of the United Nations. The U.N. satellite system, France has said, could remove some of the obstacles on the path of international safeguards and inspection for disarmament agreements. "This satellite monitoring agency would become an essential adjunct to disarmament agreements and to measures to increase international confidence and security." The monitoring agency "shall be responsible for collecting, processing and disseminating information secured by means of earth observation satellites."

Under the French plan, the Security Council might take action by invoking Article 34 of the United Nations Charter which authorizes it to "investigate any dispute or any situation which might lead to international friction or give rise to a dispute." France again pressed this plan at the Committee on Disarmament in March 1980. It is a pity that France does not set an example by stopping its atmospheric and leaky underground tests in the Pacific and declare that ocean a Zone of Peace!

Proposals from other countries come crowding in. There is no longer any excuse for the Big Nuclear Powers to hide their silos, their troop movements, their storage depots—*because they can't*. There is no longer any possibility for either Americans or Russians to shield behind lethal secrets hidden in tunnels!

A new era has begun. The Outer Space Treaty of 1967, which over 70 nations have signed, can now be effectively enlarged and equipped with the International Satellite Verification Agency, in fulfillment of Article III, which reads: "State Parties to the Treaty shall carry on activities in the exploration and use of outer space...in accordance with international law...in the interest of maintaining international peace and security and promoting international cooperation and understanding."

When the European and other "peace movements" decide to move their policies forward from protests against recalcitrant governments to implement the positive programs grounded on the 35 years experience of the United Nations Charter, they will be able to avail themselves of the latest gifts of contemporary science and the fast-expanding resources of modern technology. The "peace movements" will then inherit a new earth. The American movements, in particular, must move in the 1980s from mere protests against outmoded national weaponry to a call to revise American technology in the service of world security.

VIII
Peace Soldiers Arrive

This book began by calling for "a plague on both their houses"—i.e. America's so-called "capitalism" and Russia's alleged "communism," whose bomb-devoted diplomacy has long since become irrelevant to human needs and international security. We have adduced ample evidence in the intervening chapters deploring the egoistic pretensions of the military bullies on both sides to dominate large areas of this planet in their self interests. Well over a hundred small and medium-sized nations now stand between the nuclear rivals as neutral or unaligned powers, seeking to replace an obsolete arms race with an enhanced U.N. role in peacemaking and peacekeeping.

It is significant that Mr. Reagan's speech of 18 November 1981 (e.g., "Today I have announced an agenda that can help to achieve peace, security, and freedom across the globe") is totally devoid of any *global* sense of what peace means. He said:

> But today a new generation is emerging on both sides of the Atlantic. Its members were not present at the creation

of the North Atlantic Alliance. Many of them do not fully understand its roots in defending freedom and rebuilding a war-torn continent. Some young people question why we need weapons—particularly nuclear weapons—to deter war and to assure peaceful development.

Whereas the speech referred over thirty times to the crumbling North Atlantic Alliance, there was only one passing reference—to a past President "addressing the United Nations twenty years ago"—that the U.N. existed at all! Certainly no acknowledgement was made that the Third World existed; certainly no grasp of the fact that, for 35 years, the United States had been committed to the principles and practices of the U.N. Charter. We can, therefore, look in this chapter at just one of the most obvious *global* requirements of peacekeeping that matter most for that new generation.

At 4 o'clock in the morning of 4 November 1956, the Canadian representative, the Hon. Lester Pearson, introduced into the General Assembly debate that had been going on heatedly all the previous day and night, a proposal to send a contingent of "neutral" soldiers, selected from some half-dozen smaller states, to stand between the Israelis and the Egyptians who were then fighting as a result of Israel's aggression in Sinai, backed by the British and French Governments.

Thus, UNEF (U.N. Emergency Force) was born. It was actually a child of Dag Hammarskjöld's brain, for he planned its "modalities." And it stayed in position as a go-between along the Israeli-Egyptian border of Gaza and Sinai for eleven years, until the fateful day on 4 June 1967 when peace was broken again and another Arab-Israeli war had begun.

These remarkable U.N.-controlled "police" forces, selected from friendly nations, have now been in operation—as we have seen in earlier chapters—for a quarter of a century. They have been peacekeepers in Kashmir, Cyprus, Congo, Syria and Egypt and now in Lebanon and on the Golan Heights. Their role has not always been a safe or easy one and they have thus far been assembled on an *ad hoc* basis. But in that quarter of a century, techniques have been improvised and developed, political obstacles have been overcome, and finances have been provided by the Security Council. Thus, the world community has gained a new and flexible instrument to stop the peacebreakers and the warmongers. So the U.N. peacekeepers are here to stay.

This is only a beginning. Many proposals are on foot to develop U.N.-peacekeeping operations into an effective and *permanent stand-by policing system* to outwit and, one day, replace the militarists altogether.

Such U.N. peacekeepers differ *fundamentally* from national military forces, though for the time being they are being drawn from them. Here is a capsule list of some of the ways in which they are to be differentiated from national armies:

(1) They are servants of the world.

(2) They do not take sides in an armed struggle.

(3) They are selected from national forces having no direct interest in the conflict.

(4) They are a *global* institution.

(5) They "police" the local situation, while the Security Council decides on the *political* issues involved.

(6) They serve under a U.N. Commander, who is responsible to the Secretary-General.

(7) They must not shoot or use military weapons, except when under attack and in self-defense.

(8) They are selected and specially trained in techniques to anticipate and prevent local violence.

(9) They come at the invitation of the country concerned, not as an "occupation" army.

(10) They represent a new step toward world security that does not endanger the security of anyone.

(1) Policing the Middle East

No one assumes that this crucial experiment in peacekeeping is without blemishes. Some governments that prefer their own futile methods of military force have obstructed or opposed the U.N. peacekeeping operation from the beginning, or they have refused to allocate material or men or finances to support it. Nonetheless, this dramatic challenge to the hoary war system has already marked up some remarkable achievements during the last dozen or so years. The following three specific examples are taken from the Middle East alone. They are likely to continue until the Israeli leaders decide to eschew their present military policies and fulfill their obligations under the U.N. Charter and international law.

(1) *Egypt.* Following the Yom Kippur War in 1973 a U.N. agreement called for the establishment of an *ad hoc* UNEF-manned buffer zone, separating Israeli and Egyptian security zones. The disengagement required the withdrawal of Israeli

forces holding territory west of the Canal. At Kilometer 101, the parties agreed on 24 January 1974 on plans for the successive phases of disengagement. A timetable was worked out for redeployment by the military forces on the two sides. This U.N. achievement was barely noticed by the newspapers, but it brought the war to an end.

The Chiefs of Staff of Israel and Egypt signed a map entitled "Plan of separation of forces." General Ensio Siilasvuo, the former UNEF Commander, who chaired the meetings, also signed the map. "Thus, we have successfully concluded these meetings at Kilometer 101," he declared: "I would hope that history may record one day that the initial step toward understanding, reconciliation and peace in the Middle East began here at Kilometer 101."

From the time the process began, the military situation remained quiet. There were 6,000 UNEF troops involved. Meantime, successive Security Council and General Assembly resolutions since 1974 have insisted—but in vain—that Israel gets completely off Egyptian soil (including Gaza). Had this been done *there would have been no need for "Camp David"* and all the confusions that followed. An overall settlement is still awaited. We forget that.

(2) *Sinai*. In addition to the original UNEF presence in Sinai, the United States (playing a mediatory role between Israelis and Egyptians) worked out an "early warning" system to ensure that military outposts would not become military strong points. The U.S. also contributed $10 million in equipment to help the U.N. hold this line firm, all the way south from Gaza to Suez. Observers could detect vehicle movements up to 15 kilometers through electronic sensors—optics during the day and infra-red at night. The total system, if developed for later contingencies, has also a "strategic" early warning capability. An analogous operation on the Golan Heights still continues, in spite of Israel's threat of annexation of this Syrian territory. The U.N. marches silently on without advertisement or big headlines.

(3) *Lebanon*. The most speedy U.N. peacekeeping mission to date was mounted within 48 hours of Israel's lightning invasion of South Lebanon on 15 March 1978. The Security Council had called an emergency meeting and passed *unanimously* Resolution 425 demanding Israel's immediate and complete withdrawal. It also provided for the handing over of the occupied territory to the care of UNIFIL (U.N. Interim Force

in Lebanon) on behalf of the sovereign Lebanese Government. *UNIFIL received clear guarantees from the PLO not to return to the southern frontier*, subject to Israeli soldiers returning home themselves.

Israel was finally pressured by the Western powers to leave Lebanon after a 91-day occupation. Instead of handing over control to UNIFIL, however, which then had 6,000 troops under the command of Major-General E. A. Erskine of Ghana, Israel pursued its own military control in opposition to the U.N. by transferring the territories it had overrun to a "Christian" rebel army of about 800 irregulars, supported and equipped by Israel. Not unnaturally, the PLO withdrew their guarantee, given to the U.N., to leave Northern Israel alone. The raids recommenced. UNIFIL was stymied. The Lebanese delegate at the U.N., Ambassador Tueni, pleaded with the Security Council for help in defending Lebanese sovereignty, made precarious by both PLO and Israel's front men, as well as earlier Syrian incursions to put down a savage two-year civil war.

But for UNIFIL's skillful strategy, as directed by the Security Council, Lebanon would have been split and dismembered by these three outside aggressors. This story has been all too soon forgotten or never known. Approximately 6,000 troops from nine United Nations members (Canada, Fiji, France, Iran, Ireland, Nepal, Nigeria, Norway and Senegal) still remain on extremely delicate service, effectively denying infiltration by Palestinians with a combination of persuasion and coercion. They have tried to confine the Israeli-armed "Christian" militia in Israeli uniforms to a local nuisance value. But Major Haddad, a rebel-traitor to his own country, Lebanon, maintains his private army of some 800 rebel soldiers in a six-mile wide enclave on the Israeli-Lebanon border, financed and controlled by the Israeli Government, in defiance of U.N. decisions and the decent opinion of mankind.

Thanks to the presence of UNIFIL, half a million Lebanese have been given, for the first time in many years, security of the kind which enables crops to be harvested, children to attend school, villagers to meet without fear. One of the first Lebanese children born in the South after the U.N. peacekeeping force took the matter in hand was gratefully named Unifil.

Once again this is a holding action, until the Geneva Conference of all parties meets to restore the Palestinians to their own territory and effect a just and definitive settlement of the

Arab-Israeli conflict, as laid down in Resolution 242 sixteen years ago.

The former chief of Israeli military intelligence, General Yehoshafat Harkabi, a reformed hawk, who supports the "Peace Now" movement in Israel, has declared: "I am for finalizing the conflict. But you can't do that without recognizing that the Palestinians, like any other human group, deserve self-determination. I am for a Palestinian State" (*Herald Tribune*, 7 May 1980).

(2) Peace training for the 1980s

It seems extraordinary that people should need training to conduct war but not to construct peace. Our previous chapters have shown that we are on the edge of new techniques, new remedies for overcoming violence and war. But we have a long way to go yet. Most people—statesmen, generals, journalists, the common man—are not ready for it. It is this lack of knowledge, this failure to understand how *international* violence between sovereign states can be transformed into an ordered peace, that keeps this cruel and absurd arms race going at full tilt. National leaders like Ronald Reagan and Leonid Brezhnev are, by ideology and training, totally incapable of thinking of security except in terms of military "deterrence."

But peace organizations and peace research institutes (see names in Appendix (B)) are multiplying as the war danger grows more ominous. What has not yet been attempted is a viable "network" organization to link together on a global basis these burgeoning anti-war groups. The U.N. General Assembly in December 1980, however, resolved to establish a "World Disarmament Campaign" to strengthen and coordinate NGO action. What are our governments doing about it? Are they working with it?

Let us review, in brief, what some writers have been saying about this. Dr. Albert Einstein, shortly before his death, was quite clear about it: "So long as security is sought through national armament, no country is likely to renounce any weapon that seems to promise it victory in the event of war. In my opinion, security can be attained only by renouncing all national military defense."

With the founding of the United Nations, a new world order began quickly to emerge. Theory began to be put into hard practice. In *Foundation of Peace and Freedom* (1975) Antony

C. Gilpin described his active part in the vast U.N. peace-keeping operations in the Congo during the chaos and tribal violence erupting over the Katanga conflict of the 1960s. He writes:

In practice, the first task of the U.N. Forces was to restore law and order and thus remove any excuse for Belgium to retain troops in the Congo . . . These developments brought the U.N. face to face with the internal political problems of the Congo, a situation made even more difficult some two months later by the split that occurred between President Kasavubu and Prime Minister Lumumba, followed by the seizure of power by the then Colonel Mobutu.

The heavy responsibility the U.N. administration undertook in stabilizing the Congo nation (Zaire)—in which operation Dag Hammarskjöld met his death—brought the U.N. intervention a big step forward from merely holding the line, as in Sinai or Cyprus, or now in Lebanon, to an all-round reestablishment and administration of an immense African territory, which otherwise could have led to an internecine African war.

The *peaceful* transition of Namibia, following along similar lines to the successful Zimbabwe example—from colonization to independence and from South Africa's *apartheid* to multiracial nationhood—would be a further extension into the 1980s of "preventative peacekeeping." These U.N. Charter principles have happily been supported by the West's comprehension and cooperation.

Hence, more and more attention is being given today to the selection and training of peacemakers and peacekeepers. One of these supporting organizations, the International Peace Academy, directed by General Indar Rikhye, one-time military adviser to the Secretary-General, operates on the basis that "U.N. peacekeeping is essential to any future settlement"—anywhere in the world. General Rikhye says:

Peacemaking is defined as the process of using all peaceful means to resolve conflicts. This may require direct and bilateral negotiations or the mobilization of regional and multinational institutions in support of such efforts. But . . . the International Peace Academy has devoted its primary attention to the study of peacekeeping and peacemaking.

The Academy designs and conducts professional international training seminars for diplomats, military officers, academicians, and policy-makers in the subjects of peacekeeping, mediation and negotiation. It also produces publications and teaching materials of immediate practical use by professionals in governments, and teachers at institutes of higher education, both national and private.

Just how revolutionary this training has to be is shown by one of the Academy's expert advisers. Brigadier Michael Harbottle, former chief of staff in Cyprus, and now director of the British Disarmament Campaign, based in London, sums it up in his *The Blue Berets* (1971) as follows:

> It might be hard to believe that without the authority of a rifle a soldier can achieve very much in the way of peacekeeping, when the contestants are so obviously anxious to get at each other's throats; but he can and he does. The rifle he carries provides him with his means of self-protection, not a passport for violence . . . Peacekeeping is an impartial act and impartiality in this context means non-alignment with either side in a dispute, ideally to the extent of total detachment from the controversial issues at stake.

(3) Education for disarmament

But peace soldiering goes far beyond the work of professionals on the spot; it goes into the homes of the common people, into their work places, and into their schools. *The importance of public education in stopping the arms race must by now be clear*. There are many obstacles to the realization of disarmament and the establishment of a new order of mutual respect and toleration between nations of different histories and social systems. Obsolete ways of thinking *must* be changed if these objectives are to be achieved. The peace race is the most ambitious global undertaking of our time. It is a marathon in which millions of ordinary people can take part.

Unfortunately, many people are not prepared to accept the practical consequences of peacemaking. Transforming such mental attitudes to fit together in a global perspective will require an immense effort in all educational and information fields. The very imbecility of the arms race has already forced us to look at the world differently from even a generation ago. The implications of peace and security for the common man must be shown in this new light. Education and information thus have a crucial role in training *all* people to live together as modern societies in One World. The paranoid fear of something called "Communism," which has distorted American domestic and foreign policies for a generation, and, similarly, the crude distortions of Marxist theories and teachings that have defiled so many anxious peoples in search of the good life, must both come to accept a higher loyalty than any man-made dogma or national creed can offer its citizens for the future.

In developing school education in the West about security through disarmament, the difficulties will be complicated by special technical problems. Curricula and syllabuses must be opened up to accommodate new subject-matter. Suitable teaching in this field will require special preparation and the mastering of new bodies of information, as well as adapting teaching approaches to new purposes. Teacher training courses must be adapted for peace education and textbooks must reflect modern thinking about world cooperation.

Education aimed at developing a loyalty to the principles of peace and disarmament cannot, however, be a purely cognitive process. It must also have an effective moral impact, which cannot be achieved simply by transmitting information. The school should be a place where a mature attitude toward a warless world should *begin*.

At the university level, a central problem is to develop coherent programs of teaching the principles and techniques of peace. Specialized courses on the subject, although increasingly offered, are still very rare. The part played by universities, however, in producing community leaders and shaping the intellectual character of society makes it particularly urgent that they should present programs broad enough to reach all students, regardless of their specialization. World citizenship should become a normal teaching subject at all levels.

Happily, for our generation, a whole new range of global institutions is arising, within and around the United Nations family of organizations, which are laying the foundations of a new world order. All this is rendering the phobia for more and more weapons more irrelevant and ridiculous as each new institution comes into focus.

One of these global institutions is UNESCO. At a consultation in Paris in January 1980, attended by several hundred educators from across the world on the subject "Education for Disarmament," Mr. Frank Field, from the World Federation of U.N. Associations, with branches in some 55 countries, said:

> Education for peace and for disarmament is based on the belief that if attitudes can be changed, wars can be prevented, or at least the chances of armed conflict greatly reduced. The Constitution of UNESCO (1946) states that "since wars begin in the minds of men, it is in the minds of men that the defenses of peace must be constructed."

Historically, power has been the accepted basis on which international relations have been conducted. "Managing Soviet power," as we noted earlier, is the kind of evil dream that has brought our planet to the brink of self-immolation. War is *accepted* as a "continuation of diplomacy by other means." Military conflict once was deplored, but taken for granted in the society of nations, *because it posed no threats to its continuance*. But in 1945 all that changed. A nuclear war, as we have seen, would kill in the first "strike" between 200 and 300 million people. The basic nature of war—the ultimate end of State power—has therefore changed to the point where it threatens the very existence of all our states. That is where education for peace and disarmament must begin.

Since its establishment in 1946, UNESCO has undertaken a vast amount of research on education for peace. It has become a global storehouse of experience and information on the education of the world's citizens. Education for Peace includes a wide range of objectives, such as the development of attitudes of cooperation and universal solidarity, coupled with a determination that *international disputes should be settled without resort to armed conflict*.

Education for Disarmament is part of this larger issue of understanding the arms race and the contemporary efforts to halt it. Its subject-matter consists not only of details of weaponry, military expenditures, and arms negotiations, as we have outlined earlier in this book; but campaigning on *specific* issues such as SALT, Nuclear Proliferation, a Comprehensive Test Ban Treaty, Peacekeeping Operations, and General and Complete Disarmament; and above all, campaigning for a New International Economic Order (NIEO) as a means towards the Third World's peace and prosperity.

We therefore must seek education for disarmament in schools, beginning at the secondary level, as part of Education for Peace, and in colleges of teacher education, universities and other educational institutions, *including military staff colleges*. On the secondary level and in a wide range of nongovernmental organizations, as well as in the mass media, disarmament education would have a far greater effect if it were presented deliberately and treated as a subject of public importance *in its own right*.

The General Assembly in December 1980 voted to create a University for Peace in San José. President Rodrigo Carazo of Costa Rica said: "In the final analysis, peace in the world will depend essentially on education for peace as its indispensable instrument. It will depend on justice in international economic relations as a permanent token of goodwill. It will depend on an unyielding determination to disarm, as a necessary precondition."

Finally, a war planned and carried on with the weapons of mass murder raises questions not only of legality in the formal sense, but basic moral questions of a deeply personal character that every individual must answer for himself alone. The General Assembly received from the Human Rights Commission in 1975 a recommendation for the fulfilling (as it stated) of youth's "hope and aspiration for bringing about universal peace." It included the following appeal from youth organizations in 27 countries: "not to conscript arbitrarily any youth to join the armed forces of his country, if such youth conscientiously objects to being involved in war." In support of this appeal the hundreds of sponsoring youth organizations contended:

Young people who opt out of all modern war because of the possibility of the nuclear cremation of millions of human beings are often treated punitively.... It is a tenable assumption, however, that *no war can be just in the nuclear age* when a just cause can be vitiated by anti-human and genocidal weaponry. Thus, the decision to serve or to object can only rest with the human being called upon to take part in military service or war.

How appropriate, then, was the unprompted response of Anawara Khan, a little girl aged 15, of Dacca, Bangladesh, who replied thus to the test question: "MY WORLD IN THE YEAR 2000" which was posed by the International Year of the Child campaign:

In the Year 2000 I would be 38. There is every possibility that I may not still be alive. But if I am, I will be an architect. I want to build buildings which will not only beautify the world but bring happiness. People who live in my buildings cannot help but smile and be happy.

Finally, I aspire that in the Year AD 2000 there will be one nation, and that is human beings; that there is one race and that is the human race; and that there is one religion and that is humanity; that there is one country and that is the earth; and lastly, that the entire mankind may lead a harmonious life of peaceful existence and tolerance.

If all of us just loved and cared for one person each. That is all it takes. Love breeds love. Maybe then, we will be able to prevent each other from going insane. Maybe then, we will be able to prevent each other from becoming violent, as violence is in our hearts and not in the weapons. Guilt is not in the one who pulls the trigger, but in each of us who allows it. (Yoko Ono Lennon)

CONCLUSION:
Organizing for Survival

How can YOU play a part in rescuing your civilization from the perils of this runaway arms race? That is the question that remains. There is no easy answer to it, as the foregoing chapters must have revealed. But there is a mounting public consciousness and collective activity that is beginning to push the warmongers back to the Dark Ages where they belong. So we conclude by citing, briefly, some of the plans of those leaders of thought and action who are pressing for a worldwide campaign to defeat the arms race and those who are promoting it by "deterrence" and more rearmament. Groups and organizations who are already mobilizing their members to win the greatest battle of this fast-receding century—the battle of peace and security through disarmament and development.

But first we might eliminate a familiar trip-line which has been rolled across the pathway of the disarmers ever since the evil of international war has challenged individual consciences. This hoary fallacy was phrased in the following way during a BBC program which reviewed the hardback edition of this present book on 14 November 1980: "... there is no way in which a general popular initiative can be mobilized in the Soviet Union independently of the Party and Government, who control the media. Until the debate can be conducted as freely in the Soviet Union as it is in the West, the prospects of general disarmament as advocated are poor. And disarmament by one side only is no guarantee of peace." There we have it again: push the responsibility onto the monolithic Communists! Not only does this *non sequitur* break every rule of formal logic, but it is self-contradictory since it assumes that people, party and government are of one mind. The last public expression of that fallacy was transmitted to President Ronald Reagan on 23 February 1981 in a speech by President Leonid Brezhnev calling for *mutual disarmament and an immediate halt to the arms race*. The frequent contention of this book that the mass media in the West have become a built-in segment of the arms race itself could not have been more convincingly demonstrated, by the "enemy"! What more do we want?

There are certain requisites which have also found a place in the foregoing pages that have been demonstrated over and over again during the last 35 years. They include these three:

(1) full use must be made of the developing United Nations system, without which all General and Complete Disarmament becomes meaningless;

(2) decisions and proposals already agreed at the U.N. (see the outline of some of these in Appendix (A)) must be followed through by decisions at the *national* level to implement them;

(3) the 20th-century contest between capitalism (U.S.A.) and communism (U.S.S.R.) must be diverted from a military confrontation to commonsense cooperation via the U.N. and other global mechanisms. "Conversion capability" should replace "dissuasion capability," i.e., replace bombs by jobs!

This immense effort is something quite new in global history. But the initiative for it *must* come from the West, since the U.N. is itself the West's most important contribution to peace and its chosen structure for solving global problems. We can't wait for the Russians to change; but we can show them *how* it can be done by changing ourselves.

Disarmament must be conceived today not as a negative act but in terms of *preventive* politics. We have preventive health care for the individual. Why not the preventive politics of disarmament for the wellbeing of the human race?

Here are some broad axioms to guide the burgeoning present-day campaigns that have overflowed Europe to America:

(1) National security advances as international disarmament advances;

(2) Alternative programs for arms reduction have to be built stage by stage, nationally and globally;

(3) The U.N. Security Council, charged with world security questions, should be resorted to habitually to *prevent* wars;

(4) The U.N.'s ample and flexible machinery of peace settlement of disputes must become the normal center for dealing with each crisis as it arises;

(5) The U.N.'s peacekeeping forces must be equipped and financed by the world's governments along the lines repeatedly proposed by independent peacekeeping experts;

(6) The formal relationship existing between the U.N. system of security and disarmament and its peacemaking and peacekeeping procedures, on the one hand, and the world's sovereign governments, on the other hand, must now be implemented as agreed at the 1978 Special Session.

The World Disarmament Campaign

The World Disarmament Campaign, launched at a convention in London on 12 April 1980, accepted as its policy basis the decisions made at the Special Assembly in 1978. Representatives of forty nations, now forming the U.N. Committee on Disarmament (including all the nuclear powers) have been mandated by the General Assembly to carry those 1978 decisions further by:

(1) measures to abolish all armed forces, *except those needed for internal security* and a U.N. Peacekeeping Force, and

(2) preparing proposals for the reduction of armaments, leading to General and Complete Disarmament.

All governments pledged themselves openly in 1978 to cooperate in seeking disarmament along these drastic lines and the timetable for this revolutionary change in "defense" policies were put on the agenda of the 1982 Second Special Session. Meanwhile, President Brezhnev has repeated his long-advocated plea for the destruction of all weapons of mass destruction. But these clear statements by governments will not be fulfilled unless there is considerable pressure from peoples. Now is the time to ACT.

We can read Leonid Brezhnev's book, *Socialism, Democracy and Human Rights* (Pergamon Press, New York, 1980), and note his preface addressed "To my American and British readers" in these terms: "I hope this book will satisfy the curiosity of those readers who wish to know what Soviet socialist democracy is really like, how we view human rights and how these rights are exercised in the Soviet Union." We may profoundly disagree with some of the things he says, quite apart from our abhorrence of his brutal miscalculations over Afghanistan. But at least we can choose dialogue rather than *war*! Threats of punishment will not harm him, but they do harm us. His country and Western countries must live *together*, or not at all.

This challenge of new ways of global thinking, even from Communist regimes, has been emphasized by Dr. Lucille Green of California, President of the World Citizens Movement, who writes:

In the words of Albert Einstein, "we drift toward unparalleled catastrophe . . . a new type of thinking is essential if mankind is to survive and move toward higher levels." Unfortunately, national leaders are the ones most absorbed in the old type of thinking—that is, "winning" the race at any cost, rather than changing the game.

International disarmament goals have been marked recently by the mounting campaigns in Rumania and other "East" countries, as well as in the West. We, therefore, call on all peoples [say the organizers of the London-based Campaign] to unite in a world-wide campaign to achieve these goals:

(1) The participation of all sections of the community, including the Churches, Trade Unions, Political Parties, Peace Organizations, Universities, the Arts, Professions, Women, Youth, and the Trades Union Congress (as already approved by the latter's Congress);

(2) Enrollment of Sponsors, including MPs, Peers, Ministers of Religion, Councillors, Academics and representatives of other sections of the community;

(3) Formation of Local Councils in every locality to carry on the Campaign by meeting, marches, letters to the Press, and other constitutional means, such as deputations to the

Government, Political Parties, Members of Parliament and Managements of National Authorities, including the Media, Television and Radio;

(4) A National Convention to plan expanding action in preparation for the renewed U.N. Special Assembly in 1982; and an international meeting of Parliamentary representatives to plan united action for disarmament, as proposed by Deputies in France and Japan, together with the national disarmament movements in many other countries, thus to initiate a coordinated Campaign on a worldwide scale.

(5) The organization of an international petition or ballot, incorporating many millions of signatures, urging the adoption of measures outlawing weapons of mass destruction, the ending of the arms trade, and phased progress toward complete disarmament, as well as the utilization of the present expenditure on armaments for alternative employment and to bridge the global gulf between riches and poverty.

Smaller countries must lead

But why cannot these burgeoning *voluntary* movements, such as the above, look for one or more governments' official votes somewhere, speaking for the world's conscience? Should we not seek this initiative from several of the Scandinavian or "neutral" countries? For example, the Netherlands Government might well decide to implement their significant opposition to provide bases for the 572 American nuclear missiles. The vote by the Dutch Parliament to reject the new missile plans has surely presented the Dutch Government with a unique opportunity to propose a series of phased and specific reductions, focused on the 1982 Special Session program. Denmark, too, had not even been asked to accept missiles, after calling for a postponement of the NATO decision. Norway also strongly favored negotiating first. Here is fertile soil for boycotting the missile race in the 1980s. Japan, too, is in the lead.

While Defense Secretary Caspar Weinberger was saying that what the Reagan administration wants from Japan "would be to provide for self-defense of the Japanese islands and defense of the airspace and the sealanes up to a thousand miles from the shoreline" (so as to bottle up the Russian fleet), a massive demonstration of the World Assembly of Religious Workers for General and Nuclear Disarmament took place in Tokyo in April 1981. It stated that "today it is more urgent than ever that correct information about the damage and after-effects of the atomic bombing of Hiroshima and Nagasaki should be disseminated throughout the world. The new generation and the policy-makers are not well informed about the effects of atomic bombing. This ignorance promotes the 'legitimacy' of nuclear weapons and their use. The assumed legitimacy of nuclear weapons has given rise to the concepts of nuclear deterrence and nuclear alliances and thus to nuclear confrontation." Could there be a greater contrast of attitudes between Washington and Tokyo?

They went on to say that "Japanese religious workers have been trying to disseminate this knowledge." The leading voice of the Assembly, the Most Venerable Nichidatsu Fujii, Patriarch of Nihonzan Myohoji, declared:

Approximately 100,000 people were instantaneously charred to death by a single atomic bomb unleashed on Hiroshima by the United States at the end of the World War II. Today, the U.S.A. and the U.S.S.R. together have a nuclear stockpile equivalent in explosive force to one million Hiroshima bombs. Should all these nuclear weapons be unleashed in the Ultimate Global War, 100 *billion* people could be killed instantaneously.

The Patriarch stressed the contrast by stating: "Let us now turn our eyes to Japan. The Japanese ruling circles have been in support of the U.S. war policies for three decades through the Japan-U.S. Security Treaty. They now want to revise our Constitution to legitimize the existence of the 'Self Defense Force' and to remove Article 9, which completely denounces armed force, war potential of all kinds, including the production of armaments, and the governmental right to declare war." And to demonstrate the link between Japan and Europe, Lord Philip Noel-Baker, who was among the distinguished guests, declared: "A frenzied arms race, ever-rising expenditures on military plans, lying and distorted propaganda, with the dark cloud of nuclear war coming nearer every day—that is the picture of our World Society in the last quarter of the 20th Century after Christ! Unless we face the truth, and find a cure for this disease, our species—*homo sapiens*—will perish; our heritage of human genius: letters, music, art, architecture, science, will vanish without a trace; our lovely planet, Earth, will become as desolate and silent as the moon."

At the same time, NATO arms control proposals do, at

least, envisage talks on *limiting* Soviet SS-20 medium-range missiles and the Backfire Bomber as against limits on comparable NATO weapons in Europe. These plans could be paralleled by renewed talks in Vienna on reducing troops—especially BAOR—as well as conventional and tactical nuclear weapons in Central Europe.

Mr. Arthur F. Burns, in an address to the German Foreign Policy Association, referred to the 350,000 U.S. troops stationed in and around Europe, saying, "They will not stay if they are not welcome." He said that if the Europeans were not willing to reaffirm their alliance with the United States, "there may well be a growing sentiment in America to turn back upon itself and let Europe depend for its security and freedom upon its own resources or upon Soviet good will." (*The New York Times*, 23 December 1981.) .

NATO officials have argued, of course, that the decision on deploying the new American missiles would "strengthen the West's hand in negotiation" (as though nuclear weapons were playing cards!). So the big NATO generals would be hoisted on their own petard if smaller NATO members put forward their reduction plans as a contribution to that "negotiation." In any case, the deployment of the "572" could not be completed until 1983. So what are we waiting for? Time is running out for peace.

And it is the ex-generals of NATO who (in reflective retirement) have seen the light. A former admiral and six retired generals from NATO countries have called on the alliance to remove *all* nuclear weapons from the arsenals of Western European nations. In a 19-page memorandum to the NATO command, the retired officers, from France, West Germany, Norway, Portugal, Greece, Italy, and the Netherlands, urged renewal of détente with the Soviet Union instead of "hazardous confrontation policies." Moreover, European countries should end their "vassalage" to the United States, starting with a rejection of a plan to deploy new American-made medium-range missiles in 1983.

The retired generals' memorandum continued: "Political prejudice and factual inaccuracy within NATO" had created an exaggerated perception of the Soviet threat. The concept of military superiority was outdated and futile, and would only exacerbate the arms spiral.

The officers, who have been active in their own countries,

said that they had banded together to lend some military expertise to the campaign for arms control. They said their participation would help show that a broad cross-section of Europeans, and not just the far left, opposes the arms race. For example, Signor Nino Pasti, a retired Italian Air Force general, now a senator and a former NATO deputy-commander for nuclear affairs in Brussels, said: "It is absolute nonsense to suggest that millions of people in Europe, who are not favorable to the Soviet regime, are being influenced by Soviet propaganda. The real issue is not between a socialist way of living or a capitalist way of living, it is between life and death." (*The Times*, London, 26 November 1981)

Meanwhile, the Russians do not admit that they have done anything provocative by deploying SS-20 missiles and Backfire Bombers. They point out that they *tried* to bring weapons of this sort into the SALT talks with the United States, but that the Americans objected. The Soviet Union made a concession—recognized as such by the Americans—when it went along with this. They feel that the new U.S. weapons do, however, represent an unequal threat, for the weapons will be able to strike Soviet territory, while the SS-20 and the Backfire Bombers cannot hit the United States. This destroys the myth of "balance."

However, in 1980, *unilateral* disarmament as a first step in Britain and some European countries began to assume national campaign status. Mr. Frank Allaun, former Labour Party Chairman, said: "Outside Parliament there has been a dramatic swing in support of unilateral arms reduction. The CND demonstration drew more than 70,000 marchers on to the streets. People are ready for our policies." He added that, while backing multilateral disarmament, "we feel that a limited unilateral step *divesting nuclear weapons is the most practical way to achieve it*. In Vienna the governments have been negotiating conventional disarmament. After seven years they have not even agreed to reduce armaments by a single rifle. We cannot afford to wait another seven years." And in November 1980 Michael Foot, leader of the Parliamentary Labour Party, who might become Prime Minister in 1984, declared an intention to cancel existing nuclear arms contracts. The newspaper magnates prophesied that this would mean disaster for his party, but public opinion polls have since shown a Labour lead over the Conservative Government of 10.5 percent.

Moving forward

At its General Conference held at Helsinki in September 1981, the International Peace Bureau, founded in 1892 (which has no Communist members or affiliations), decided to initiate in-depth studies as to the ethical morality and as to the legality under international law of the use of weapons of mass destruction, and, in particular, of nuclear weapons. It stated: "While most Church and Religious leaders have at different times and with different emphasis condemned nuclear weapons and decried wars, they have stopped short of formally declaring them to be a violation of ethical morality."

Nobel Peace Prize laureate Sean MacBride, the IPB President, who is preparing these studies, has pointed out that in the juridical domain a trend can be identified since the Declaration of St. Petersburg (1868) to limit the scope and extent of what belligerents are *permitted to do* under international law. That Declaration laid down that the purpose of war "would be clearly exceeded by the employment of arms which unnecessarily aggravate the sufferings of disabled men, or render their deaths inevitable." It goes on to declare that the employment of some arms "would therefore be contrary to the laws of humanity." Moreover, the Hague Conventions of 1899 and 1907 lay down that "the right of belligerents to adopt means of injuring the enemy is not unlimited" and outlawed "the throwing of explosives from balloons, the use of dum-dum bullets and the use of poison and other chemicals."

The destructive nature of World War I, when 10 million people were killed, prompted the formulation of the Briand-Kellog Pact of 1928. This treaty for the first time *outlawed* war and the use of force in international affairs. The Nuremberg Tribunal in 1946, which condemned and executed the Nazi war criminals, relied on the provisions of the 1928 treaty. Its judgment laid down:

> The solemn renunciation of war as an instrument of national policy necessarily involves the proposition that such a war is illegal in international law; and that those who plan and wage such a war with its inevitable and terrible consequences *are committing a crime in so doing*.

In 1950, the United Nations unanimously approved of the seven Principles of the Nuremberg Jurisdiction. Principle Number Six laid down as punishable under international law (our italics):

(a) Crimes against Peace:
   (i) Planning, preparation, initiation or waging of a war of aggression *or a war in violation of international treaties, agreements, or assurances*;
   (ii) Participation in a *common plan or conspiracy* for the accomplishment of any of the acts mentioned;
(b) War Crimes:
   Violations of the laws or customs of war which include . . . *wanton destruction* of cities, towns, or devastation not justified by military necessity.

U.S. Arms Control and Disarmament Agency former Director, Mr. William C. Foster, has wisely said:

Every step that helped to move us toward the control of nuclear weapons was important. Among such steps was the Test Ban Treaty of 1963. Though limited, it successfully reduced atmospheric testing and the contamination of the environment by radioactive substances. Another step of great importance was the Treaty on the Non-Proliferation of Nuclear Weapons in 1968 . . . Now in SALT II one more such opportunity presents itself . . . This is an awesome task *that we have begun*, and it is of supreme importance that we continue the effort step by step.

Then, throughout Western Europe, in Australia and Canada, as well as in the U.S., large-scale demonstrations against nuclear sites and facilities are rapidly on the increase. Weapons sales bazaars have received adverse public notice for the first time, and are picketed. In May 1979, Washington witnessed its largest mass demonstration since the Vietnam War, as 90,000 people marched against nuclear power *and* nuclear weapons. Also in 1979 there was initiated a new citizen development in the coalition of church, peace and women's groups with environmentalists, scientists, and labor unions.

This could well be the start of the first serious public challenge to the arms race in many years, allied to the new World Disarmament Campaign inaugurated in London under the Chairmanship of Lord Gardiner, former Lord Chancellor, supported by Lord Noel-Baker and other Nobel Prize winners. To claim that this global movement of intelligent opinion is Moscow-inspired reveals the blight that has fallen upon our Western civilization and faith.

"The United States now has its great opportunity. Hardline bully-boys have failed ignominiously, playing cops-and-robbers. We have lost world respect, world confidence. Let us grow up, stop playing the giant without a soul, and begin working hard for peace and cooperation on this little planet. Anybody, even the most mediocre, can make war. It takes intellect, maturity, statesmanship, to make peace." said William Winter in *The Churchman* (November 1980).

This *moral* revolt against the more-arms advocates is finding its voice at last in some unusual places across the earth. No one can stop it. For example, at what was termed the greatest Christian demonstration in the history of Fiji, attended by the Governor-General of Fiji and broadcast throughout the Pacific area, over 30,000 people gathered together to hear Dr. Alan Walker of the World Methodist Council say: "Humanity is only a pushbutton away from atomic weapons killing millions and destroying the centers of the world's life." He went on: "Irreligion is steadily destroying the Western world. Without faith in God, respect for human life, moral standards, family life and ideals of service are undermined . . . 'Feed the hungry, set the poverty-captives free,' is the call of the new decade." And Dr. Walker added: "A new world economic order must be found. The present world order is collapsing. We call for the launching of a vast crusade against poverty, not for charity or aid, but for justice."

If this was a Protestant plea from the other side of the planet, it shared the same moral urgency as Pope John Paul's courageous and piercing words when visiting the NATO Defense College in 1979: "Sensitivity to the immense needs of humanity brings with it a spontaneous rejection of the arms race, which is incompatible with the all-out struggle against hunger, sickness, underdevelopment and illiteracy."

Europe comes to its senses

A further chance on the governmental level came at the last Conference on Security and Cooperation in Europe (CSCE), meeting in Madrid in November 1980. This time, "security" has acquired a new emphasis. Confidence-building measures and invitations to observers to watch maneuvers have worked well, as mentioned above, since the 1975 Helsinki agreements and have reduced the chances of miscalculation and surprise attack between NATO and WAPO. The CSCE, founded in Helsinki as a *permanent* European organization, includes *all* the European states (except Albania), plus the United States and Canada—a total of 35 signatories.

The French, for instance, are fairly confident that, from the way the Russians have been publicizing their own schemes for "a European military détente," the time has come to develop a *European Disarmament Conference*. This French disarmament plan has two phases and is only a beginning. The first spreads the scope of reporting measures as far back as the Urals. The second phase calls for actual cuts in armaments. Such ideas are now being fitted into the Madrid Scheme, but the U.S. delegate spends his time in attacking the Russians!

There is also ample evidence, reinforced by a recent Warsaw Pact Foreign Ministers' meeting in East Berlin, of a Rumanian and Yugoslav lead in a Russian *arms limitation campaign*. The French think that the same kind of human rights emphasis that the West placed on the Russians at Helsinki should be repeated after Madrid, if balanced by Western arms reductions that the Russians clearly want. Some NATO allies, especially the West Germans, are in favor of the French approach, on the understanding that the Alliance links security to human rights. Thus, CSCE might eventually come *to replace NATO and WAPO by an All-European Security System*. Why not? The Madrid meetings are not an East/West boxing match!

We have already deplored the Cold War behavior of some Western governments in distorting the purposes of the 1975 Helsinki Agreement and using it as a negative human rights weapon against the Soviet Union. But there is a positive movement now afoot. A Conference of Non-Governmental Organizations met in Madrid alongside the Revision Conference in November 1980 to urge the implementation of the CSCE Final Act in terms of peace and security, without which human rights cannot endure. Representatives of 32 international NGOs and 14 United Nations Associations and national NGOs reflected a broad spectrum of public opinion including trade unions, women's groups, students' and youth movements, human rights activists, veterans, scientists, social workers, lawyers, journalists, churches and other religious bodies, representing millions of ordinary people from all parts of the world.

This grass-roots assembly noted that the deterioration of

relations between the signatory governments endangered the Final Act, the only existing and acceptable basis for peace and security *in Europe*. For it offers the people of Europe an antidote to the external pressures coming from the Kremlin and the Pentagon to turn their continent into a nuclear battlefield.

The NGO Conference pressed their governments to return to the atmosphere of goodwill which had produced the original Helsinki guiding principles, including: respect for the rights inherent in sovereignty and territorial integrity; refraining from the threat or use of force; inviolability of frontiers; peaceful settlement of disputes; non-intervention in internal affairs; respect for human rights and self-determination of peoples; co-operation among states; and, above all, "fulfillment in good faith of obligations under international law."

It is not possible in a book of this kind, dealing with the arms race, to present a full blueprint of a viable world peace system, other than by sketching a few simple guidelines, as we have attempted to do in these recent chapters. But all men and women of good faith and goodwill must acknowledge our primary need, in the declining years of this Century of Anxiety, to seek and encourage more sensible co-existence patterns between the rival imperialisms of Russia and America, which are the taproot of the arms race.

There is a clear call in the 1980s for a global homecoming between the United States and the Soviet Union, to which reconciliation the British and European peoples—both East and West—should be expected to contribute an essential part. A leading U.S. businessman who knows Russia well has written: "Sooner or later we will reverse our alleged hostility towards the Soviet Union and recognize that country as our natural ally and trading partner. We have never warred with Russia; we have been partners in conflict . . . The new president may just seize the opportunity to lead America to a successful, peaceful world" (Edward Lamb of Toledo, Ohio, in the *New York Times*). The U.S. President has still this chance.

The 35 brief years that have been misspent in pursuing this criminal exercise in military suicide, which gives the title to this book, is only a tiny segment of man's long existence on this planet. During the three million years or more that have elapsed since *homo sapiens* emerged from his animal ancestry as the crown of God's creation, more than one "crisis" has threatened his race with extinction. It cannot surely be beyond the wit of the leaders of this generation to range themselves and their peoples on the side of life.

One Moment in Annihilation's Waste,
One Moment of the Well of Life to taste—
The Stars are setting, and the Caravan
Starts for the Dawn of Nothing—Oh, make haste.

(Omar Khayyám, Rubáiyát)

APPENDIX (A)
A Short History of Arms Pacts*

Arms reduction agreements concluded in the post-World War II period have had the following objectives: (1) prevention of the militarization, or military nuclearization, of certain areas or environments; (2) freeze or limitation on the numbers and characteristics of nuclear delivery vehicles; (3) restrictions on weapons tests; (4) prevention of the spread of specified weapons among nations; (5) prohibition of the production as well as elimination of stocks of certain types of weapons; (6) prohibition of certain methods of warfare; (7) reduction of the risk of an accidental outbreak of nuclear war; (8) observance of the rules of conduct in war; (9) notification of certain military activities; and (10) verification of obligations contracted under previously signed treaties.

This concise list shows what can be done. The 1980s can show more progress in real disarmament.

*Josef Goldblat, *Arms Control: A Survey and Appraisal of Multilateral Agreements*, SIPRI, 1978

The 1959 Antarctic Treaty has declared that Antarctica shall be used exclusively for peaceful purposes. It is an important demilitarization measure. But it will be in constant jeopardy so long as the question of territorial sovereignty in Antarctica has not been definitely resolved. (Signed: 1 December 1959; entered into force: 23 June 1961. Number of parties as of 31 December 1978: 19.)

The 1963 Partial Test Ban Treaty has banned nuclear weapon tests in the atmosphere, in outer space and under water. It has helped to curb radioactive pollution caused by nuclear explosions. But continued testing underground has made it possible for the nuclear weapon parties to the Treaty to develop new generations of nuclear warheads. They have carried out more explosions since this Treaty than before it. (Signed: 5 August 1963; entered into force: 10 October 1963. Number of parties as of 31 December 1978: 109.)

The 1967 Outer Space Treaty has prohibited the placing of nuclear or other weapons of mass destruction in orbit around the Earth and also established that celestial bodies are to be used exclusively for peaceful purposes. But weapons of mass-destruction in outer space present apparently insurmountable problems of maintenance, command and control, making it easy for the nuclear-weapon powers to forego them. Moreover, outer space has remained open for ballistic missiles carrying nuclear weapons; and the deployment in outer space of weapons not capable of mass destruction is subject to no restrictions. The major powers are also engaged in developing devices capable of destroying satellites in orbit, adding a new dimension to the arms race. (Signed: 27 January 1967; entered into force: 10 October 1967. Number of parties as of 31 December 1978: 78.)

The 1967 Treaty of Tlatelolco prohibits nuclear weapons in Latin America. It has established the first nuclear-weapon-free zone in a populated region of the world. But it will not achieve its principal goal until Argentina and Brazil, the only countries in the area with any nuclear potential and aspirations, are bound by its provisions. (Signed: 14 February 1967; entered into force: 22 April 1968. Number of parties as of 31 December 1978: 22.) Additional Protocols were in the course of ratification during 1980.

The 1968 Non-Proliferation Treaty prohibits the transfer of nuclear weapons by nuclear-weapon states and the acquisition of such weapons by non-nuclear-weapon states. It grew out of the realization that the possession of nuclear weapons by many countries would increase the threat to world security. But it is being gradually eroded because of the inconsistent policies of the nuclear-material suppliers, the non-fulfillment of the obligations undertaken by the nuclear-weapon powers, and the lack of guarantees that nuclear weapons will not be used against non-nuclear-weapon states. (Signed: 1 July 1968; entered into force: 5 March 1970. Number of parties as of 24 March 1980: 114.)

The 1971 Sea-Bed Treaty has prohibited the emplacement of nuclear weapons on the seabed beyond a 12-mile zone. But because of the vulnerability of fixed devices, such emplacement is not militarily attractive. And since the Treaty permits the use of the seabed for facilities that service free-swimming nuclear weapon systems, it presents no obstacle to a nuclear arms race in the whole of the marine environment. (Signed: 11 February 1971; entered into force: 18 May 1972. Number of parties as of 31 December 1978: 65.)

The 1974 Threshold Test Ban Treaty has limited the size of U.S. and Soviet nuclear-weapon test explosions to 150 kilotons. But the threshold is so high (ten times higher than the yield of the Hiroshima bomb) that the parties cannot be experiencing onerous restraint in continuing their nuclear-weapon development programs. (Signed: 3 July 1974; *not* in force by 31 December 1977.)

The 1972 Biological Weapons Convention has prohibited biological means of warfare. But in view of their uncontrolability and unpredictability, these weapons have always been considered of little utility. On the other hand, chemical weapons, which are more predictable and which have been used on a large scale in war, are still the subject of disarmament negotiations. (Signed: 10 April 1972; entered into force: 26 March 1975. Number of parties as of 21 March 1978: 87.)

The 1972 SALT ABM Treaty has imposed limitations on U.S. and Soviet anti-ballistic missile defenses. But the type of ABMs the Treaty deals with cannot offer meaningful resistance to the penetration of offensive missiles. The development of new ABMs continues. (Signed: 26 May 1972; entered into force: 3 October 1972.)

The 1972 SALT Interim Agreement has frozen the aggregate number of U.S. and Soviet ballistic missile launchers. But it has not restricted the qualitative improvement of nuclear weapons—their survivability, accuracy, penetrativity and range. Moreover, the number of nuclear charges carried by each missile has been allowed to proliferate. (Signed: 26 May 1972; entered into force: 2 October 1972. Number of parties: 28.)

The 1975 Document on Confidence-building Measures contained in the Final Act of the Conference on Security and Cooperation in Europe provides for notification of major military maneuvers in Europe. But it does not restrict these activities. Moreover, military movements, other than maneuvers, do not have to be notified, even though transfers of combat-ready units outside their permanent garrison or base areas, especially over long distances and close to the borders of other states, may cause greater concern than maneuvers. (Signed: 1 August 1975.)

The 1976 Peaceful Nuclear Explosions Treaty regulates the U.S. and Soviet explosions carried out outside the nuclear-weapon test sites and therefore presumed to be for peaceful purposes. But, apart from being a complement to the 1974 Threshold Test Ban Treaty, it has no arms control value. On the contrary, in emphasizing the importance of peaceful nuclear explosions it may have had a negative impact on the policy of presenting nuclear-weapon proliferation by providing added justification and encouragement for some non-nuclear-weapon countries to plan for an indigenous development of nuclear explosives. (Signed: 28 May 1976; *not* in force by 31 December 1978.)

The 1977 Environmental Modification Convention prohibits the hostile use of techniques which could produce substantial environmental modifications. But essentially only those techniques have been forbidden which are still the subject of scientific speculation and which, if proved feasible, seem hardly usable as rational weapons of war. Manipulation of the environment with techniques which are already in existence, and which can be useful in tactical military operations, has escaped proscription. (Signed: 18 May 1977; entered into force: 5 October 1978.)

The 1977 Protocols Additional to the 1949 Geneva Conventions provide for the protection of victims of international and non-international armed conflicts. They constitute a step forward in the development of the humanitarian laws of war. But they have not forbidden any specific weapon which is excessively injurious or has indiscriminate effects. (Signed: 12 December 1977; *not* in force by 31 December 1978.)

THIS IS A BEGINNING FOR U.S.A.

A \$10 billion transfer from military procurement to solar power, railroads, buses and fishing fleet construction would be a start in improving our national security. The endless pile-up of overkill capacity will not run our cars, fuel our factories or heat our homes. Only a major transfusion of capital, technology and manpower into the industries which will make us energy independent will do that.

We no longer have the excess capital to fuel both the arms race and to provide the capital for our energy needs. The measures suggested in this report are a beginning. The economic impact of transferring capital out of the inflation-causing military budget into solar power, gasohol and railroads will be positive. Inflation will go down, employment will go up, and the nation can begin the long path back to economic health (Marion Anderson, *Converting the Work Force*).

APPENDIX (B)
Organizations *You* Can Join

These non-governmental organizations are seeking to promote a planetary consciousness in a divided world. There is always a time lag in social change. Christianity did not spread at once. Three centuries were to pass before the persecuted few in the catacombs sat on the throne of the Caesars. Darwin's evolutionary impact took a generation to challenge the old creation story. Now, for the first time since history began, a planetary consciousness is spreading—more powerful than any "ism" or creed that threatens world unity. As Arthur Koestler reminds us, mankind has always had to live with the idea of individual death; but, from now on, mankind will have to live with the idea of death as a *species*.

Concerned with peace and disarmament, the following list of addresses has been selected with permission from the *Peace Diary* published by Housmans, 5 Caledonian Road, London N1, England (01-837 4473).

United States

American Civil Liberties Union, 22 E. 40th St., New York, N.Y. 10016.

American Friends Service Committee, 1515 Cherry St., Philadelphia, Pa. 19102.

Amnesty International, 2112 Broadway, Office 309, New York, N.Y. 10023

Baptist Peace Fellowship, 3448 Rainbow Dr., Palo Alto, Ca. 94306.

Carnegie Endowment for International Peace, 345 East 46th Street, New York, N.Y. 10017.

Catholic Peace Fellowship, 339 Lafayette St., New York, N.Y. 10012.

Catholic Worker Movement, 36 E. 1st St., New York, N.Y. 10003

CCCO (Draft and Military Counseling), 2016 Walnut St., Philadelphia, Pa. 19103.

Center for Global Perspectives, 218 East 18th St., New York, N.Y. 10003.

Center for Study of Armament and Disarmament, California State College, 5151 State University Dr., Los Angeles, California 90032.

Coalition for a New Foreign and Military Policy, 122 Maryland Ave., Washington D.C. 20002.

Conference on Peace Research in History, University of Toledo, Toledo, Ohio 43606.

Consortium Peace Research, Education and Development, Gustavus Adolphus College, St. Peter, Minnesota 56082.

Episcopal Peace Fellowship, 61 Gramercy Park N., New York, N.Y. 10010.

Fellowship of Reconciliation, Box 271, Nyack, N.Y. 10960.

Friends Committee on National Legislation, 245 Second St. N.E., Washington D.C. 20002.

Friends of the Earth, 529 Commercial St., San Francisco.

Friends Peace Committee, 1515 Cherry St., Philadelphia, Pa. 19102.

Ground Zero, 806 15th St. N.W., Suite 421, Washington, D.C. 20005.

Institute for International Policy, 120 Maryland Ave., Washington D.C. 20002.

Jewish Peace Fellowship, Box 271, Nyack, N.Y. 10960.

Liberation, 136 Hampshire St., Cambridge, Mass. 02139.

Lutheran Peace Fellowship, 168 W. 100th St., New York, N.Y. 10025.

Mobilization for Survival, 198 Broadway (Rm. 302), New York, N.Y. 10038.

Movement for a New Society, 4722 Baltimore Ave., Philadelphia, Pa. 19143 (215 724 1464).

National Action/Research on the Military Industrial Complex, c/o AFSC Philadelphia.

Pax Christi, c/o Peace Studies Institute, Manhattan College, Bronx, New York, N.Y. 10471.

Peace Digest, Lamplighter Lane, Newington, Conn. 06111.

Peace Science Society (International), 3718 Locust Walk, CR, McNeill Bldg., University of Pennsylvania, Philadelphia, Pa 19174.

Physicians for Social Responsibility, P.O. Box 144, 23 Main St., Watertown, Mass. 02172.

Progressive, 408 West Gorham St., Madison, Wis. 53703.

Society for Social Responsibility in Science, 221 Rock Hill Road, Bala Cynwyd, Pa. 19004.

Swarthmore College Peace Collection, Swarthmore, Pa. 19081.

Unitarian Universalist Association, Dept. of Education and Social Concern, 25 Beacon St., Boston, Mass. 02188.

United Farmworkers Union, Logan Ave., San Diego, Ca. 92113.

United Methodist Church, Division of World Peace, 100 Maryland Ave. N.E., Washington, D.C. 20002.

United Nations Association, 345 East 46th St., New York, N.Y. 10017.

War Resisters' League, 339 Lafayette St., New York, N.Y. 10012.

Women's International League for Peace and Freedom, 1213 Race St., Philadelphia, Pa. 19107.

World Council of Churches, 475 Riverside Drive, New York, N.Y. 10027.

World Federalists Association, 1424 16th St. N.W., Washington D.C. 20036.

World Peace News, 777 U.N. Plaza, 11th Floor, New York, N.Y. 10017.

World Without War Council, 175 Fifth Ave., New York, N.Y. 10010.

Canada

Amnesty International, POB 6033, 2101 Algonquin Ave., Ottawa, Ontario K2A 1TI.

Canadian Peace Research Institute, 25 Dundana Ave., Dundas. Ontario L9H 4E5.

Christian Movement for Peace, 24 Alexandra Blvd., Toronto M4R 1L7.

Fellowship of Reconciliation, 126A St. Ocean Pk., Surrey, B.C.

Friends (Quaker) Centre, 60 Lowther Ave., Toronto, Ontario M5R 1C7.

Project Ploughshares, School for Peace and Conflict Studies, Conrad Grebel College, Waterloo, Ontario N2L 3G6.

United Nations Association in Canada, 63 Sparks Street, Ottawa K1P 5A6, Ontario.

Voice of Women/La Voix des Femmes, 175 Charlton St., Toronto, Ontario M5A 2K3.

Women's International League, 1768 West 11th Ave., Vancouver B.C., V6J 2C3.

World Federalists, 46 Elgin St., Rm. 32, Ottawa, Ontario K1P 5K6.

Great Britain

Africa Bureau, 48 Grafton Way, London W1P 5LB (01-387 3182).

African National Congress of South Africa, 49 Rathbone St., London W1A
4NL (01-580 5303).

Amnesty International, British Section, 8-14 Southampton St., London
WC2E 7HF (01-836 5621).

Anglican Pacifist Fellowship, St. Mary's Church House, Bayswater Rd.,
Headington, Oxford OX3 9EY.

Anti-Apartheid Movement, 89 Charlotte St., London W1P 2DQ.

Association of World Federalists, 40 Shaftesbury Ave., London W1V 8HJ
(01-969 2803).

Baha'i National Spiritual Assembly, 27 Rutland Gate, London SW7 1RD.

J. D. Bernal Peace Library, 44 Albert St., London NW1.

Bertrand Russell Peace Foundation, 45 Gamble St., Nottingham NG7 4ET.

Birmingham Peace Centre, 18 Moor St., Queensway, Birmingham B4
7UB.

British Society for Social Responsibility in Science, 9 Poland St., London
W1V 3DG.

British Soviet Friendship Society, 36 St. John's Square, London EC1V
4JH.

Campaign Against the Arms Trade, 5 Caledonian Rd., London NI 9DX.

Campaign for Nuclear Disarmament, 29 Gt. James St., London WC1N
3EY.

Central Board for Conscientious Objectors, c/o 6 Endsleigh St., London
WC1.

Christian Action, 15 Blackfriars La., London SE1.

Christian Movement for Peace, Stowford House, Bayswater Rd., Oxford
OX3 95A.

Commission for International Justice and Peace, 44 Grays Inn Rd., London
WC1X 8LR.

Concerns Against Nuclear Technology, 19 Cheyne Walk, London SW3.

Cooperative Women's Guild, Pioneer House, 342 Hoe St., London E17
9PX.

Council for Education in World Citizenship, 43 Russell Sq., London
WC1B 5DA.

Danilo Dolci Trust, 29 Gt. James St., London WC1N 3EY.

Fellowship of Reconciliation, 9 Coombe Rd., New Malden, Surrey KT3
4QA.

FOR in Scotland, 53 Kelvinside Gdns., Glasgow G20 6BQ.

Friends, Peace and International Relations Committee, Friends House,
Euston Rd., London NW1 2BJ.

Friends World Committee, London.

Greenpeace, c/o Peace Pledge Union.

International Confederation for Disarmament and Peace, London (*see* National Peace Council).

International Friendship League, 3 Creswick Rd., London W3 9HE.

International Voluntary Service, Ceresole Ho., 53 Regent Rd., Leicester LE1 6YL.

Labour Action for Peace, 81 Orchard Ave., Croydon CR0 7NF, Surrey.

Liaison Committee of Women's Peace Groups, 44 Albert St., London NW1 7NU.

Liberation, 313 Caledonian Rd., London N7.

Medical Association for the Prevention of War, c/o Richardson Institute, 158 N. Gower St., London NW1.

Mennonite Centre (London), 14 Shepherds Hill, London N6 5AQ (01-340 8775).

Methodist Peace Fellowship, c/o FOR.

Minority Rights Group, 36 Craven St., London WC2N 5NG.

National Council for Civil Liberties and Cobden Trust, 186 Kings Cross Rd., London WC1X 9DE.

National Peace Council and United World Trust, 29 Gt. James St., London WC1N 3ES.

New Internationalist, 62 High St., Wallingford, Oxford OX10 OEE.

New Left Review, 7 Carlisle St., London W1.

Northern Friends Peace Board, 30 Gledhowwood Grove, Leeds, LS8 1NZ.

Nuclear Information Network, c/o Nat. Peace Council.

Overseas Development Institute, 10/11 Percy St., London W1P OJP.

Oxfam, 274 Banbury Road, Oxford OX2 7DZ.

Pax Christi, Blackfriars Hall, Southampton Rd., London NW5.

Peace News, 5 Caledonian Rd., London N1 9DX.

Peace Pledge Union, Dick Sheppard House, 6 Endsleigh St., London WC1H ODX.

Religious Society of Friends, Friends House, Euston Rd., London NW1 2BJ.

Richardson Institute for Conflict Research, 158 N. Gower St., London NW1 2ND.

School of Peace Studies, University of Bradford, Bradford, BD7 1DP, W. Yorks.

Student Christian Movement, Wick Ct., Wick, nr Bristol BS15 5RD.

Tribune, 24 St. John St., London EC1.

Unitarian and Free Christian Peace Fellowship, 53 Kelvinside Gdns., Glasgow G20 6BQ.

United Nations Assoc., 3 Whitehall Ct., London SW1A 2EL.

Voluntary Service Overseas, 14 Bishops Bridge Rd., London W2 6AA.

War on Want, 467 Caledonian Rd., London N7 9BE.

Women for World Disarmament, North Curry, Taunton, Somerset TA3 6HL.

Women's International League for Peace and Freedom, 29 Gt. James St., London WC1N 3ES.
World Development Movement, Bedford Chambers, Covent Gdn., London WC2E 8HA.
World Disarmament Campaign, 21 Little Russell St., London WC2.
Young Liberals Movement, 1 Whitehall Pl., London WC2.

Australia

Amnesty International, St. Kilda 3182, Victoria.
Association for International Co-operation and Disarmament, PB A243, Sydney South PO, NSW 2000.
Catholic Commission for Justice and Peace, POB J124, Brickfield Hill, NSW 2000.
Congress for International Co-operation and Disarmament, 208 Lt. Lonsdale St., Melbourne 3000.
Federal Pacifist Council, Box 2598, Sydney, NSW 2001.
Friends (Quaker) Centre, 631 Orrang Rd., Toorak, Melbourne 3142.
Pax Christi, 31 Carlton South, Victoria 3053.
Peace Institute, 306 Murray St., Perth, WA 6008.
Peace Pledge Union, 3 Euston Ave., Highgate, S. Australia.
Transnational Co-operative, 232 Castlereagh St., Syndey, NSW 2001.
United Nations Association, 66 Turbot St., Brisbane 4001.
Women's International League, PB 35, Fairfield, Victoria 3078.

New Zealand

Anglican Pacifist Fellowship, 56a Wai-iti, Cres, Lower Hutt (Wellington 698125).
Catholic Peace Fellowship, Box 12224, Wellington.
Christian Pacifist Society, 9 Grove Rd., Kelburn, Wellington.
New Zealand Foundation for Peace Studies, PB 4110, Auckland.
Society of Friends Peace Committee, 14 Sunnynook Rd., Takapuna North, Auckland 10.
Student Christian Movement, POB 9792, Courtenay Pl., Wellington.
United Nations Association, 1011, 10 Brandon St., Wellington.
Voice of Women, 21 Ravelston St., Dunedin.
Women's International League for Peace and Freedom, 7A Queenstown Rd., Auckland 6.

Japan

Amnesty International, Rm. 54, 3–18 Nishi-Waseda 2-chome, Shinjuku-ku, Tokyo 160.

Asahi Shimbun Peace Research Center, c/o Research Room, Asahi Shimbun, 2–6–1, Yuraku-eho, Chiyodaku, Tokyo.

Civil Liberties Union, 7F Nankai-Tokyo Bldg., 5–15–1, Ginza Chuo-ku, Tokyo 104.

Friends Center (SoF), 8–19 Mita 4-chome, Minato-ku, Tokyo 108.

Gensuikin (Japan Congress against A and H Bombs) (I), 4th Floor, Akimoto Bldg., 2–19 Tsukasa-cho, Kanda, Chivoda-ku, Tokyo.

Gensuikyo (Japan Council Against A and H Bombs), 6–19–23 Shimbasi, Minato-ku, Tokyo 105.

Japan Buddha Sangha, 8-7 Shinsen-cho, Shibuya-ku, Tokyo 150.

Japan Communes Assoc., 10 Sangubashi Haitsu, 4-5-14 Yoyogi Shibuya-ku, Tokyo 151.

Japan Peace Research Group, 1–15–23 Hogashikaigan Tsujido, Fujisawa-shi, Kanagawa.

Mosakusha (Information Center), Nakae Bldg., Shinjuko 2–4–9, Shinojuko-ku, Tokyo.

Nihon Heiwa Kenkyu Kondankai (R), c/o Prof. Y. Sakamoto, Fac. of Law, Univ. of Tokyo, Bunkyoku, Tokyo 13.

Pacific Asia Resource Center, Rm. 403, A. Omotemachi Bldg., 4–8–19 Akasaka, Minato-ku, Tokyo.

Peace Studies Association of Japan, c/o Mitsuo Okamoto, Shikoko Gakuin University, 765 Zentsuji-shi, Kagawa Ken.

Quaker International Affairs Program in East Asia (SoF), Sendagaya Apts., Room 606, 9–9, Sendagaya 1-chome, Shibuya-ku, Tokyo 151.

Servas, 21–22, 6-chome, Todoroki, Setagaya-ku, Tokyo 158.

Service Civil International, 249 Iidaoka, Odawarashi, Kanagawa-ken 250.

United Nations Association and Student Assoc., 521 Nippon Bldg., 6–2, 2-chome Ohtemachi, Chiyoda-ku, Tokyo 100.

United World Federalists, 1–15–10, Uchikanda, Chiyoda-ku, Tokyo 101.

Utsunomiya Disarmament Research Institute, Tokyo.

War Resisters' International Group, 354 Kameyama, Himeji-shi Hyogo-ken.

Union of Soviet Socialist Republics

Assotsiatsiya Sodeistviya Oon V SSSR, Kirovst 24, Moskva 101000.

Institute of World Economy and International Relations, Dept. of Peace Research, 2 Jaroslavskaya Ulitsa, d.3 korpus 8, Moskva 1–243.

KMO-CCP, Bogdan Khmeinisky 7/8, Moskva.

Soviet Peace Committee, U1 Kropotkine 10, Moskva 634.

International Organizations

This section includes organizations which coordinate their national groups and those primarily international.

Amnesty International, 8–14 Southampton St., London WC2E 7HF, Gt. Britain.

Baha'i International Community, 345 E. 46th St., New York, N.Y. 10017, U.S.A.

Christian Movement of Peace, rue Louvrex, 36, 4000 Liège, Belgium.

Christian Peace Conference, Jungmannova 9, 111 21 Praha 1, Czechoslovakia.

Eirene, 545 Neuwied 1, Engerserstr. 74B, West Germany.

Friends of the Earth, 9 Poland St., London W1V 3D9, Gt. Britain.

Friends World Committee for Consultation, 30 Gordon St., London WC1H OAX, Gt. Britain.

International Committee of the Red Cross, 17 Avenue de la Paix, 1211 Genève, Switzerland.

International Confederation for Disarmament and Peace, 6 Endsleigh St., London WC1H 0DX, Gt. Britain.

International Court of Justice, Peace Palace, The Hague, Netherlands.

International Fellowship of Reconciliation, Hof van Sonoy, Veerstraat 1, Alkmar, Netherlands.

International Labor Organization, 4 route des Morillons, CH 1211 Genève 22, Switzerland.

International League for Human Rights (HR), 777 United Nations Plaza, Suite 6F, New York, N.Y. 10017, U.S.A.

International Peace Academy, 777 United Nations Plaza, New York, N.Y. 10017, U.S.A.

International Peace Bureau, rue de Zurich 41, CH-1202 Genève, Switzerland.

International Peace Research Association, PO Box 70, 33101 Tampere 10, Finland.

International Registry of World Citizens, 55 rue Lacépède, Paris 75005, France.

International Youth and Student Movement for the United Nations, 5 Chemin des Iris, 1216 Cointrin, Genève, Switzerland.

Pax Christi International, PO Box 85627, NL-2040, Den Haag, Celebesstr. 60, Netherlands.

Pax Romana, 1 route de Jura, PB 1062, CH-1701 Fribourg, Switzerland.

Servas International, 268 W. 12th St., New York, N.Y. 10014, U.S.A.

Service Civil International, 35 ave. Gaston Diderich, Luxembourg.

Transnational Institute, Paulus Potterstr., Amsterdam, Netherlands.

United Nations, New York, N.Y. 10017, U.S.A.

United Nations Educational, Scientific and Cultural Organization, Place de Fontenoy, 75700 Paris, France.

War Resisters' International, 35 rue van Elewyck, 1050 Bruxelles, Belgium.

Women's International League for Peace and Freedom, 1 rue de Varembé, 1211 Genève 20, Switzerland.

World Association of World Federalists and World Federalist Youth, Leliegracht 21, Amsterdam, C. Netherlands.

World Conference of Religion for Peace, 777 United Nations Plaza, New York, N.Y. 10017, U.S.A.

World Council of Churches, 150 route de Ferney, 1211 Genève 20, Switzerland.

World Federation of Scientific Workers, 40 Goodge St., London W1P 1FH, Gt. Britain.

World Federation of United Nations Associations, Palais des Nations, 1202 Genève, Switzerland.

World Peace Council, Lönnrethinkatu, 25 Helsinki 18, Finland.

World Peace Through Law Center, 400 Hill Bldgs., Washington, D.C. 20006, U.S.A.

World Student Christian Federation, 37 Quai Wilson, 1201 Genève, Switzerland.

AMERICAN WOMEN CHALLENGE THE WAR LORDS

Women know all too well the *machismo* determination to force—win and kill, if necessary, to achieve and maintain prominence and power. Some women know it as domestic violence. The women and children of Cambodia, Nicaragua, Vietnam and the ravaged lands of World War II know it as war. They know that civilian casualties outweigh military casualties in confrontation, and that violence in a society means violence to women.

Today's economic realities are that increased military programs and spending are impractical, unaffordable, *and disastrous for women*. Military increases must be scrutinized as closely as domestic programs. The critical questions of what we are buying and why, what are the military's roles and missions within a foreign policy framework must be addressed before spending begins.

From the moon only one man-made object is visible—the Great Wall of China. It stands as the pre-eminent symbol of defensive attempts at national security. Recent satellite photos show that pieces of the wall are being broken away by citizens who use the stones to build and repair houses.

Unmet human needs will chip away at all security plans that exclude the needs of the people. Women know this best and feel it most (Nancy Ramsey, Executive Director of The Committee for National Security, Women's Building, San Francisco, California, U.S.A., 27 September 1980).

Further Reading

Books on Disarmament and those mentioned in the text

Blainley, G., *The Causes of War*, Free Press, 1973.

Boserup and Mack, *War and Weapons*, Pinter, 1974.

Booth and Wright, *American Thinking about Peace and War*, Harvester Press, 1978.

Burns, E. L. M., *Megamurder*, Harrap, 1966.

Burns, R. D., *Arms Control and Disarmament, A Bibliography*, ABC Clio, 1979.

Collins, J. M., *Imbalance of Power*, Presidio Press, 1978.

Benoit, Emile and Boulding, *Disarmament and the Economy*, 1963.

Cervenka and Rogers, *The Nuclear Axis*, Friedmann Books, 1978.

Cox, J., *Overkill*, Penguin, 1977.

Center for Study of Developing Societies, *Disarmament, Development and a Just World Order*, New Delhi, 1978.

Eide and Thee, *Problems of Contemporary Militarism*, Croom-Helm, 1980.

Falk, R. A., and Mendlovitz, S. H., *The Strategy of World Order—Disarmament and Economic Development*, Praeger, 1966.

Gilpin, A. C., from *Foundation of Peace and Freedom*, Christopher Davies, 1975.

Ground Zero, *Nuclear War: What's in It for You?*, Pocket Books, 1982.

Hackett, J., *The Third World War, August 1985*, Sidgwick and Jackson, 1978.

Harbottle, M., *The Blue Berets*, Leo Cooper, 1971.

Jolly, Richard, *Disarmament and World Development*, 1978.

Joyce, J. A., *End of an Illusion*, Allen and Unwin, 1969.

Kaldor, M., *European Defence Industries*, Sussex University, 1972.

Kaldor, M., *World Military Order*, Macmillan, 1979.

Kennedy, G., *The Military in the Third World*, Duckworth, 1974.

Labour Party Defence Study Group, *Sense About Defence*, Quartet Books, 1977.

Lall, B. G., *Prosperity without Guns*, Cornell, 1978.

Lloyd and Sims, *British Writing on Disarmament*, Bibliography, Pinter, 1979.

SIPRI, *Military Research and Development*, Stockholm, 1972.

Thee, M., *Armaments and Disarmament in the Nuclear Age*, IPRI Stockholm, 1976.

Mitrany, D., *A Working Peace System*, Chicago, 1966.

Perlmutter, A., *The Military and Politics in Modern Times*, Yale, 1977.

Sampson, A., *The Arms Bazaar*, Coronet, 1978.

Schell, Jonathan, *The Fate of the Earth*, Knopf, 1982; paperback reprint, Avon Books, 1982.

Sims, Nicholas A., *Approaches to Disarmament*, 1979.

Suter, Keith, *Uranium, the Law and You*, Friends of the Earth, 1978, Sydney, Australia.

United Nations and Disarmament Yearbook, Annual, 1978.

U.N. Documents

Economic and Social Consequences of the Armaments Race and its Extremely Harmful Effects on World Peace and Security (A/32/88 Rev. 1) (Sales Wo.: E 78 IX 1).

Report of Ad-Hoc Group of the Special Session on Disarmament on the Relationship between Disarmament and Development (A/S-10/9).

Final Document of the Special Session on Disarmament (1978).

Document of the General Assembly 33rd Session on Disarmament and Development (A/C.1/33/L.12/Rev.1).

Report of the Group of Governmental Experts on the Relationship between Disarmament and Development (A/33/317).

Document of the General Assembly, 34th Session: Relationship between Disarmament and Development (A/34/534).

ECOSOC: Committee for Development Planning—Disarmament and Development: An Analytical Survey (E/AC.54/L.90).

Disarmament and Science and Technology for Development (A/CONF.81/5/Add.2).

Reports and Studies

Anderson, Marion, *Converting the Work Force*, 1980.

Arms Production and Employment in the Netherlands, Peace Research Center, University of Nijmegen.

Asquith, Phil, *A Contribution to Disarmament and the Reduction of Social Conflict*, The Lucas Aerospace Corporate Plan, U.K., 1979.

Ball, Nicole and Leitenberg, M., *Disarmament and Development*.

Scientific Symposium on "Problems of the Conversion from War to Peace Production," Vienna, March—April 1979.

Emelyanov, Vasily, *Disarmament and Reconversion of the Defence Industry*.

Faramazyan, R. A., *Economic and Social Problems of Conversion*, Vienna, 1979.

Knorr, Lorenz, *The Political Aspect of Conversion from War to Peace Production*.

Leitenberg, M., *Defence Industry Conversion in the United States; USSR Economy, Defence Industry and Military Expenditure*, Cornell University, 1979.

Lock, P., *Obstacles to Disarmament*, UNESCO Expert Meeting, Paris, 1978.

Rölling, B. V. A., *Disarmament and Development—Perspective of Security*.

SIPRI, *The Arms Trade with the Third World*, Penguin, 1974.

Soukup, Miroslav, *Principles of Establishing a Comprehensive Programme of Global Development*, Supplementary Resources Gained from Disarmament.

Värynen, Raimo, *Employment, Economic Policy and Military Production*, Tampere, 1979.

POSTSCRIPT:
The Security Myth

A state's armaments are determined by its sense of security. It will not want to reduce its arms budget unless it can gain a greater sense of security. That is, at least, the theory. *Yet a state cannot gain a greater sense of security by adding to its armaments.* Excessive armaments lead to—always have led to—"a war-like state of mind." The arms race is itself a token of insecurity.

But as the U.N. takes over problems which cannot be solved by sovereign states—settling disputes about frontiers, such as those of Palestine or Namibia, or by prohibiting certain weaponry, such as seabed and space installations—peacebuilding procedures become accepted as the *normal* method of conducting inter-state differences. Security has therefore to be centralized in the U.N., not in national military establishments or rival alliances.

Security can, of course, be developed between two previously hostile neighboring countries, such as East and West Germany. Yet it can also be multilateral. This is the very essence of the U.N. security system. Security and disarmament are the twin pillars of world peace. But security cannot come *first*, as some people tell us. Security and disarmament belong together. Disarmament inevitably brings with it a sense of security.

The Helsinki Final Act of 1975 belongs to this process of promoting security. The contribution of Helsinki to all-round European security has not received the appreciation it deserves. That is why this book has advocated an all-European Disarmament Conference to *implement* "Helsinki."

The universal quest for "security" is not simply a matter of conflict *between* states, but rather of opposition between policies and personalities *within* states. Throughout history this has been so—a war party versus a peace party. Though we do not call them by those names, many instances show this still to be true.

In every country certain men and institutions make up a war party that deliberately promotes the arms race for their private benefit. Military bodies manipulate deep-seated fears within the population against past or potential enemies or rival political systems, as well as commercial competitors. They thus promote insecurity. *National* security can no longer be envisaged as a democratic process. Ordinary citizens of a country have to rely for their sense of security on what they *are told* by a political élite. They are told continually that the arms race is necessary for their security.

A vast nationwide apparatus of public persuasion is at the service of its martial traditions, war-prone personalities, and money-making interests. Public opinion is formed less by the external facts of foreign relations—which are too complicated to be grasped—than by selective interpretations that these internal interest groups put upon them. Commercialized press and media present a frightening shop-window of insecurity.

Addressing the 96 nations of the Non-aligned Conference at New Delhi on 11 February 1981 the U.N. Secretary-General said:

> The arms race cannot either remove the threats of today or be a shield against the dangers of tomorrow. *We must all, therefore, encourage a perception of security in other than military terms*. This requires an unceasing effort to build confidence among nations which, in turn, demands that the causes of distrust should be constructively dealt with. Only through restraint and peaceful adjustment of national interests can lasting international security be achieved.

Acknowledgments

Since the first edition of this book appeared, a number of expert inter-governmental studies have been published by the United Nations, dealing specifically with the relations between Disarmament, Security and Development, and focusing on the 1982 Second Special Session on Disarmament in New York. Largely ignored by the press, some of their most relevant findings and conclusions have been included in this third edition so as to update my proposals for ending this nightmare of an insane arms race.

The American side of our story owes much to the research data published by the Center for Defense Information in Washington. I express my deep appreciation for the generous services extended to me by its Director, Rear Admiral Gene R. La Rocque (U.S. Navy, Ret.), and his indefatigable assistants who received me so warmly in the Washington office. The aerospace and aeronautical data from the Smithsonian Institution relating to missiles and their vehicles has also proved invaluable. The State Department's regular bulletins were indispensable as a source of official data and statements of policy. In New York

I have benefited especially from the careful researches of Professor Betty Lall of Cornell University and from Ruth Leger Sivard's annual survey of military expenditures. Studies and reports of the International Peace Academy, under the direction of Major-General Indar Jit Rikhye (Indian Army, Ret.) were most helpful in preparing my later chapters.

Among British sources, I found Dr. John Cox's *Overkill* a *vade mecum* on nuclear weapons, and acknowledge my indebtedness to the author and publishers, Penguin Books Ltd. The reports of the Swedish International Peace Research Institute (SIPRI) provided the foundations for the sections devoted to the arms race, and I am indebted to the Institute and Josef Goldblat for permission to reprint their survey of multilateral arms agreements as Appendix (A).

In Geneva, practical help and advice came from the International Peace Bureau (for reports of the 1977 Hiroshima seminar on radiation effects), and from Mrs. L. Waldheim-Natural, Chief of the Disarmament Center at Le Palais des Nations, and her staff. Mr. René Wadlow, Geneva representative of the Association of World Federalists has always been ready to supply me with just the data I needed.

For 30 years, the U.N. has published a considerable range of expert reports, not least the pamphlets and brochures published by its Department of Public Information, covering every possible aspect of the arms race and disarmament. These reports have been indispensable. I am indebted to Mrs. Filiz Ertan, documentalist at the Geneva Center, who helped me to update this third edition and to prepare the important list of Further Reading at the end.

From the wide variety of literature produced by non-governmental organizations for the U.N. Special Sessions on Disarmament in 1978 and 1982, I have selected much that is not yet available in more substantial publications. I have also drawn considerably on the monthly editions of *Disarmament News*, under the editorship of Richard Hudson, whose *War/Peace Report* in New York is a goldmine of facts and figures.

Harry Robertson, Secretary of Labour Action for Peace, in London, provided me with up-to-date material, particularly on U.K. trade·union activities, and he has checked some of the data that I have selected to support my proposals on British policy. Ronald Huzzard's bimonthly *Labour Peace Newsletter*, also of London, is often cited; as are several publications of the redoubtable Campaign for Nuclear Disarmament (CND) and the Campaign Against the Arms Trade. *Sense about Defence* (Quartet Books, 1977), was most useful on questions of conversion. Other books and pamphlets are acknowledged in the references, as they occur.

The maps and charts available at the Imperial War Museum, London, have been most useful. I also wish to thank Sidgwick and Jackson for permission to produce the map, "The Soviet Plan to attack Western Europe," from General Hackett's book *Third World War, August 1985*. Without the initiative and patience of Mr. Vito Mannina of Avon Books, New York, this edition would not have appeared so soon in its American dress.

Index